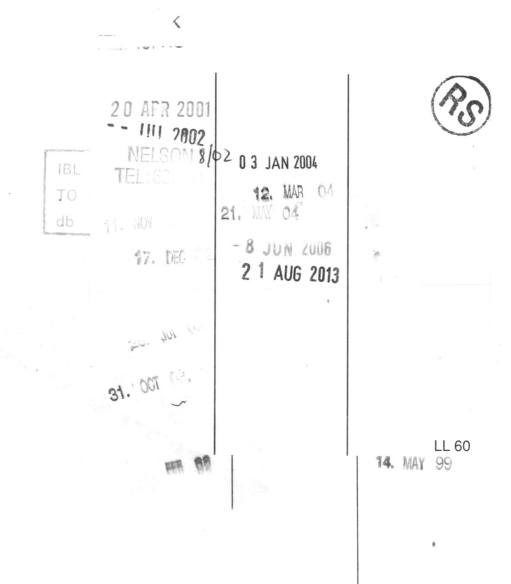

THE
JEWS OF BRITAIN

A Thousand Years of History

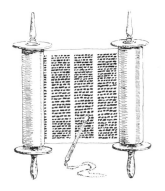

THE JEWS OF BRITAIN

A Thousand Years of History

Pamela Fletcher Jones

THE WINDRUSH PRESS · GLOUCESTERSHIRE

First published in Great Britain by
The Windrush Press,
Windrush House,
Adlestrop,
Moreton-in-Marsh,
Gloucestershire
1990

© Pamela Fletcher Jones 1990

British Library Cataloguing in Publication Data
Fletcher Jones, Pamela
    The Jews of Britain : a thousand years of history.
    1. Great Britain. Jews, history
    I. Title
    941.004924

    ISBN 0 900075 66 X

Typeset by W. G. Harrison Ltd, Grantham, Lincolnshire

Printed and bound in Great Britain by
Courier International Ltd, Tiptree, Essex

Contents

Acknowledgements

In the preparation of this book, I have received help from many people and organisations, to all of whom I am most grateful. Among them are my niece, Toinette Lippe, and Laura Barnes, both of New York, and my friend, Effie Mansfield of Lincoln, who all did research for local facts and pictures for me; Rabbi Dr Albert Friedlander, who spared the time to read the manuscript and wrote the Foreword; other friends who lent me books of reference or supplied information, including Shelley Power, John Gould, Gerald Rosen and June Wertheim; Ronald Harrison of Lincoln who took photographs of Lincoln Cathedral for me at very short notice; Norman Clarkson, Secretary of the Kingston Numismatic Society, who supplied ancient coins to be photographed and information about them and Ian Franklin, who supplied an additional coin; and Dr Edward Conway, former head of the Jews' Free School, who gave me historical details about the school.

I also appreciated the assistance of Judith Prendergast of the National Portrait Gallery; the Bursers' Department of the West London Institute of Higher Education and Doris Jones, the Institute's Archivist; the staff of Kingston Library; Dahlia Tracz, Librarian of the Moccatta Library in University College, London; Hyam Maccoby, Librarian of the Leo Baeck College; The Jewish Museum, London; Paul Bookbinder, Archivist of Marks and Spencer; Rita Freedman, York City Archivist, and Dorothy Lee, Press/PR Officer of York Minster; Carolyn Wingfield, Archaeological Officer of the Bedford Museum; Linda Greenlick, Librarian of The Jewish Chronicle; Simone Mace, Archivist of N.M. Rothschild and Sons Limited; and Rickie Burman, Curator of the London Museum of Jewish Life. Assistance was also given by the Board of Deputies of British Jews, Jewish Care, Jews' College, the Union of Liberal and Progressive Synagogues and the West London Synagogue.

My particular thanks, however, go to four people without whose help and encouragement this book might never have been written. First, to my husband, Norman Fletcher Jones, not only for contributing many of the drawings, but also for his long suffering support and enthusiasm throughout the whole operation – often into the small hours. Secondly, to Rabbi Danny Rich of Kingston Liberal Synagogue, who not only lent me many books of reference, but also gave me the benefit of his knowledge and scholarship whenever I needed it. Thirdly, to Ken Simmons, who spent a great deal of his time and energy on new photography to help illustrate this book. And lastly, to the late George Grafton Green, who taught me the craft of writing.

P.F.J. April 1990

Picture Credits

Page 1: Bedford Museum/Miles Birch (North Bedfordshire Borough Council). Page 7: reproduced by kind permission of the Dean and Chapter of York (photographer: Jim Kershaw). Pages 11, 30 and 54: Press Agency (Yorkshire) Ltd. Page 15: Lincoln City Council. Pages 41, 73, 79, 91, 92, 101, 106, 108, 140 and 176: National Portrait Gallery, London. Page 57: Public Record Office. Page 63: Ronald Harrison, Lincoln. Page 68: British Library. Page 69: Bodleian Library and the Ashmolean Museum, Oxford. Pages 82 and 84: Courtesy of Leo Baeck College Library, London. Page 102: from an engraving by P. van Gunst. Page 109: Spanish and Portuguese Jews Congregation, London. Pages 116 and 117: Jewish Museum, London. Pages 118, 124, 129 and 134 (bottom): Print Collection, Miriam & Ira D. Wallach Division of Art, Prints and Photographs, The New York Public Library, Astor, Lenox and Tilden Foundations. Pages 134 (top) and 142: Jewish Theological Seminary of America. Page 146: a painting by Henry Barraud reproduced by kind permission of Lord Rothschild. Page 147: Courtesy of Gerald Rosen. Pages 149 and 154: Tower Hamlets Local History Library and Archives. Page 150: courtesy of Vicki Simmons. Page 156: courtesy of the West London Synagogue. Pages 157, 182 and 185: Jewish Chronicle. Page 158: courtesy of Jews' College, London. Page 161, 172 (bottom), 173 (left) and 183: London Museum of Jewish Life, Finchley, London. Page 162: courtesy of Ken Simmons. Page 165, 166 and 167: courtesy of Marks & Spencer. Page 168 and 169 (left): courtesy of Union of Liberal and Progressives Synagogues. Page 169 (right): courtesy of Kingston Liberal Synagogue, Surrey. Page 171: Imperial War Museum. Page 172 (top): courtesy of Pamela Fletcher Jones. Page 173 (right): courtesy of Shelley Power. Page 177, 178, 184 and 188: Associated Press, London. Page 186: courtesy of International Stoke Mandeville Games Federation. Page 189: photo by Astrid Zydower reproduced by courtesy of Rambert Dance Company. Page 190: courtesy of EMI and Jacqueline du Pré Memorial Fund.

Additional photographs by Ken Simmonds
Additional line drawings by Norman Fletcher Jones

While every effort has been made to trace copyright owners of the material used in this book, the publishers take this opportunity of apologising to any owners whose rights may have been unwittingly infringed.

Foreword

The doyen of Anglo-Jewish historians, Lucien Wolf, founded the Jewish Historical Society of England almost a century ago. Since then, there has been no dearth of outstanding historians who have chronicled Jewish life in Great Britain and who have examined almost every facet of a Jewish community which became so much part of British life that its present Chief Rabbi sits in the House of Lords.

There is a ready reception given to such texts by a public which finds the tale of Anglo-Jewish assimilation and symbiosis, of rejection and of acceptance, to be of absorbing interest. A country is mirrored and revealed by the treatment it metes out to the minority groups who come to it as a place of refuge. How does it respond to the stranger? There is a dark side of its soul which can show itself and which will become known even when the records have been lost. The literature of the land, the plays of Marlowe and Shakespeare, then become as relevant to our study of history as documents slumbering in some corner of the British Library. In this text, Pamela Fletcher Jones points to the mistreatment of the Jews during an early epoch; its cruelties exceeded much of what was taking place in the rest of Europe. At the same time, one must point out that she also notes the over-riding decency of later years. And the strange quirks of history, accidents that are not accidents but move against prevailing tendencies – these are recorded as well: the 'happy pragmatism of Oliver Cromwell' (so Antonia Fraser) followed by Charles II and his 'good natured indifference' (as Cecil Roth saw it) permitted the Jews to return to the tolerant atmosphere of immediate post-Restoration England. The rest, as they say, is history.

There is also the paradigmatic story of the Jewish community, once it had become established, and its own view of the arriving immigrants. Over 100,000 East European Jews came in the 1880s and were integrated within an Anglo-Jewish community of less than half their number. It changed the pattern of Jewish life in Great

Britain; but it did not destroy it. Anglo-Jewry was enlarged; it gained in richness and colour. Half a century later, the German Jewish refugees fleeing from Hitler also brought a new and deeper cultural and religious dimension into a Jewish world where the Sephardi and Eastern Jewish establishments had learned to live next to one another, if not with one another.

The Jews of Britain is written for the inquiring lay-person, for Jews and for non-Jews who want a general introduction rather than solutions to the puzzles of history which still plague the scholars examining the by-ways of Anglo-Jewish history. Any book is a challenge to readers: they must add to it. But that is the way it should be. Jews never finish a book. Once the text is written, the commentaries begin. This is the essence of Jewish history: it is *toldot*, the continuing story of the generations who transmit what was past into the present, and who, through their lives, move forward into the future.

Rabbi Dr Albert H. Friedlander
Dean, *Leo Baeck College*
Rabbi, *Westminster Synagogue.*

PROLOGUE
Who are the Jews?

This book tells the story of a varied group of people who have lived in Britain for over a thousand years – from Roman times to the present day. It treats as 'Jews' anyone who is born of a Jewish mother, whether they profess the Jewish faith or not, plus a comparatively few converts to Judaism.

The origin of what has come to be called 'The Jewish People' lies in the days of the Hebrew Bible, when their ancestors – the Hebrews and the Israelites – lived in the Middle East, eventually reaching Palestine; the Promised Land. They lived and thrived there for more than 1,500 years until they were forcibly dispersed over the whole of the Roman Empire by the Romans after the fall of the Second Temple in Jerusalem in 70 AD. Their situation in Europe was as slaves, mercenaries in the Roman army or just displaced persons scraping a living as best they could. Those refugees formed the beginning of what is now called the Diaspora – the dispersed Jews. Bit by bit, the Jews spread all over Europe, into the Far East and even back into the Middle East, mainly because of persecution in many countries – persecution which persisted in a major fashion right up to and throughout the Second World War.

On the whole, wherever Jews have settled, they have integrated well with their non-Jewish neighbours, but seldom actually assimilated to the extent of losing either their Jewish identity or their religious faith. This is true, to a greater or lesser degree, of the bulk of the Jewish community living in the United Kingdom.

There has always been controversy among both Jews and non-Jews as to exactly *what* Jews *are*. What they are *not* is a 'nation', though they are certainly 'a People'. Being Jewish is certainly *not* a nationality, though it *is* 'a heritage' of which most Jews are proud. Judaism, however, is *certainly* a religion (the first monotheistic faith) *and* a tradition.

Who or what *are* the Jews? That may well depend on the viewpoint, or the prejudice, of those evaluating them!

P.F.J.

CHAPTER ONE
In the Beginning

There were Jews living in Britain as early as Roman times. Most people, including many British Jews, would be surprised to learn that a few Jews came to England during the period from 43 AD to 400 AD (or Common Era, as Jews term it). Indeed, the finding of three Jewish coins lends credence to this, although not certainty. The earliest coin, and probably the most important, was found in 1948 at Bingley Moor in the West Riding of Yorkshire. It was a coin of Herod Agrippa I and was struck in the year 42–43 AD, the date of the invasion and occupation of Britain. It is thought that it was probably brought by a Jew, who was perhaps a Roman soldier and who came to Britain in Hadrian's time. The second coin, found at Melandra Castle in Derbyshire, was dated 66–72 AD, and the third, found at the old General Post Office site in London's St Martins-le-Grand, was a 'second revolt' coin struck to celebrate a victory of Bar Kokhba, the Jewish leader, in Jerusalem over the Romans during his ultimately

This pottery lamp was found in a sandpit in Flitwick, Bedfordshire, in 1924. It is believed to be a fourth-century lamp from Palestine, particularly because of the Jewish menorah (candlestick) which is moulded near the spout. It is possible that there was a small Jewish community in Bedfordshire during the fourth century.

unsuccessful uprising to save Jerusalem from the Romans in 132–135 AD.

A Jewish lamp was found in Bedfordshire dated the fourth century AD and there is a possibility of a small early Jewish community there and also at Exeter, possibly started by Jewish soldiers in oriental units of the Roman army or by Jewish traders travelling with those armies. It is possible, too, that some of those merchants were concerned with the import of pottery, glass and oriental wares to England and they may have been the founders of small Jewish communities at such places as Colchester, York, Corbridge and even London. There is also a theory among historians that a few Jews found their way to London, possibly, though not necessarily, as slaves, after the tragic end of the Bar Kokhba uprising in Palestine. Furthermore, one or two Jews were actually mentioned as officials in Britain in the fourth century. There may even have been some itinerant Jews in Anglo-Saxon England, but there is no firm evidence of any actual settlers.

It was not, however, until the Norman Invasion of England in 1066 that a settled Jewish community was started. They were Normandy Jews and many may have been brought over from Rouen by William the Conqueror shortly after he was established as King William I, while others followed not much later.

Although from the start most Jews lived in London, there is a reference to some living in Oxford as early as 1075. Anthony à Wood, a historian of the seventeenth century, recorded that they were mentioned in several surviving letters and deeds of that year. One, in particular, was written by Brumman le Riche to the church of St George in Oxford. It gave the right of their land to the canons of the church in Walton, a northern suburb of Oxford, and guaranteed that it would not be transferred to Jews. This was, in fact, to prevent the rights of the land being claimed by the Crown, because, in England, as in Normandy, the Jews themselves were regarded as the property of the king.

It was this negative note that was to castigate the Jews as second class citizens, non-citizens, for a variety of reasons, from the time their English community started – and this was to be the pattern of Jewish life in England for the following two centuries.

In 1086, when Jews were actually mentioned in the Domesday Book, the outlook was not exactly encouraging:

Alwi sherriff hold from the King two hides [approximately ten acres] and a half at Blicestone [Oxfordshire]. This land Manasses [a corruption of Mannasseh] brought from him without

A settled Jewish community started in England very shortly after the Norman Conquest. William the Conqueror probably brought a number of the Jews over from Rouen in Normandy very soon after he was established as King William I. This portrait is after an illustration in the Bayeux Tapestry.

licence of the King. The same bishop holds Staplebridge [in Dorset]. Of the same land Manasses holds three virgates [approximately 30 acres] which William, the King's son, took from the church without the consent of the bishops and monks.

Mannasseh, it seems, had transgressed because he had not obtained the licence from the monarch which was necessary for land transactions, marriages, custody of children and other legal matters engaged in by the Jews.

Indeed, from the foundation of the settled – or fairly settled – Jewish community in England (and later in Wales and Ireland), the Jews were so hedged round with legal regulations and prohibitions on their liberty, that it is quite astonishing that, as the years passed, more and more of them crossed the English Channel from mainland Europe to find a new life in the British Isles.

When William the Conqueror's son, William Rufus, came to the throne in 1087, he actively encouraged the Jews to settle in his realm. By now, more had arrived from Normandy following a massacre of Jews in Rouen by crusading knights – and many members of the fairly large Jewish community who escaped death probably came to England to seek refuge in their Lord's dominions across the sea, especially since England was as yet untouched by the crusading frenzy which was to hit it about a hundred years later. It is likely that the settled and quite sizeable English Jewish community which followed owed its origin to the massacre in Rouen.

William II was not a loved monarch and there seems to have been little sorrow among his people when he met his death in 1100 after being hit by an arrow in the New Forest. Yet Rufus the Red, so-called because of his red hair, must have had some warmth and even a sense of humour, as chronicled by William of Malmesbury in his *Gesta Rerum Anglicanarum*:

> The Jews who dwelt in London, whom his [Rufus's] father brought thither from Rouen, approached on a certain solemn occasion, bringing him gifts; he bent down to them and even dared to animate them to a conflict [a debate] against the Christians. 'By the face of Luke', quoth he, declaring that if they conquered he would join their sect.

These debates or dialogues, mainly on the relative merits of Judaism and Christianity, were encouraged during this and some later reigns by both kings and clerics. There were generally good relations between Jews and non-Jews in the early years of Jewish settlement and they had also considerable economic and social contact with gentiles, such as drinking with their Christian neighbours, using their medical skills for the benefit of the gentile population and even becoming involved in monastic politics. Nevertheless, the Jews had their own religious and cultural institutions from the early days and they mostly mixed with members of their own community. Jews would often live together in the same street or area, but, in those days, they were not limited to living in particular areas and they and their non-Jewish neighbours could and did visit each other's homes socially.

Details of a friendly debate between Christian and Jew were sent to St Anselm about this time. The debate was between Brother Gilbert Crispin, proctor and servant of Westminster Abbey, and an unnamed Jew who had been educated at Mayence in France. Brother Gilbert wrote in a letter to 'The Rev. Father and Lord Anselm', who was then Archbishop of Canterbury,

As early as William II's reign, there were many friendly debates between Jews and Christians on the relative merits of Judaism and Christianity. This modern impression of such a dialogue shows the Christians on the left and the Jews, wearing distinctive hats, on the right.

I send you a little work to be submitted to your fatherly prudence. I wrote it recently putting to paper what a Jew said when formerly disputing with me against our faith in defence of his own law, and what I replied in favour of the faith against his objections. I know not where he was born, but he was educated at Mayence; he was well versed even in our law and literature, and had a mind practised in the Scriptures and in disputes against us. He often used to come to me as a friend both for business and to see me, since in certain things I was very necessary to him, and as often as we came together we would soon get talking in a friendly spirit about the Scriptures and our faith. Now on a certain day God granted both him and me greater leisure than usual, and soon we began questioning as usual. And as his objections were consequent and logical, and as he explained with equal consequence his former objections, while our reply met his objections foot to foot, and by his own confession seemed equally supported by the testimony of the Scriptures, some of the bystanders requested me to preserve our disputes as likely to be of use to others in the future.

Alas, the 'little work' containing details of the debate does not appear to have survived, but Gilbert's letter to the Archbishop sheds light on the tolerant attitude and friendly relations between Christians and Jews in this period and also makes it clear that such disputations were held in public.

It is likely that when William II's brother, Henry I, came to the throne in 1100, he issued a charter of protection, either to the Jews generally or, at least, to certain of them. Though the text of this charter no longer exists, it must have been so important that it was continually referred to in later records as a model document and was imitated by English monarchs for nearly two centuries. It was, in fact, the fundamental charter of liberties for medieval English Jewry. Most importantly, it guaranteed for Jews freedom of movement throughout the country, relief from ordinary tolls and protection from being misused. It also permitted them to keep land taken in pledge as security and made special provisions for them to have fair trials and it gave Jews free recourse to royal justice and responsibility to no one other than the king. What this charter achieved for English Jewry was the establishment of a community in a privileged position as a separate entity – even though it was an entity which existed for the advantage of the king. It was, however, protected by him and answerable to him alone in all legitimate transactions.

Henry I's nephew, Stephen, became king in 1135 and the nineteen years of his reign were not, on the whole, to be very happy ones for the Jews. Money was urgently needed by the Crown and the king imposed levies on his Jewish subjects which were both unfair and extortionate.

There was a double instance of this during the civil war between Stephen and his cousin, Henry I's daughter, Empress Matilda, Countess of Anjou, who had laid claim to the throne. In 1141, Matilda and her troops occupied Oxford and immediately imposed a levy on the Jews there. When the town was recaptured by Stephen, as punishment for their payments to his rival, the king demanded from them three and a half times as much tax as his cousin had taken from them. It is believed that because the Jews were unwilling to pay up, Stephen sent his retainers with lighted torches to set fire to all the Jewish houses in the town. One of the finest houses was owned by a rich Jewish businessman, Aaron fil' Isaac (the earliest named Jew in Oxford), and it was not until his house had been burnt down that the Jews paid the sum the king demanded.

The 'blood libel', which has always been one of the greatest lies and injustices perpetrated against Jews, originated in England with the case of William of Norwich in 1144. According to the libel, which differed slightly, but not substantially, from case to case, the Jews demonstrated their hatred of Christianity by re-enacting the Crucifixion and murdering a Christian child at Easter time. Later, it was also alleged that the Jews used the child's blood to make mat-

The 'blood libel', accusing the Jews of showing their hatred of Christianity by re-enacting the Crucifixion and murdering a Christian child at Easter time, originated in England. The first, in 1144, concerned the case of William of Norwich, whose body was found in a wood on the eve of Easter. This picture, probably created long after the event, shows the so-called crucifixion and two Jews draining the child's blood.

zot (unleavened bread) for the celebration of the Jewish Festival of Passover, which often occurs at the same time as Easter. Despite being condemned by several Popes in the medieval period, the blood libel idea spread throughout Europe and actually continued into the twentieth century. There was a horrifying instance of it in Poland in August 1946, when more than forty Polish Jews were massacred by Polish Christians, who claimed that local Jews had killed a Christian child to use its blood to make matzot.

The facts of the first case which gave rise to all the future blood libel accusations were that on the eve of Easter in 1144, the body of a young skinner's apprentice, named William, was found in a wood near Norwich. It is now believed that the child probably lost consciousness in some kind of fit and his relatives, believing him dead, promptly buried him and, in doing so, finished him off, but immediately rumours were put about that he was a victim of the local Jews, who had enticed him away from his family and, in mockery of the Passion of Jesus, had crucified him after a service in the Synagogue on the second day of Passover.

The version of the story in old English chronicles is very much in the same vein:

> Now we will say something of what befel in King Stephen's time. In his time the Jews of Norwich bought a Christian child before Easter and tortured him with all the tortures wherewith our Lord was tortured, and on Long Friday hanged him on a rood in hatred of our Lord, and afterwards buried him. They thought it would be concealed, but our Lord showed that he was a holy martyr. And the monks took him and buried him honourably in the monastery, and through our Lord he makes wonderful and manifold miracles, and he is hight Saint William.

There was not actually enough evidence against the Jews to justify a trial and the Sheriff of Norwich refused to hold one. Indeed, he permitted local Jews to seek refuge in Norwich Castle. Nevertheless, when they ventured out of it, one of them was killed by the followers of a knight who owed him money and there may have been other similar murders.

However, the removal of young William's body to Norwich Cathedral was a popular move made by the local clergy, who encouraged belief in the libel, probably because the shrine brought many visitors – and consequently funds – to them. Indeed, William of Norwich was venerated as a saint and martyr up to the time of the

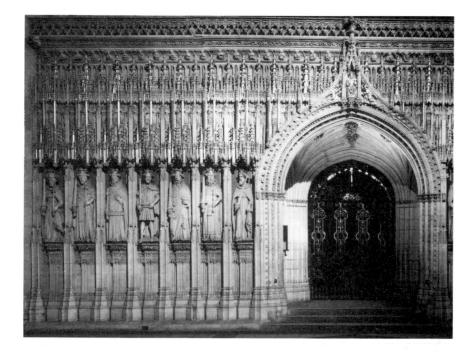

King Stephen did his best to protect the Jews of his realm and issued edicts that neither they nor their property were to be molested or violated in any way. A stone statue of this king decorates the left side of the choir screen in York Minster along with six other English Kings who had much to do with the lives of the Jews in medieval England. They are, from left to right, William I, William II, Henry I, Stephen, Henry II, Richard I and John.

Reformation in the sixteenth century. So prevalent was the blood libel idea that, despite the fact that the Jews were expelled from England in 1290, there appears in the Prioress' Tale in *The Canterbury Tales* (which Chaucer did not write until 1386) ten verses written about another 'blood libel martyr', Little Saint Hugh of Lincoln, whom the Jews were accused and convicted of killing in 1255.

Though it is unlikely that there were *no* verbal and possibly physical attacks on individual Jews or small Jewish communities, there are no records of any other outbreaks of blood libel accusations in England following the episode of William of Norwich. Indeed, only two years later, in 1146, during the Second Crusade, Bernard of Clairvaux actually made a strong appeal against the molestations of the Jews of England, as well as those in Germany and France. Encouraged perhaps by this, King Stephen, a contemporary Jewish chronicler recorded, was apparently inspired to protect the Jews of his realm and issued edicts that neither they nor their property were to be molested or violated in any way.

This *volte face* on the part of the monarch enabled the Anglo-Jewish communities to strengthen and settle more comfortably and considerably more safely and to consolidate themselves, so that, by the next generation, they had reached what was to be the height of their prosperity during the following hundred or so years.

*　*　*　*

What were the day-to-day lives of those early English settlers really like? How – and in what kind of dwellings – did the majority live? What did they wear? How did they follow the strict rules of Judaism, particularly *kashrut* (the ritual dietary laws)? What was the role – and the education – of the Jewish child? What was the pattern of English Jewish life in the early Middle Ages?

Little detailed information is available about the domestic, social or even religious lives of the people of those first eighty-odd years of Jewish settlement in England. Just as there is a paucity of documentary material about the general conditions of all people in the England of the mid-eleventh to the mid-twelfth centuries, so there is a proportionate – or even greater – dearth of information about the intimate lives of England's Jews in the same period.

Two facts that do emerge, however, are that the way of life of those early settlers from Normandy and, somewhat later, from other parts of Western Europe, differed little from life for Jews in the countries they had left and that, because of the introspective and necessarily enclosed nature of Jewish domestic and religious life, it actually changed little throughout Europe (including England) from about the ninth to fourteenth centuries.

It is clear that the early settlers, particularly those who were actually brought over by William of Normandy, were fairly well-to-do by the standards of the time. It was they who, in the following few years, became the prosperous money-lenders on whom the king and the barons depended. Their homes would have been fairly opulent ones. In Norwich, for instance, where there was definitely a settled Jewish community by 1144 – and it is likely that its origins dated from as much as nine years earlier – a rich Jew, Jurnet, owned quite a large stone house. Indeed, it is believed that the first people to build stone houses in England were Jews, anxious to protect themselves both from their debtors and any other 'invaders' who might do them harm. A very small number of those houses, mostly built towards the end of the twelfth century, still survive in Norwich, Lincoln and York.

Probably most Jewish houses, however, would have been built of wood and plaster, as were the homes of many of their fellow citizens. Few of the less wealthy Jews owned their own houses; they rented them from Christian landlords, who would have charged them high rents for that time, because, like most immigrants, they were in no position to argue.

Jurnet's house, some of the walls of which are still standing, would have been similar to those of the fairly wealthy Christian merchants of the town. It had an area of 18 feet, 9 inches by 52 feet,

6 inches, the narrow frontage or gable end was to the street and the house stretched back towards the river. What survives today is thought to be only part of the original stone house, which was owned by one of the most important Jewish families in England in the second half of the twelfth century. What remains of what was thought to be an L-shaped building is an arched and vaulted cellar (probably near street level in the Middle Ages) which formed two rooms separated by a stone wall, with a newel stairway in the north-east angle at the rear, leading to the floor above. There were two narrow windows on the eastern side and an entrance porch at the side of the house. This was clearly the home of a well-to-do family and was similar to a small manor house of the same period. We have far less idea of what the wood and plaster houses would have been like, except that they would have naturally resembled the dwellings in which the Jews' Christian neighbours resided.

Although it is known what kind of homes Jews lived in, it is much more difficult to form a picture of what a so-called 'Jewish street' would have looked like. It is believed that most less well-off Jews, whose occupation was trading, rather than money-lending, lived near markets or in streets where there would be shops and stalls. Few records remain, but a scholarly, though nonetheless imaginative, description of the Jewish quarter of Oxford, about this time or a little later, is given by the historian, Cecil Roth, in his book on the subject:

> We have to imagine a roadway a good deal narrower than the present one – unpaved, fetid, ankle deep in refuse. The Jews' houses were exceptionally well built, some of them being of stone... All probably had gardens or at least strips of land which could have been used for this purpose.... They would have been divided from the street in some cases by shops... In front of these again were the stands of fishmongers, greengrocers, and so on...

Throughout post-biblical Jewish history, Jews have tended to adopt the dress of the lands in which they were living (often for a tragically short time). Sometimes they wore distinguishing marks (though these came later than the period with which this chapter deals) – the conical Jews' hat and the Jew badge showing the tablets of the Ten Commandments, for instance, which were both imposed on Jews by the administration of the European countries in which they lived. But, by and large, any early pictures that survive show Jews in contemporary dress, such as those depicted in two twelfth-century

Most Jews wore the contempory dress of the lands in which they settled, though some, such as the Jew in this picture, tended to wear more traditional garments and sometimes the pointed Jewish hat.

drawings made by monks in Bury (later Bury St Edmunds) in Suffolk. The pictures show two scenes from the New Testament, one of Jesus driving the money-lenders from the Temple in Jerusalem and the other of Jews preparing to stone Jesus in the porch of the Temple. In both pictures, the Jews (including Jesus) are wearing medieval English costume, which suggests that the illustrations reflected the everyday dress of the English Jews whom the monks were used to seeing.

What is certain about the Jewish way of life in eleventh and twelfth century England is that *religiously* it would have been virtually unchanged from before they crossed the English Channel to settle in a new land. Their lives were ruled by the *Halacha* (the Jewish religious law), which told them when and how to pray, how to comport themselves virtuously, how to keep and enforce the dietary laws (known as *kashrut*), how to educate their children – in fact, how to lead a truly religious life. Most of this would have presented few difficulties. Judaism is a religion of the home as well as the synagogue, so, even if they did not have a central place in which to gather, they could continue to follow their religion in family groups.

One factor, however, must have presented problems to them in their early days in England (particularly to those who lived in the centre of the cities, which most of the new settlers did) – and that was the ritual slaughter of animals. There was little doubt that, among each small Jewish community, there would have been at least one man trained as a *shochet* (a ritual slaughterer). The problem was not that the animals could not be killed in the approved way, but whether they could be procured alive in the first place. It is true that there would have been cattle market days even in the centre of London, but meat was expensive and very likely in short supply. Cattle, sheep and goats were the only animals permissible for Jews to eat and it is more than possible that several not so well off families would have had to club together to pay for each animal and, when it had been slaughtered, would have shared it out.

Education has, from earliest days, been a high Jewish priority and the families which settled in England in the eleventh, twelfth and thirteenth centuries carried on the practice of educating not only their sons, but also their daughters (although not perhaps to the same standard of scholarship on the distaff side). Surviving Jewish papers in British archives of this period do not show any signs of illiteracy – indeed, very much the opposite. One of the reasons for this was that even an isolated Jewish family, perhaps living in a country village, would have employed a tutor to teach their children. As a rule, however, Jews were unable to write in Latin characters, but they could usually decipher the meaning of Latin deeds and most could speak French, English and, of course, Hebrew fluently. Cecil Roth tells us that all contracts between Jews (and their own set of rolls recording their transactions) were drawn up in Hebrew, in which tongue they usually, when necessary, endorsed Latin deeds. It is likely, however, that relatively few of them could write literately in French or English and they mostly used Hebrew characters instead.

At the end of the twelfth century, it is recorded that Morell, a Jew of Norfolk (who probably lived in Norwich), died leaving books. So important were they to his heirs that his two daughters and other heirs paid 100 shillings to have their share of those books. Because Jewish children were often betrothed at birth and married as soon as the boys reached puberty, bridegrooms often needed to continue their education after the wedding – especially if they were to become efficient businessmen. This is evident in a twelfth century betrothal contract between members of two middle class Jewish families in Norwich, which stipulated that the father-in-law must engage a teacher for the bridegroom for a year after the marriage took place.

Local centres which added to the Jews' sense of security and also aided their administration in those early years of settlement – and, indeed, until almost the day when they were eventually expelled from Britain at the end of the thirteenth century – were the castles.

Castles, which were local centres in medieval England, added to the Jews' sense of security and also aided their administration. Clifford's Tower, which still stands in York, was built somewhat later, but is similar to the style of many castles of those days.

There were three categories of castles: those which William the Conqueror had built and directly controlled; those which he had built, but placed under the jurisdiction of his barons whom he allowed to live in them; and many others built by barons and others with royal consent. The castles, both royal and otherwise, impinged on the lives of medieval Jews in certainly three and possibly four ways. The castle was a refuge in time of trouble; it was the administrative centre from which their lives were governed; and it was often a prison in which they were detained. Moreover, a 'private' castle – one owned by a private person, possibly a member of the nobility, but not the king – might well be the residence of a valuable client and this, apart from the first two reasons for living close to castles, might well have attracted Jews to settle near the private variety. During the twelfth century, castles were springing up in many English towns and it was certainly not accidental that the Jewish quarters in those towns were sited near enough to local castles, of one kind or another, for Jews in fear or danger of local persecution to take shelter in them.

The situation of England's Jews at the end of King Stephen's reign was therefore one that appeared to offer hope of permanent settlement and peaceful, if financially expensive, progress. Peace during the thirty-five year reign of the next king they did achieve, but it was to be the lull before a storm of persecution.

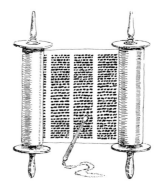

CHAPTER TWO
Prosperity and After

The years leading up to the final expulsion of the Jews from Britain were to be full of drama and tragedy for them, with distressingly regular blood libel accusations in London and other cities and towns in which, by now, there were sizeable Jewish communities. Nevertheless, the long reign of King Henry II, 1154 to 1189, was paradoxically also a time of peace for the Jewish community, as, indeed, it was for the whole country.

Like his predecessors, however, the king not only fined the Jews, he also taxed them heavily, but, at the same time, he protected and even encouraged them. For instance, he both confirmed and extended the charter of protection that his grandfather, Henry I, had given them, by formally granting the Jews of England the privilege of internal jurisdiction in accordance with their Talmudic Law, except in cases of offence against public order. In fact, they still had to observe that 'the law of the land was the law' and that it would in civil matters therefore supersede the Jewish law. That rule has been observed by Jews in Britain (and, indeed, throughout Europe and wherever else in the world they live) ever since.

Jews could now hold property as tenants-in-chief of the Crown, though they were not allowed to discharge their financial obligations, as did other Englishmen, by doing military service. They were, however, treated with great tolerance by most churchmen who, though there were laws forbidding such transactions, frequently borrowed money from Jewish financiers by pledging as security holy plate and vessels used in divine worship and even relics of saints! Perhaps in gratitude for the great sums the Church had taken from the Jews at this time, Jewish womenfolk and children were allowed to take shelter in the monasteries for safety from the fairly frequent outbursts of local persecution. Furthermore, Jews were also allowed to keep their valuable business deeds in the cathedral treasuries.

Not only that. In Canterbury and Bury St Edmunds, they even took part – indeed, took sides – in monastic politics and actually prayed in their synagogues for the success of the candidate they favoured. Surprisingly enough, perhaps, Jews were familiar figures in St Paul's Cathedral, because they often went there in search of their debtors. Many Jews still spoke Norman French and it is recorded that they often travelled with Christian clerics and talked to them in that language – often badly.

The king's and the Church's tolerant treatment of the Jews aroused widespread jealousy among some members of the gentile population, who often exaggerated their descriptions of Jewish behaviour. One bitter contemporary chronicler, William of Newburgh, wrote: 'By an absurd arrangement, they were happy and renowned far more than the Christians, and swelling very impudently against Christ through their good fortune, did much injury to Christians'.

At the beginning of Henry II's reign, according to official Treasury records, Jews were settled not only in London, but also in Norwich, Winchester, Cambridge, Northampton, Oxford, Gloucester, Lincoln, Thetford (Norfolk), Bury (presumably Bury St Edmunds), Bedford, Devizes, Ipswich, Canterbury, Hereford, Dunstable, Chichester, Newport (presumably in Monmouthshire) and in some smaller places.

One of the most famous Jews of the twelfth century – and reputed to be the richest man in England at that time – was Aaron of Lincoln. He was born in 1125, and, by the time he died in 1186, he had assisted financially in the construction of no fewer than nine of the Cistercian monasteries of England, in addition to Lincoln and Peterborough Cathedrals and the important St Albans Abbey. As the country's most prosperous and successful money-lender, Aaron was not only in demand for financial assistance to the Crown, he was the main source of loans for the successful completion of any major undertaking. Indeed, his financial operations extended to twenty-five of Britain's counties and he maintained agents in nineteen of them.

It was not until Aaron was forty-one that his financial transactions were first mentioned officially. In common with other Jewish financiers, he made fairly regular loans to the king on the security of local taxation and it was recorded in 1166 that these amounted to £600. He also, of course, lent money to many private individuals on such security as corn, estates, houses and even armour. As already stated, his assistance in the construction of St Albans Abbey was so vital that he used to boast – not very tactfully – that he had made the great window in the church and prepared a home for the saint when he had been without one. It is proof of the power at that time of the possession of money in general, and Aaron's in particular, that he could make an abrasive statement such as this in regard to the Christian Church and go unpunished.

Because the bishopric of Lincoln Minster had fallen into great financial difficulties early in Henry II's reign, Bishop Chesney had borrowed money from Aaron pledging some of the church ornaments. After that bishop's death, his archdeacon succeeded him in 1173 and this new bishop, perhaps because he was the king's natural son, Godfrey, made sure that one of the first things *he* did was to redeem the ornaments from Aaron!

For a long time, Aaron and his family were believed to have lived in one of Lincoln's earliest stone houses (situated on Steep Hill) which is still standing and which was possibly owned by a Jew. J.W.F. Hill, in *Medieval Lincoln*, debunks that theory, which, he says, arose by misunderstanding only towards the end of the nineteenth century. He points out that, according to a list of escheats, taken in 1226–8, (escheats were the lapsed properties of owners who died intestate and without heirs, which were legally confiscated by the king or the lord of the manor), the house (*domus*) of Aaron the Jew in the Bail [now known as Bailgate] was worth 6s. yearly. '... it had escheated to the king and was held by Nicholaa de Haya the constable for the purposes of the castle (*occasione castri*). This modest annual value does not point to a large house, and indeed *domus* may mean only an office or room.' There are, Mr Hill points out, several references to Aaron in the Hundred Rolls. One says that Aaron the Jew 'encroached on the king's wall', another that land 'formerly of Aaron the rich on the west side of the gate of the Bail had escheated and was worth 40s. yearly' and a third 'that all the houses situate within the old gate of the Bail on the west side had escheated from Aaron the rich to the king, extending from opposite the castle gate to the castle ditch.' It is clear that a large part of Aaron's business was in Lincolnshire and that he made Lincoln his headquarters, but it is Mr Hill's view that, in later years, he may have found it necessary to spend much of his time in London. He adds: 'The heavy fine imposed on him in the London and Middlesex Exchequer accounts points to this conclusion and it is to be noted that he had a house in Lothbury, near Walbrook.' From this detailed research, it seems likely that Aaron's family home was in Bailgate. Little – indeed, almost nothing – is known about his family life, although he certainly had one son, Samuel, who was later known as Samuel Molkin.

Immediately after Aaron's death, because he was probably the country's wealthiest person, King Henry exercised his legal right

The Jew's House in Steep Hill, Lincoln, in which Aaron of Lincoln, reputed to be the richest man in England in the middle of the twelfth century, was originally thought to have lived with his family. Although it is one of Lincoln's earliest stone houses and it is likely it was owned by another Jew, it is now thought that Aaron lived in the Bail, now known as Bailgate.

and declared all Aaron's property forfeit to the Crown. A year later, the king sent Aaron's bullion and other treasure to France to be used to help finance the war over Normandy against the French king, Philip Augustus. But the ship sank with all hands – and the king's booty. Nevertheless, bills of credit of £15,000 of Aaron's money were still in the king's coffers – equivalent to three-quarters of the royal income for a year! This vast sum was owed by some 430 people living up and down the country and, to collect the outstanding debts, a special branch of the Exchequer had to be created. It was called *Scaccarium Aronis* and run by two treasurers and two clerks. Even with those four officials working full time, the sorting out of debts due to the Crown took nearly five years.

More and more Jews were now arriving from Europe, not perhaps in large numbers, but significant enough for them to be recorded in the 1186 roll of the London Jewish community that there were Jews from both France and Spain. In addition, some Jews from Paris and elsewhere in France had settled in York and some from Italy (known as Lombard) in Lincoln, Nottingham and Winchester. There was even one Jewish immigrant noted as coming from Russia.

By the close of Henry II's reign, some three hundred Jewish businessmen and householders were scattered about the country, all of them prosperous enough to make quite sizeable contributions to the Royal Exchequer.

A year before Henry's death, when he was planning to finance a crusade to the Holy Land to fight against the Mohammedan 'infidel', Saladin, the first English tax on personal property, appropriately called the Saladin Tithe, was ruthlessly levied throughout the kingdom. This hit the Jews particularly hard, because their share of the tax was not a tenth of their property, as it was for their Christian neighbours; it was a quarter. This tax on the Jews was expected to bring in £60,000, though only £70,000 was expected from the levy on all the other inhabitants of Britain. Sixty thousand pounds was a vast sum in that day – equivalent to about twelve million pounds today – and its collection was not, in fact, completed by the time the king died.

Henry II was succeeded by his son, Richard I – the Richard who is reputed to have said that he would sell London to finance the crusades, if he could find someone rich enough to buy it! Pledging himself to go on the crusade that had been his father's dream, Richard, the so-called Lionheart, started his reign full of 'Christian' zeal and a determination to raise the money to pay for his holy war – one way or another. It was inevitable that, as enthusiasm for the

At the start of his reign, King Richard I pledged himself to go on the Crusade which his father, Henry II, had failed to lead. The enthusiasm that spread through England for the Crusade also increased the feeling against, and persecution of, the Jews.

crusade spread through England among all classes, the feeling against the Jews would increase. The fact that a large number of them were still wealthy, despite the heavy taxes extorted from them in the previous reign, inflamed people more and more against them. Jealousy of the Jews grew, and, with it, the conviction that they, too, were infidels, every bit as dangerous to the Christian cause as the Mohammedans.

A relatively trivial episode at Richard's coronation on 3 September 1189, set off a horrific massacre of a number of London's Jews. An order had been given that no woman and no Jew should be admitted to the long coronation ceremony, but, nevertheless, on the afternoon of the coronation day, a deputation representing the kingdom's Jewish community approached the gateway of Westminster Hall, bearing gifts for the king – probably in the hope of a renewal of the charter of privileges originally given to them by Henry I. Then one or two members of the deputation quietly slipped in among the crowds, hoping to glimpse the magnificent scene. Here is what followed, reported by that learned canon from Yorkshire's Newburgh Priory, though rather biased observer, William of Newburgh, in his contemporary work *Historia Rerum Anglicanarum*:

Richard then the only King thus named for a century, was hallowed to King at London and solemnly crowned by Baldwin, archbishop of Canterbury, on September 3. There had come together for the solemn anointing of the Christian prince from all quarters of England, not alone Christian nobles, but likewise the chiefs of the Jews. For these enemies of truth fearing that the good luck they had under the former King might be less favourable to them under the new, brought first fruits most decorous and honourable, and hoped to find favour equal to the multitude of their gifts. But he, either because he was less favourable to them than his father, or having some premonition, a certain superstitious foreboding about the plans of certain persons, by an edict, it is said, forbade them entry either into the church where he was being crowned or to the palace where he was banqueting after the coronation. Now it happened that while he was at the repast with all the assembly of nobles, the people watching round the palace began rioting. Some Jews mixed among the crowd by this means entered the royal doors. Whereat a Christian being, it is said, indignant, struck a Jew with his palm and so drove him away from the entrance of the door, thus recalling the King's edict. And many being excited by this sample drove away the Jews with insults, and a tumult arising a disorderly crowd came up and believing the King had commanded such treatment, as if relying on the authority of the King, rushed together upon the crowd of Jews waiting at the palace gates. And at first indeed they struck them with the fist but afterwards being more savagely enraged they brought sticks and stones. Then the Jews began to flee, some during their flight being beaten unto death or some of them even being crushed, perished. Now there had come thither with the rest two noble Jews of York, viz., Joce and Benedict, of whom the first escaped, but the other was caught as he fled but tardily from the strokes laid upon him: in order to escape death, he was compelled to confess Christ and being led in to the Church was baptised on the spot. In the meantime a pleasing rumour spread with incredible rapidity through all London, namely that the King had ordered all the Jews to be exterminated. And soon a huge mob of disorderly persons both from the city as well as those of whom the ceremony of the hallowing of the King had attracted from the provinces, run up all armed, and breathing slaughter and spoil against the people of God's judgement hated by all. Then the Jewish citizens, of whom a multitude is known to dwell in London, together with those who had flocked together from all parts withdrew into their own houses. These houses were surrounded by the roaring people, and were stoutly besieged from 9 o'clock till sunset, and as they could not be broken into owing to their strong build and because the madmen had not tools, fire was thrown on the [thatched] roof, and a terrible fire quickly broke out which was fatal to the Jews as they strove [to put it out] and offered the aid of light to the raging Christians at their night work. And the fire kindled against the Jews did not hurt them alone but likewise seized hold of the neighbouring houses of Christians. You might see all of a sudden the best known places of the city wretchedly alight through fires of citizens acting as if they had been enemies. But the Jews were either roasted in their own houses or if they came out of them were received with swords. Much blood was shed in a brief space. But soon the lust after booty burning higher brought on a repletion of slaughter and avarice got the better of cruelty. Thereupon leaving the butchery, their greedy rage betook itself to stripping the houses and snatching their riches. But this in turn made Christians oppose Christians, for each envied what the other may have seized, and in the eagerness of plunder the rivalry of avarice forgetting all natural ties spared neither friend or comrades.

The new King, however, being of a great and fierce spirit, was indignant and grieved that such things should have occurred at the ceremony of his coronation, and the beginning of his reign. He was angry, and yet perplexed to know what was to be done in the matter. To pass over such a breach of the royal majesty without any example, and to dismiss it unavenged, seemed unworthy of a King and harmful to the state, since passing over such an atrocity would encourage bold and wicked persons to attempt similar misdeeds in confidence of being able to do so with impunity. But on the other hand to exercise the rigour of the royal displeasure against such a multitude of criminals was plainly impossible. For except the nobles banqueting with the King, whose number was such that the breadth of the royal palace seemed narrow, hatred of the Jews and the temptation to plunder had attracted to the perpetration of the deed above-mentioned almost the whole body of the citizens, and almost all the families of the nobles who had come up with the nobles themselves to the ceremony of the King's coronation. He had, therefore to dissemble where vengeance was impossible. God doubtless arranging that those who had stood forth as the ministers of Divine vengeance against blaspheming infidels should not suffer human justice on that account. For the reasons of the heavenly example demanded that those blasphemers who in the time of the preceding reign had been too stiff-necked and haughty towards Christians should be humbled at the beginning of its successor. But the prince guaranteed peace to the Jews by an edict after the slaughter; but as will be narrated in its place, they did not enjoy this long, heaven's judgement demanding that the pride of the blaspheming people should be chastised most severely.

As William of Newburgh stated, the king was horrified when he heard what had happened and he immediately sent his justiciar, Ranulph de Glanville, to stop the carnage, but Ranulph was unsuccessful. It was not thought possible to take proceedings against all those who had taken part in the persecution, but some of the ringleaders were arrested and three were hanged – one for robbing a Christian and two because the fire they lit burned down a house owned by a Christian! Letters were also sent from the king to all parts of his kingdom ordering that the Jews should be left in peace.

The day after the coronation, the king sent for Benedict of York, who had allowed himself to be baptised, and Benedict admitted that he had agreed to adopt Christianity only to escape death. Richard asked the Archbishop of Canterbury how he should deal with Benedict and William of Newburgh reported that the Archbishop replied contemptuously: 'If he will not serve God, let him serve the devil'. So Benedict was allowed to return to York without punishment, but his freedom was short-lived, because he died from the wounds he had sustained during the coronation on his way back from London to York.

Whether the news of the affair in London reaching other towns helped to start up the spate of Jew baiting, which followed a few months after the king's coronation, is not clear. The igniting spark was certainly the result of the preparations in England for the crusade. In December, 1189, Richard travelled to France and remained there for six months, gathering his forces for the Third Crusade. At the same time, in almost every English town, crusading detachments were assembling in readiness to go overseas and it is certain that many of them were the ringleaders in the Jewish persecution at the time, using the excuse that it was wrong that Jewish infidels should stay at home and enjoy their ill-gotten gains while the 'Soldiers of the Cross' were risking their lives fighting the Mohammedan infidels overseas.

Early in February, 1190, the first outbreak of anti-Jewish violence took place in the port of Lynn (later King's Lynn) in Norfolk. Here, the story goes, a recent Christian convert from Judaism took refuge from the insults of his former co-religionists in a local church. (It was Cecil Roth's opinion – and is also the writer's – that this is an unlikely story, because, as Roth says, 'the medieval Jew may not always have been tolerant, but experience had taught him to be circumspect!') Whether the story was true or not, an uproar swiftly turned into a riot, led probably by foreign sailors who were in the port. The Jewish community of Lynn was almost exterminated as Jewish houses were attacked and pillaged. Most of the families in the houses were butchered or burned in the flames, which also destroyed quite a large part of what cannot have been a very big town.

Norwich was the principal town in the eastern counties and the news of the massacre in Lynn reached there within a day or two. On 6 February, a similar attack on a Jewish community commenced there, though many of Norwich's Jews, fearing what was coming, had already taken refuge in the royal castle. It is not known how many members of the community died in this uprising, but certainly all those Jews who were found in their own houses were butchered. Among those who survived were members of the wealthy Jurnet family. Not only was this family the foremost Jewish family in Norwich, it was, as already stated, one of the most outstanding Jewish families in England between 1170 and 1240.

Jurnet, whose Hebrew name was Eliab, was the second generation of his family. By the 1160s, he had become a very successful national financier and money-lender. He and his wife, Muriel, had a son, Isaac, who eventually became a partner in his father's business. Jurnet had married Muriel (or Miryld), a Christian heiress, in 1170 and the story of what happened, the clues to which were first discovered in 1745 by a Christian minister, the Reverend Francis Blomefield, was recounted in some detail by a Jewish minister, the Rev. Michael Adler, in *The Jews of Medieval England*.

> Few marriages created quite such a stir in English Jewry as when Jurnet (Jacob), the son of Moses of Norwich, about the year 1170 married Miryld (Muriel), the heiress of Sir Humphrey de Herlham, and she became a Jewess. This is the only example known in medieval records of the admission of a Christian woman to the faith. As a result of her apostasy, Muriel was deprived of all her lands, and her daring husband was mulcted in the sum of 6,000 marks (equal in modern value to £120,000). Their romantic marriage reduced them to utter poverty, and they left England for a few years. As Jurnet had been unable to meet the extortionate royal demands, his marriage fine was levied upon the whole Jewish community, which must have been none too happy at the entry of the high-born convert into the fold of Israel. Later on, the circumstances of the family improved, and their son Isaac and their daughter Margaret both became well-known financiers.

There are doubts of the authenticity of this story in the mind of another historian, H.G. Richardson, who says in *The English Jewry under Angevin Kings* that a marriage between a Christian and Jew in the Middle Ages seemed to be out of the question and that such a marriage would have been abhorrent both to the Church and the Jewish community. In addition, he points out, Justinian's Code in Roman law forbade such marriages. It was more than possible that an unmarried Jew who converted to Christianity might make a Christian marriage, but there is no suggestion that Jurnet converted. The third possibility, he concludes, is that a Christian could marry a Jew if he or she became a proselyte. Indeed, the firm implication has always been that Muriel *did* convert to Judaism before she married Jurnet. Certainly, despite the rather bitter fact that members of the Jewish community had to pay Jurnet's punishment fine, he and his descendants were always regarded as Jewish by their co-religionists.

Persecution is contagious and, even in those days of very slow communication, it spread, in greater or lesser degree, throughout East Anglia. Within a month of the Norwich uprising, a large number of people, including some crusaders, assembled in Stamford for the annual Lent fair. William of Newburgh is, once again, the reporter and commentator:

> They were indignant that the enemies of the cross of Christ who dwelt there should possess so much when they had not enough for the expenses of so great a journey. They considered they ought to extort from them as unjust possessions whatever they could apply to the necessary uses of the pilgrimage they had undertaken. Considering, therefore, that they could be doing honour to Christ if they attacked his enemies, whose goods they were longing for, they boldly rushed upon them, nobody either of the inhabitants of the place or of those who had come to the fair opposing such daring persons and some even helping them. Some of the Jews were slain, but the rest escaped with some difficulty by retreating to the Castle. Their homes were pillaged and a great quantity of money captured....

In Lincoln, in the same month, William of Newburgh further tells us, the Jews fearing that a similar thing could happen to them and

> ... rendered more cautious by knowing the fate or the terror of their fellows in various places, had betaken themselves betimes with their money to the fortified part of the town. And so nothing much being done, though much investigation was carried on by the royal officials, that vain rising quickly subsided.

There were probably further attacks in Colchester, Thetford and Ospringe and perhaps some other nearby towns, because a contemporary chronicler reported that it was only at Winchester 'thanks to the phlegmatic nature of the citizens, that the Jews were unscathed'. (It is a sad fact, however, that the respite for Winchester's Jews lasted for only two years and then the city was the scene of a ritual murder accusation with subsequent tragic results).

But the worst tragedy and the most unforgettable – was yet to come. York's Christians had become increasingly jealous and fearful of the well-established Jewish community there – a settlement which, although it was first recorded in 1130, had only in latter years become really prosperous. The citizens of York were particularly suspicious of two very wealthy Jews, Benedict and Joce, both usurers. This was the same Benedict who had been allowed to return to York after forswearing his Christian conversion during the king's coronation, but who died on the journey home. Joce, however, survived and, says William, '...as the King after the London riot issued a decree for the protection of the Jews, he, together with the rest of the Jews throughout England, continued to act confidently according to their old ways'.

As the tide of Jewish persecution spread throughout eastern England, the people of York saw their opportunity to rid the city, once and for all, of the hated race. What happened on Friday, 16 March 1190 (the eve of the Great Sabbath before the important Jewish festival of Passover) was graphically – and with considerably less bias than usual – described by William of Newburgh shortly after it happened.

But the men of York were restrained neither by fear of the hot-tempered King nor the vigour of the laws, nor by feelings of humanity, from satiating their fury with the total ruin of their perfidious fellow-citizens and from rooting out the whole race in their city. And as this was a very remarkable occurrence, it ought to be transmitted to posterity at greater length. Of the Jews of York, as we said, the foremost were Benedict and Joce, men of great riches and great usurers. Now they had built in the middle of the city at very great expense large houses, like royal palaces, and there they dwelt like two princes of their own people and tyrants of the Christians, behaving with almost royal state and pomp and exercising harsh tyranny against those whom they oppressed with their usuries. And when they were at London at the solemnity of the anointing of the King, Benedict, as we mentioned above, by the judgement of God, met with a most wretched end and might be called Maledict. But Joce, escaping with difficulty on that occasion, returned to York, and as the King after the London riot issued a decree for the protection of the Jews, he, together with the rest of the Jews throughout England, continued to act confidently according to their old ways. But when the King had established himself across the sea many of the province of York plotted against the Jews, not being able to suffer their opulence when they themselves were in need, and without any scruple of Christian conscience thirsting for the blood of infidels from greed for booty.

The leaders of the plot against the Jews were some of the nobles who were in debt to the Jewish money-lenders for very large sums. Some, indeed, had been forced to forfeit their estates in payment of these debts, some were now greatly impoverished and a number were preparing to start out on the crusades, which would get them safely away from the scene of their crimes. They were led by Richard Malebisse, whose surname appropriately meant 'evil beast'. Malebisse and his followers waited until one stormy night and then set fire to quite a large number of buildings in the city; thus making sure that their Christian fellow citizens were too occupied with their own troubles to worry about what was happening to their Jewish neighbours.

'There was nothing, therefore, in the way of the robbers,' William of Newburgh explains,

> and an armed band of the conspirators, with great violence and tools prepared for the purpose, burst into the house of the before-mentioned Benedict, who had miserably died at London as mentioned above. There his widow and children with many others dwelt; all of these who were in it were slain and the roof put on fire. And while the fire gloomily increased in strength, the robbers seized their booty and left the burning house, and by help of the darkness retired unobserved and heavy laden. The Jews, and especially their leader Joce, in consternation at this misdeed having begged the assistance of the Warden of the royal castle, carried into it huge weights of their monies equal to royal treasures, and took more vigilant guard of the rest at their houses. But after a few days these nocturnal thieves returned with greater confidence and boldness and many joined them, they boldly besieged Joce's house which rivalled a noble citadel in the scale and stoutness of its construction. At length they captured and pillaged it, and then set it on fire after having removed by sword or fire all those whom an unlucky chance had kept in it. For Joce a little before had wisely anticipated this mischance and had removed with his wife and children into the Castle, and the rest of the Jews did the same, only a few remaining outside as victims.

After the thieves had left at daybreak with their valuable spoils from what remained of Joce's house, the mob took over and completed the destruction of the Jewish homes and contents that had survived the fire. Soon, those who hated the Jews most, knowing that they would not be punished, began, as William of Newburgh reports, 'to rage against them openly and with abundant license'. Furthermore, any Jew who had not gained the sanctuary of the castle was captured by the mob and offered the alternatives of instant baptism or death. Some, to save their lives, were baptised and appeared to accept Christianity. Those who refused baptism were cruelly put to death.

It might seem that those who had managed to reach the sanctuary of the castle would be safe, but it was not to be. William of Newburgh continues the gruesome story:

But the warden of the castle having gone out on some business, when he wished to return was not re-admitted by the trembling multitude, uncertain in whom to trust and fearing that perchance his fidelity to them was tottering, and that being bribed he was about to give up to their enemies those whom he should protect. But he immediately went to the sheriff of the county who happened to be at York with a large body of the county soldiers, and complained to him that the Jews had cheated him out of the castle entrusted to him. The sheriff became indignant and raged against the Jews. The leaders of the conspiracy fanned his fury alleging that the timid precaution of those poor wretches was an insolent seizure of the royal castle and would cause injury to our Lord, the King. And when many declared that such traitors were to be got at by some means or another, and the royal castle taken out of their hands, the sheriff ordered the people to be summoned and the castle to be besieged. The irrevocable word went forth, the zeal of the Christian folk was inflamed, immense masses of armed men both from the town and the country were clustered round the citadel. Then the sheriff struck with regret at his order tried in vain to recall it and wished to prohibit the siege of the castle. But he could by no influence of reason or authority keep back their inflamed minds from carrying out what they had begun. It is true the nobles of the city and the more weighty citizens fearing the danger of a royal movement cautiously declined such a great transgression. But the whole of the workpeople and all the youth of the town and a large number of the country folk, together with soldiers not a few, came with such alacrity and joined in the cruel business as if each man was seeking his own gain. And there were not lacking many clergymen, among whom a certain hermit seemed more vehement than the rest.

Whether, as William of Newburgh stated, the populace of York 'thought they would be doing a great act of devotion to God' or whether they were merely actuated by hatred and jealousy, the people brought uninhibited enthusiasm to the task of besieging the castle and, as the Jews had little food to sustain themselves in Clifford's Tower, nor enough weapons to protect themselves, they were, indeed, in a sorry plight.

The tower was besieged for several days and then, as William of Newburgh says: '... the machines which had been prepared for the purpose were brought into position.' What these siege machines actually were is not clear, either from William of Newburgh's account or that of Roger of Howden, another contemporary commentator. It is probable that one was a battering ram to break down the door of the castle and that there were also stone-throwing catapaults or ballistas, a rock from which may well have caused the death of the vicious hermit who, while urging on the crowd, was so imbued with his self-appointed task of 'crushing Christ's enemies' that he got in the way of a missile that was fired at the castle and bounced off. A third kind of siege machine could have been a siege tower, which would have been drawn up beside the castle walls so that an attack could have been made over the turrets at the top by means of a form of gangplank.

Once these 'machines' were in position, the taking of the tower became certain and, as William of Newburgh continues.

It was no longer doubtful that the fatal hour was nearing for the besieged. On the following night the besiegers were quiet,

More than 150 of York's Jews took refuge in Clifford's Tower to avoid being murdered by their fellow citizens. the tower was besieged for several days and then 'siege machines' which had been prepared for that purpose were brought into position. The machines, which were to be used to break into the tower would probably have looked like those pictured here. A battering ram is seen on the left, a form of ballista (a catapult) is in the centre and a siege tower to enable the walls to be scaled is on the right.

rejoicing in the certainty of their approaching victory. But the Jews were brave, and braced up by their very despair, had little rest, discussing what they should do in such an extremity. Now there was a certain old man, a most famous Doctor of the Law, according to the letter that kills, who, it is said had come from parts beyond the sea to teach the English Jews. He was honoured by all and was obeyed by all as if he had been one of the prophets. When, therefore, he was asked his advice on that occasion, he replied, 'God to whom none shall say 'Why dost Thou so? (Eccles. viii. 4, Dan. iv. 35), orders us to die now for the Law. And behold our death is at the door. Unless, perchance, which God forbid, you think of deserting the sacred Law for this brief space of life, and choose a fate harder than any death to honest and manly minds, namely to live as apostates at the mercy of impious enemies in the deepest dishonour. Since then we ought to prefer a most glorious death to a very dishonest life, we ought to select the easiest and most honourable form of death. For if we fall into the hands of the enemy, we shall die at their will and amidst their jeers. And so since the life which the Creator gave us, He now demands back from us, let us willingly and devoutly render it up to Him with our own hands and let us not await the help of hostile cruelty by giving up what He demands. For many of our people in different times of tribulation are known to have done the same, preferring a form of choice most honourable for us.' When he had said this very many of them embraced his fatal advice, but to many his word seemed a hard one. Then the elder says, 'Let those whom this good and pious plan pleaseth not, seat themselves apart from this holy assembly, for to us this life on earth is now thought nothing of through our love of the Law of our fathers.' Very many of them therefore withdrew, preferring rather to try the clemency of their enemies than perish in this way with their friends. Soon at the advice of this mad elder fire consumed their richest garments in the sight of all lest the enemy should be made rich by their wealth, they passed through the fire their most precious vessels and everything they could, by their dainty envy they condemned these things to a disgraceful resting place. When this was done and fire being set to the roof which fed upon the more solid materials while the horrid deed was being done and putting in danger the lives of those who from love of life had separated themselves from them, they prepared their throats for sacrifice. At the order of that inveterate [author] of wicked days that those men whose courage was most steady should take the lives of their wives and pledges, the famous Joce cuts the throat of Anna, his dear wife, with a sharp knife, and did not spare his own sons. And when this had been done by the other men, that wretched elder cut Joce's throat so that he might be more honoured than the rest. All of them thus slain together with the author of their error, the fire which had been lighted by them before their death, as we have mentioned, began to burst out in the interior of the tower. Those who had chosen to live resisted as much as they could the fire lit by their own friends lest they too should die with them though unwillingly, betaking themselves to the extremity of the tower where they were least burnt.

At daybreak on the Saturday, the crowd of people who had gathered to storm the castle found only the pathetic remnants of the Jews at the gates, reporting, with tears in their eyes, the self-destruction of the rest during the past night. They even threw the bodies down from the walls to prove their words and, as they did so, they called out: 'Behold the bodies of the wretched men who were guilty of their own death with wicked fury and when we refused to do the same, but preferred to try Christian clemency, they set fire to the interior of this tower so that they might burn us alive.'

Christian clemency, despite the avowals from the surviving Jews that they wished to embrace the Christian faith, was shown them immediately by the evil Richard Malebisse and his followers, who promised them baptism, so that they left the safety of the castle, and then butchered them all as they emerged.

By now, the environs of the castle were strewn with bodies and blood, but, leaving them there, Malebisse and his henchmen went immediately to the cathedral and threateningly demanded all the records of the Christians' debts to the Jewish money-lenders held there. The terrified officials handed them over and the conspirators immediately set fire to the records in the middle of the cathedral.

'Which being done' William of Newburgh concludes, 'those of the conspirators who had taken the cross went on their proposed journey before any inquest; but the rest remained in the country in fear of an inquiry. Such were the tidings that happened at York at the time of the Lord's passion, that is the day before Palm Sunday 17 March 1190.'

A special messenger was dispatched to the king in France on Easter Monday carrying the news of what had happened at York three days earlier. The king and his advisors were both furious and horrified. Not only was any breach of the peace forbidden, but the Jews had been taken into the royal protection only a few months earlier. What was probably most important to them, however, was that the Royal Exchequer would certainly lose heavily, both by the impoverishment of those Jews who had survived and by the despoiling of those who had perished, at least part of whose property would have been forfeit to the Crown on their deaths.

The Bishop of Ely, William Longchamp, who was also Chancellor and Co-Justiciar of England, was with the king when the bad news was received. He was returning to England the following day and the king instructed him to take vigorous proceedings against the culprits as soon as he landed. Accordingly, at the beginning of May, the bishop sent his brother, Osbert, to York with an armed force to stamp out any remnants of disorder, following himself on about 3 May to administer justice.

Faced with possible retribution, the ringleaders, led by Richard Malebisse, fled – some to Scotland, some to other remote parts of the country and some to the Continent to join the crusade. The remaining prominent citizens of York, now terrified, categorically denied being implicated in what had happened to their Jewish neighbours. What was more, William of Newburgh tells us, they stressed that 'with slender resources they could not prevent the unbridled attack of an undisciplined mob'. Nevertheless, Bishop Longchamp imposed fines on about fifty of the city's burghers, the estates of some of the fugitive barons were confiscated (though later restored to them) and some hostages for good conduct were sent in custody to Northampton. In addition, the sheriff was removed from office and replaced by Longchamp's own brother. But the main perpetrators of the outrage, 'the promiscuous and numberless mob, whose untrained zeal had been the principal cause of the deed', had quickly melted away and could not be brought to justice. Perhaps because it was impossible to pinpoint the main culprits, not one execution for murder took place, but nevertheless, very few physical crimes against the Jews in medieval times had been treated and dealt with so drastically. Longchamp then left York and proceeded with 'sixty pairs of fetters' to Lincoln to punish those who had persecuted the Jews there. It is recorded that in Lincoln he found no fewer than eighty miscreants, all of whom were fined.

Clifford's Tower, the fortress of the royal castle where the mass suicide took place, which was built of wood, was almost completely destroyed and more than £200 was spent during the next twelve months to restore it. The restored wooden tower was demolished and rebuilt in stone in the middle of the thirteenth century along with the rest of the castle, on the site of the original one. It still stands in the grounds of York's Castle Museum. Today, visitors will find a memorial plaque (the cost of which was defrayed by both Jews and Christians) by the tower, put there by the City of

Britain's Chief Rabbi, Dr (now Lord) Immanuel Jakobovits (centre left) and the Archbishop of York, Dr Stuart Blanch (centre right) watch Dr Aubrey Newman, President of the Jewish Historical Society of England, unveil a plaque on 31 October 1978 at the foot of Clifford's Tower, which stands in the grounds of York's Castle Museum. The plaque (enlarged here) records the story of the massacre of the Jews in 1190 and ends with a quotation in Hebrew from the Book of Isaiah, which means: 'They ascribe glory to the Lord and His praise in the Isles.'

On the night of Friday 16 March 1190 some 150 Jews and Jewesses of York having sought protection in the Royal Castle on this site from a mob incited by Richard Malebisse and others chose to die at each other's hands rather than renounce their faith

שימו לד כבוד ותהלתו באיים

ISAIAH XLII 12

York, and unveiled on 31 October 1978, in the presence of Britain's Chief Rabbi, Dr (now Lord) Immanuel Jakobovits, and by Dr Stuart Blanch, then Archbishop of York. This plaque records publicly, for the first time, the fact of the massacre in 1190.

'On the night of Friday 16th March 1190 some 150 Jews and Jewesses of York having sought protection in the royal castle on this site from a mob incited by Richard Malebisse and others chose to die at each other's hands rather than renounce their faith.'

Also on the plaque is a quotation in Hebrew from the prophet Isaiah: 'They ascribe glory to the Lord and His praise in the Isles.' While this plaque and ceremony certainly did not redress the balance, it put on visual record the admission by the City of York of one of the worst incidents of Jewish persecution in medieval England.

King Richard was now immersed in the final preparations for his crusade, but, on his behalf, Bishop Longchamp took steps to ensure that the king's authority with regard to the Jews should not be flouted again. On 22 March 1190, a charter was issued 'by which many liberties are granted and confirmed to the Jews.'

The charter confirmed 'to Ysaac, son of Rabbi Joce, and his sons and their men, all their customs and liberties just as the Lord King Henry, our father, granted and by his charter confirmed to the Jews of England and Normandy.' It then restated that they could reside in the king's land 'freely and honourably' and they were permitted to continue to hold everything that King Henry had granted them 'in lands and fiefs, and pledges and gifts, and purchases'.

The new charter also granted to the Jew a right of appeal in a legal quarrel with a Christian, providing an honest Jewish witness was produced. A Christian plaintiff would be treated in the same way. It granted rights to Jewish heirs with regard to inherited money and debts and allowed them to buy any goods offered to them 'except things of the church or bloodstained garments'.

It further permitted Jews who could not produce a witness in an argument to swear on the Torah (the scroll of the Jewish law) on the honesty of their own evidence. And it said: 'If there be any dissension between a Christian and any of the aforesaid Jews or their children about the settlement of any money, the Jew shall prove the capital and the Christian the interest.' It also allowed Jews to sell their pledges, if they wished, after they had held them for a year and a day.

The two final clauses in the charter were probably the most important so far as the Jews were concerned. The first ruled that Jews could go wherever they wished in the king's realm, unmolested and taking their possessions with them – and it also stated that if a Christian debtor to a Jew died leaving an heir, the debt should be paid to the Jew even if the heir was a minor, unless the land was held by the Crown.

The second clause ordered that all Jews in England and Normandy should be free of all customs and tolls '... just like our own chattels' and concluded: 'and we command and order you to ward and defend and protect them and we forbid any one against this charter about the aforesaid to put the said Jews into plea or on forfeit'.

The Third Crusade opened officially at the beginning of July. Hailed as a brilliant military achievement at the time, it was nevertheless not very successful and was concluded in 1192 by a three-year truce with Saladin. Alas, King Richard did not even have the satisfaction of returning in partial triumph to England, because, on his return journey, he was captured by the Duke of Austria, his old enemy, who handed him over to the Emperor of Austria, Henry VI. The Emperor demanded a ransom for King Richard of £100,000, as well as insisting on a humiliating treaty with England. Once again, the nation was leaned on to produce this prodigious amount and, once again, the Jews had to contribute disproportionately, being taxed at 5,000 marks – three times as much as the London burghers.

Representatives of the Jews were summoned to meet at Northampton on 30 March 1194, to decide how much each of the country's Jewish communities should contribute towards this sum. A document called the Northampton Donum records the outcome of this meeting and it confirms the presence at that time of Jews living in about twenty major communities, as well as in a number of smaller places up and down the country. The most important

The Third Crusade opened at the beginning of July 1190. This contemporary illustration drawn on the foot of a relevant document shows King Richard I (on right) tearing the cross from Saladin, the ruler of the Saracens.

centres were now London, Lincoln, Canterbury, Northampton and Gloucester, each with between twenty and forty contributors – obviously wealthy Jewish businessmen. Many of them clearly lived in London, because the capital's Jewish contribution was more than that of Lincoln and Northampton combined. York, Stamford, Dunstable, Lynn and Bury, where the most terrible outbreaks of violence against the Jews had happened in 1190, were not mentioned as contributing anything. In the end, the sum actually raised was only about half of what had been demanded from the Jews.

Shortly after the king at last returned to England, he ordered the Archbishop of Canterbury, Hubert Walter, to devise a definitive means of preventing a repetition of the disastrous attacks on the Jews, attacks which not only disobeyed the royal edict, but resulted in a great loss to the king's Exchequer.

An enquiry into the events of 1190 was conducted by the justices, during which any person who had been implicated in the attacks, and had not yet been punished for his offence, was arrested. A searching enquiry was then made into the state of affairs of the Jewish victims before their deaths, including what money had been owing to them and what pledges they had held. All this was 'taken into the king's hands', so that those responsible should not be able to profit from their crimes. Finally, two exchequer officials were instructed, among their other duties, to supervise the affairs of the Jews to ensure the safeguarding of royal rights, in case any similar disaster happened again.

William of Sainte-Mere-Eglise (later Bishop of London) and William de Chimille, the two officials, ordered all Jewish possessions and credits to be registered and for six or seven cities (probably London, Lincoln, Norwich, Winchester, Canterbury and Oxford and either Northampton, Cambridge, Gloucester, Nottingham or Bristol) to be the centres for all business operations in future. In each designated town, a bureau, run by two reputable Jews, two Christians and two clerks, was to be set up under the supervision of a representative of the central authority. All deeds and contracts must in future be produced in duplicate, in the presence of those officials, and the second copies of each placed in a chest (known as an *archa*, *huche* or chirograph) which had to have three locks and seals, so that no one person alone could open it without his fellow key-holders being there.

As if that was not safeguard enough, in addition, every Jewish financier had to take a solemn oath upon the Hebrew Torah (the Scroll of the Jewish Law, containing the five books of Moses) that he would register all his transactions without concealment and would denounce to the authorities all forgeries or evasions that came to his notice. The result of all this was that, however badly the Jews of England might be treated by their fellow citizens in the future, the Treasury and its claims were safe – because the death of their creditors would place the debtors in the hands of the king, who would be informed exactly of all outstanding claims. It also made it possible for the Crown or its agents to control Jewish affairs – and this made the new system of arbitrary taxation dangerously simple.

Once set up, the progress of the organisation was like a large stone rolling downhill. Four years later, in 1198, the central authority was extended into the institution of Wardens, or Justices, of the Jews. When the organisation was first set up, it was run by three Christians working in collaboration with one Jew (Benedict of Talmont).

But the king under whose rule the Jews had been treated so brutally did not live much longer to profit by his Jewish subjects. In 1199, when he was only forty-two, while fighting the ongoing war against the French king, Philip Augustus, Richard I was killed in Normandy, during the besieging of a small castle in Chalus, resulting from a wound from a crossbow which struck him in the shoulder.

He was succeeded by his brother John, whose reign was to prove almost as dangerous for the Jews of Britain as Richard's had been.

CHAPTER THREE
The Downward Slide

The following seventeen years, during which King John ruled England, were to see many changes in the way of life for the Jewish community. John, a rapacious and grasping monarch, benefited greatly from the exploitation of the Jews, set up, however tolerantly, by his brother. At the start of his reign, the Jews' contributions to the Exchequer were considerable, but not, in fact, beyond their means, so they paid up with good grace and were rewarded with special privileges.

In July, 1199, the first Archpriest (or Archpresbyter) of the Jews was appointed by the king. His name was Jacob of London. The deed, dated 31 July, was witnessed by William Marshal, the realm's Rector Regni. A clause in it suggests that Jacob had already been appointed to this office (the highest civil office to which a Jew could aspire) by King Richard I, but this appears to be the first documentary confirmation of it. Despite its title, the office does not seem to have been a religious one – it was certainly primarily a secular administrative post. Describing it in the Crown's Memoranda Rolls, Jacob states that he is answerable for the great debts of the English Jewry, 'the *cummune* of the Jews of England' – from the time of Henry II and Richard I. It is believed that by the term 'great debts', he meant taxes, fines, payable for charters and other common responsibilities. He did not hold himself responsible, however, for personal fines and other small debts, though his clerk, Abraham, did record them on a roll. The fact that Jacob declared his responsibility to ensure that the Jews' great debts were settled from the time of Henry II, further suggests that Henry's son, Richard, *had* appointed him Archpresbyter during his reign.

A change not for the better, was that, after 1 April 1200, no Jew was listed among the institution of Wardens, or Justiciars, of the Jews which had been set up by Richard I, to be administered by three Christians and one Jew. Justices from 1200, who were all Christians, were sometimes as few as two; at others, though not often, as many as eight. By this time, the office was coveted by Christians, not only

The seventeen years during which King John ruled England were to see many changes in the way of life of the Jewish community. John was a rapacious and grasping monarch and he benefited greatly from his exploitation of his Jewish subjects.

for the fee, but because it had become a distinguished one, and, later on, highly important people in England's administration were sometimes appointed to it, though without giving up their other duties. These officials presided over what by then had become known as the Exchequer of the Jews – a department of the country's Great Exchequer, and, as time went on, it grew into an organisation which was considerably more important than the original plan had implied. The *Scaccarium Judaeorum*, as it was eventually named, was not just fiscal (i.e. a method of obtaining public revenue), it was, for Jewish affairs, both administrative and judicial. Consequently, the half dozen or so centres for all Jewish business operations which had been specified in the original organisation were not found to be enough, perhaps more because communication was slow, than through increased business. Ultimately, *archae* were set up in the main Jewish centres throughout the country. There were about twenty-seven chirograph chests established and though some of the Jewish communities were relatively small, they were commercially important because of the wealth and business activity of perhaps only one Jewish businessman in them.

For some time, however, providing it 'kept to the rules', Britain's surprisingly far-flung Jewish community, enjoyed a fairly calm existence – certainly a much less violent one than it did in the last quarter of the twelfth century. Like immigrants throughout history, Jewish settlers often made their homes in or near ports of entry. By the thirteenth century, Jewish settlements had sprung up in about seventy towns in England and Wales, some as remote as Beaumaris and Newborough in Angelsey, as far north as Newcastle upon Tyne and as far south as Exeter in Devon. Some of these places would have had only a few Jewish families living in them; others many more, such as Winchester, Bury St Edmunds, Derby, Stamford, Worcester, Hereford, Lincoln, Norwich and York. For despite the York massacre, it is clear that Jews did return to the city in fairly large numbers very soon after the tragedy and, as R. B. Dobson tells us in *The Jews of Medieval York and the Massacre of March 1190*, '... they then proceed to play a more prominent role in almost every sphere (except that of scholarship) than their martyred predecessors.' And he goes on to say, 'The very combination of royal and local financial needs which had brought the Jews to York in the late twelfth century survived to ensure their renewed prosperity for years to come.'

Later, when his Treasury was empty, King John began to extort money from the Jews by a series of short-sighted and desperate expedients, as his successor was also to do in the following reign.

By this time, the barons, not least of them Richard Malebisse, the now reinstated ringleader of the York massacre, were very resentful of the assistance which the king derived from the Jewish community – and the relatively high positions some of them had reached. Leo, a Norwich Jew, for example, had become the royal goldsmith; others received special grants of protection and favour; and perhaps John's most controversial action, when he appointed Jacob of London, Archpresbyter, was to refer to him as *delectus et familiaris noster* (meaning either 'well-beloved' or 'our dear friend'), a phrase generally reserved for the great officers of the State.

To make matters worse, so far as the jealous baronetage was concerned, in April, 1201, the king reissued the old exemplary charter of liberties for the Jews of England and Normandy, confirming their right to dwell in the country and to enjoy all rights and liberties granted by previous sovereigns. The barons probably did not take into account that this concession cost the Jews of the realm the sum of 4,000 marks (about £2,700 at that time) – a sum so huge in their now very reduced circumstances that the Jewish community had to pay it in four instalments.

Nevertheless, the Jews became more and more identified in the barons' minds with royal oppression – and, in fact, John's reign marked the beginning of the political, as distinct from the religious, reaction among English people against Jews.

In 1205, the Jews of Lincoln were singled out by the king for another accusation, when he sent an order on 9 November to the Sheriff of Lincoln, commanding him to make known immediately:

> throughout your bailiwick at the fairs and markets, and on feast days at the porches of churches, that no one shall carry or have clipped money after the feast of St Hilary in the sixth year of our reign. ... And the man or woman who shall have such money shall be at our mercy and shall give safe pledges, and all their chattels shall be attached for obtaining our mercy. But if clipped money be found in the hand of Jew or Jewess the money shall be taken and perforated and placed in a certain safe box for our needs, and the body of the Jew or Jewess that has such money shall be taken and their goods taken and retained without bail till we order otherwise.

Jews were often accused of coin clipping in medieval England. This Jew (after a figure shown in a caricature of Norwich Jews) is carefully weighing coins to guard against coin clipping.

In fairness, it must be admitted that Jews might well have been guilty of money clipping, because, as money-lenders, they would have been able to force their debtors to take depreciated coin.

The year 1206 was a turning point, not only in English history, but also in Anglo-Jewish history, because this was the year that England

Although they were often wrongly accused of money clipping, some Jewish moneylenders might well have been guilty of clipping coins, because they would have been able to force their debtors to accept depreciated coin. Opposite are three examples of coin clipping in the reigns of Henry III and Edward I (top left, an Edward I silver penny; top right, a Henry III silver penny and, bottom left, an Edward I silver groat); the circles drawn round the coins show how much silver has been clipped from them. However, Jews were not the only coin clippers and their expulsion from Britain by Edward I certainly did not stop this crime, as the condition of the Edward III silver groat (bottom right) proves.

became politically, as well as physically, an island again. For about 125 years, the country had been closely connected with northern France – not only politically, culturally and linguistically, but also, to a certain extent, commercially.

Between the years 1204 and 1206, however, Normandy was lost through King John's incompetence and the link was irrevocably severed. It was also severed for the Jewish community, many of whom were Anglo-Normans. They were now largely cut off from the great centres on the Continent with which they had done so much business in the past years.

It was not just a question of commerce; the influx of Jewish settlers from abroad was also greatly reduced and, from that time, the names of native Jewish scholars became more prominent. Indeed, the civil authorities accentuated this tendency and forbade the Jews to appeal to Continental scholars, as they had often done previously, against the decisions of their own rabbis.

Though the Jews were now, through King John's political inexperience, somewhat more settled and 'English' (or 'Welsh'), the king in his endeavours to recover Normandy, levelled arbitrary taxation on the country as a whole – and the Jewish community in particular. This undoubtedly hastened the decline of medieval English and Welsh Jewry.

In addition to a tallage (taxation) of 4,000 marks demanded from the Jews in 1207, a levy of one-tenth of their bonds was also demanded from them. This was only a curtain-raiser, however, to plans to confiscate Jewish property and money three years later. The year 1210 was to prove a very black year for the Jews, numbering now between 2,000 and 3,000. When he returned to Bristol after a very unsuccessful campaign in Ireland, King John immediately issued instructions for the arrest of all the Jewish men of wealth in the kingdom. Their charters were also seized and investigated. Enough evidence – and, so long afterwards, there is no way of knowing how much of it was trumped up – about certain rich Jews withholding information was found to justify widespread condemnation, accompanied by the highest taxation ever levelled on the Jews. Contemporary writers reported that it was somewhere between 60,000 and 66,000 marks, but it may have been even more.

This huge sum was extracted from any Jews who were reluctant, or unable, to pay with great barbarity and cruelty. For instance, Roger of Wendover, a chronicler of the period, relates the following dreadful story:

> ... among them there was a Jew of Bristol, who refused to ransom himself by payment, though lacerated by a variety of torment. The King therefore ordered his torturers to pull out one of his molar teeth each day until he had paid the sum of 1,000 marks [the actual sum was later disputed as being unbelievably high for an individual]. For seven days a tooth was extracted with almost intolerable suffering, and on the eighth day the torturers had begun the same cruel work, when the Jew unable to hold out any further, paid the required sum, that he might save his eighth molar, having already lost seven of them.

Jewish officials were nominated in each county to distrain on debtors, while the property of those who could not pay was confiscated outright and their houses demolished so that something could be realised on the building materials. Even the poorest Jew had to pay a levy of forty shillings. If he could not, he was banished from Britain and many poorer Jews were indeed expelled at this time.

Furthermore, proceedings were taken ruthlessly against those accused of concealing assets – failing to declare how much money and how many possessions they actually had. Some were even hanged for this offence, while Isaac, son of the famous Jurnet of Norwich, purchased his pardon with an enormous fine, which was still being collected from him some years later. Inevitably, many Jews left England voluntarily at that time, realising that there was little prosperity or even security to be had there.

Hardly had members of the Jewish community recovered from paying up the Bristol Tallage, when, in 1213, a further enquiry into their property was ordered. Pressure was again brought to bear on them to pay up their arrears by the sheriffs. Those who pleaded penury were imprisoned. Members of the few Hampshire communities, for example, who still owed were sent to Bristol to be shut up in the castle, while one of the leaders of the Bristol community, Isaac, son of another Jurnet (Jacob), was, as an example to the rest, sent to the Tower of London. Southampton Jews were also dilatory in their contributions and, in 1214, they were imprisoned in Bristol Castle in order to make them pay heavily for their release.

The outbreak of civil war, set up by about forty rebellious barons against the king not long after this, made the Jews' position even more serious. Because there was much violence, the barons, considering that Jews were not only harsh creditors to Christians but also royal agents, used this as an excuse to double their attacks on them. On 17 May 1215, London was occupied and the Jewry was the first target of the invaders. They sacked it ruthlessly, demolished the houses and used the stone to repair the City walls.

When, as a result of the unrest and the king's bad administration, the barons forced King John to sign Magna Carta, the great charter of freedom, on 15 June 1215, two of the sixty-two clauses in it related to English Jewry. They concerned the part which the Jews were forced to play as passive instruments of royal behaviour and they emphasised the unpopularity which Jews earned in consequence. Clauses 10 and 11 stated:

> If any one who has borrowed from the Jews any amount, large or small, dies before the debt is repaid, it shall not carry interest as long as the heir is under age, of whomsoever he holds; and if that debt falls into our hands, [if the Jewish creditor died and the King seized his bonds] we will take nothing except the principal sum specified in the bond. And if a man dies owing a debt to the Jews, his wife may have her dower and pay nothing of that debt; and if he leaves children under age, their needs shall be met in a manner in keeping with the holding of the deceased; and the debt shall be paid out of the residue, saving the service due to the lords.

However, the second clause adds the words: 'Debts owing to other than Jews shall be dealt with likewise.', but since money-lending by Christians was still frowned upon, it is unlikely that there would have been many such cases appertaining to them.

— 40 —

There is little doubt that, if King John had not died the year after he signed Magna Carta, the Jewish position would have inevitably deteriorated as they were used as political pawns between the king and his barons.

King Henry III was only nine when his father died and his very long reign of fifty-six years saw the decline of medieval Jewry in Britain from a position of relative prosperity to one of complete ruin, caused eventually by a rapacious and ruthless royal policy and an increasingly hostile Church.

At the beginning of Henry III's reign, however, things seemed better for the Jews, though there was still some suffering for them while the embers of previous disorder were being stamped out. As part of the policy of re-establishing England's badly battered financial system, everything possible was done to renew Jewish confidence. For instance, in the confirmation of Magna Carta, which took place in November 1216, at Bristol almost immediately after John's death, the two clauses relating to the Jews were omitted, as prejudicial to the interests of the Exchequer, and were not reinserted in any of the many reissues of Magna Carta in subsequent years. Furthermore, instructions were given for the release of those Jews imprisoned at the close of John's reign or in the following unrest. In some cases, their confiscated bonds were restored and they received safe conducts.

The following year, when preparations were being made for the crusade proclaimed by the Pope in 1215, steps were taken immediately to check any repetition of the appalling treatment of the Jews that had happened in England during the preparations for the ill-fated Third Crusade. In every city and town where Jews resided in any numbers, the royal officers were instructed to select as sureties twenty-four burgesses who would be held responsible for any outrage on those placed under their care. Consequently, another outbreak of the murderous attacks on the Jews of York and London was prevented. The right of Jews to live in Hereford, Worcester, York, Lincoln, Stamford, Gloucester, Bristol, Northampton and Winchester was officially and expressly confirmed and the local officials were ordered not to molest them or allow any unauthorised people to interfere with them in any way.

Good news travelled quite fast, even in those early days, and, hearing of the improved conditions in England, immigrants began to arrive from the Continent. Indeed, some of them were undoubtedly Jews who had fled from England during the last reign and now felt it was safe to return to their former homes. The obdurate wardens of the Cinque Ports, who controlled communications with

King Henry III was only nine when his father, King John, died. He had a long reign of fifty-six years which saw the decline of medieval Jewry in Britain. This statue representing him was placed in Westminster Abbey nearly twenty years after his death in 1272.

Pope Innocent III proclaimed another crusade in 1215. The same year, he presided over the Fourth Lateran Council, the proceedings of which greatly affected the Jews, including the introduction, for the first time in the Christian world, of the 'Jew badge', the distinguishing mark which Jews of all nationalities were forced to wear.

the Continent, at first raised difficulties about admitting them and even threw some into prison, but when the royal authorities heard about this, the wardens were peremptorily instructed to set them free and to allow immigrants to be admitted without hindrance in future. Indeed, so much were the royal authorities 'bending over backwards' to re-establish the Jews' former prosperity and security, that no formality was now needed for immigrants on entry except that they had to give a guarantee that they would present themselves before the Justice of the Jews to be enrolled. None of this good treatment by the establishment was really altruistic, however; it was done merely to increase their mercenary value to the State. Proof of this was in an edict issued at the same time – that no Jews were to be allowed to leave the country without a licence. There seems little doubt that any wealthier Jewish citizens who wished to leave would not have been issued with such licences.

The policy of the Church authorities, however, was much less tolerant. Lateran councils, which were attended by Christian clerics from all over Europe, met at irregular intervals to establish and correct church policy. The Archbishop of Canterbury, Stephen Langton, had been one of the leading spirits at the Fourth Lateran Council of 1215, the proceedings of which greatly affected the Jews. It considered that their influence had been responsible for the alarming spread in Europe of heresy – opinion contrary to the orthodox doctrine of the Christian Church.

The Third Lateran Council of 1179, which had proscribed Christians from money-lending and had unwittingly helped to make the Jews rich as usurers, had prohibited Jews from having Christians in their service, or for Christians to enter into Jewish employment, even as nurses or midwives. It also 'forbade true believers to lodge amongst the infidel', thus laying the foundation for what was later to be called the ghetto system. The Fourth Lateran Council reaffirmed all these degrading restrictions on Jews, but it went considerably further and added even more stringent edicts. They included: the relieving of Christian debtors, especially crusaders, of the obligation to pay interest on debts to Jewish money-lenders; Jews were to be excluded from public office or any position which might give them the smallest authority; for the first time, Jews were ordered to pay tithes to the Church on all the property they held; converts were to be stopped from following their ancient rites. But worst of all was the introduction, for the first time in the Christian world, of the 'Jew badge', the distinguishing badge which Jews of all nationalities were forced to wear. Ostensibly, this was to prevent the strictly prohibited offence of (unwitting) sexual intercourse between people of the two faiths, which was looked on as little better than incest and was often punished by death. The badge took different forms in different countries (plus, in some lands, the wearing of a distinctively coloured hat). In England, the badge was a representation of the two tablets of stone on which the Ten Commandments were inscribed. It was probably introduced, by order of the king, as early as 1218 and certainly not later than 1222.

Despite all these curtailments on their freedom and the implacable attitude of the Church, during the royal minority, when the land was ruled for the young king by two regents (William Marshal and later Hubert de Burgh), the Jews' lives mostly remained tolerable. But, in 1232, with the fall of Hubert de Burgh, their conditions worsened.

King Henry, now twenty-five, had been the legal ruler of England since 1227 and his court, thronged with his favourites – many of them from overseas – was tremendously extravagant. In addition, his disastrous foreign policy culminated in a series of ruinously expensive and unsuccessful wars, mainly against the French in Gascony, which England still owned, and, furthermore, his insolvency was added to because he was extremely pious and supported, with a good deal of England's money, the schemes of several Popes against the Holy Roman Emperor (whose domain threatened the Popes' authority). To raise this money he increased taxation on all his subjects, but, as usual, the Jewish share was disproportionate. The old system, under which they were allowed to amass wealth as the financial agents of the Crown, was abolished and, instead, they were now regarded only as a source of revenue – and very high taxes were pitilessly extorted from them, regardless of the ultimate result. The king appointed his Treasurer, Peter des Rivalux, custody of the Jewry 'so that all the Jews of England should be intendant and accountable to him'. The Deputy Treasurer, Passelewe, was one of the Justices of the Jews, and Stephen Segrave, the Justiciar, worked in collusion with them.

In 1234, the Archbishop of Canterbury rather surprisingly forced the king, under threat of excommunication, to dismiss these three because of their appalling treatment of the Jews. The remaining Justices of the Jews were instructed to report all matters of importance direct to the king. In the enquiry which followed, no fewer than eighteen Jewish businessmen gave evidence of how their co-religionists had been fleeced by the wicked trio, particularly Passelewe, for their own enrichment. Nevertheless, these three were restored to royal favour two years later.

During the ten years from the start of the king's personal rule in

Shown above are four different forms of the 'Jew badge', which all Jews had to wear on their outer garments in the orders set out at the Fourth Lateran Council of 1215. Different forms of the badge were worn in different countries and British Jews had to wear the 'tablets of the Ten Commandments' shown at bottom left. King Henry III probably enforced the wearing of the badge as early as 1218 and certainly not later than 1222.

1227, taxes were extracted from the Jewish community to the value of at least 65,000 marks – nearly four times as much as they had to pay in the previous decade. But that was not all; the cost of the king's foreign campaigns from 1230 onwards was covered, to a considerable extent, by the remission of interest on (and even sometimes the principal of) the debts owed to the Jews by those who were willing to help the king financially, in whole or in part, whether temporarily or for good. In addition, the Jewish communities of the realm were commanded to make a joint gift of 3,000 marks to the Earl of Cornwall, the king's brother, for the financial support of his intended crusade and this was repeated whenever a member of the royal family announced his intention of going to fight the Saracens!

The administration of the Exchequer of the Jews then, for a time, passed into the hands of the king's foreign ministers, who used it as a means of patronage and extortion and, indeed, the control of the Exchequer of the Jews was the cause of much change, reorganisation and contention in the dramatic and difficult years that followed. Things went speedily from bad to worse and the only possible way for Jews to avoid paying the crippling taxes was to leave the country – and, at that time, the exodus of Jews from England reached considerable proportions. Those who stayed were more and more put upon and, by 1259, in the thirty-two years since the king had taken over personal rule, a total of 250,000 marks had been taken from the Jewish community by the Crown.

At this time, the king was desperate for another way to extort money from anyone and particularly the Jews, so it was strange and totally illogical that in 1234, probably his most impoverished year, he allowed legislation to come into force which restricted their ability to make money, by forbidding Crown tenants to borrow money on the security of their estates from Jewish money-lenders (and, four years later, this was extended to include those who held their property by military service).

Some of the ways of extorting money were particularly heartless. In 1236, for instance, ten of the kingdom's most wealthy Jews were imprisoned as security for the sum of 10,000 marks to be paid by their co-religionists. In 1239, an alleged murder in London was punished by confiscating one-third of the ten prisoners' property. In 1240, a census of every Jew and Jewess in Britain over the age of twelve was taken – it is presumed in order to assess the Jewish taxation for the following year. In 1240, too, what was called a Parliament of the Jews was summoned to meet at Worcester. The Parliament consisted of from two to six members of each of the twenty-one Jewish communities in the kingdom. One of those representatives was none other than Isaac of Bristol who, in 1213, was imprisoned in the Tower of London because he had not paid his share of the Bristol Tallage. The task of the representatives was to apportion among themselves a new tallage of no fewer than 20,000 marks (equivalent to one third of their joint property). These representatives were to be held personally responsible for the collection and delivery of this vast sum. Horrified at the size of the tax, some members of the London community protested, but the king ignored their pleas and ordered drastic treatment for any Jew who could not raise his share. Subsequently, many Jews from all over the country who could not pay in full were arrested with their wives and children, imprisoned in the Tower of London and their property confiscated to make up the deficit. To add insult to injury, in the same year, donations were obtained from some wealthy Jews to cover the expenses of the queen's 'childbed'.

Despite some arrears, the king was so pleased with the result of the 1240 tax that, three years later, he repeated it on an even larger scale – this time, the enormous sum of 60,000 marks was demanded, with the excuse that the Jews had been guilty of a ritual killing. Somehow, they raised this ransom, though six years were to elapse before it was fully paid up. Also in 1243, a 'minor levy' of 4,000 marks was extorted from them to enable the king to repay a loan he had had from some Italian merchants and, a year later, another tax of 8,000 marks was imposed to meet the unexpected cost of his Welsh war. To obtain this sum, he threatened that if it was not paid, the wealthiest Jews would be imprisoned in Ireland. Fearing a repetition of the wholesale arrests of 1241, some Jews put their wives and children in hiding and were immediately outlawed and their property confiscated.

And so the progressive bankrupting of the country's Jewish community by the king proceeded unabated. Indeed, every time he needed money for his wars, his Church allegiance or merely his expensive lifestyle, he ordered yet another special Jewish tax. In 1251, for instance, a new levy of 10,000 marks was ordered, with instructions that no Jew was to be spared. The commissioners to whom this was entrusted, among other measures, imprisoned the whole Jewish community of Wilton – and these commissioners were egged on by one unprincipled Jew, Abraham of Berkhamsted, who, presumably to save his own skin and property, threatened to denounce them if they showed any mercy. Alas, every group has its renegades.

In 1253, the king went to Gascony and, to support his continuing military skirmishes there, the Jews were made to pay another 5,000 marks. However, on 31 January of that year, Henry had also imposed new restrictions on his Jewish subjects, when he issued the following edict:

MANDATE OF THE KING TO THE JUSTICES ASSIGNED TO THE CUSTODY OF THE JEWS TOUCHING CERTAIN STATUTES RELATING TO THE JEWS IN ENGLAND WHICH ARE TO BE RIGOROUSLY OBSERVED.

The King has provided and ordained etc.: That no Jew remain in England unless he do the King service, and that from the hour of birth every Jew whether male or female, serve US in some way. And that there be no synagogues of the Jews in England save in those places in which synagogues were in the time of King John, the King's father. And that in their synagogues the Jews, one and all, subdue their voices in performing their ritual offices, that Christians may not hear them. And that all Jews answer to the rector of the church of the parish in which they dwell touching all dues parochial relating to their houses. And that no Christian nurse in future suckle or nourish the male child of any Jew, nor any Christian man or woman serve any Jew or Jewess, or eat with them or tarry in their houses. And that no Jew or Jewess eat or buy meat in Lent. And that no Jew disparage the Christian faith, or publicly dispute concerning the same. And that no Jew have secret familiar intercourse with any Christian woman, and no Christian man with a Jewess. And that every Jew wear his badge conspiciously on his breast. And that no Jew enter any church or chapel save for purpose of transit, or linger in them in dishonour of Christ. And that no Jew place any hindrance in the way of another Jew desirous of turning to the Christian faith. And that no Jew be received in any town but by special licence of the King, save only in those towns in which Jews have been wont to dwell.

And the Justices assigned to the custody of the Jews are commanded that they cause these provisions to be carried into effect, and rigorously observed on pain of forfeiture of the chattels of the said Jews. Witness the King at Westminster, on the 31st day of January. By King and Council.

The restatement in this mandate that every must Jew wear a badge was probably because, although it had been instituted in England at least thirty years earlier, the wearing of the Jewish badge had never been very seriously enforced.

In that year also, Elias le Eveske of London, who had been appointed Archpresbyter (Presbyter Judaeorum) in 1243, begged Richard, Earl of Cornwall, the king's brother, who was now responsible for levying tax on the Jews, to reduce the sum being demanded from the impoverished Jewish community and he also requested that those who wished should be allowed to leave the country. Richard refused to let any Jews leave, although he did modify his demands somewhat. But when the king returned from Gascony in 1254, desperately needing to raise money to obtain the throne of Sicily for his son, Edmund, Henry demanded that Elias should raise from his fellow Jews an immediate payment of another 8,000 marks. The unhappy Elias protested that the Jews had no money with which to meet the request and again begged that they should be allowed to leave the country. This was met with an angry refusal and, to ensure that none managed to go *without* permission, the wardens of the Cinque Ports were instructed to arrest any Jews who tried to leave.

Head over heels in debt, it was now obvious to the king that there was very little chance of his being able to raise any more revenue from the Jewish community, so, as their suzerain (feudal lord), he mortgaged the whole community, as security for a loan of 5,000 marks, to his wealthy brother, Richard. This amount, plus another thousand marks as *douceur* (a gratuity or bribe), was to be paid by the Jews in instalments over two years, during which, two of the most able Jewish financiers were appointed to administer the affairs of their co-religionists – rather like receivers of an estate in bankruptcy today.

In fact, Richard, who had always had quite good relations with the Jews, proved a fairly kind master. Alas, this situation lasted only for those two years. As soon as those two years, and the repayment of the debt were completed, the king handed over the mortgage of the Jewish community to his son, Edward, the heir to the throne, for a further three years, together with the whole mechanism of the Jewish Exchequer, to secure Edward's loyalty to his father, plus the annual sum of 3,000 marks from *his* estates. In 1262, Edward was granted another favour from his crafty father – he was allowed to maintain his own prison to keep Jews in, when necessary.

After barely a year, Edward 'sold' the Jews yet again; this time, to their own business competitiors, the Italian Lombards (also known as Cahorsins), who were acquiring a very bad reputation for *their* methods of usury. By now, as a community, the Jews had so little left

Aaron, son of Leo of Colchester, who is wearing the 'Jew badge', or the 'badge of shame', as it came to be called, stood bail for one of a group of Colchester Jews who were prosecuted for chasing a doe from the forest through the streets of the city. He was sketched in the margin of the relevant court roll labelled 'fil diaboli' (son of the devil).

to give that it may seem that they were hardly worth the buying and selling, though some rich Jewish financiers there still were and throughout the 1240s and 1250s, huge sums were still being extracted from them.

In 1245, for instance, when Westminster Abbey was rebuilt, the Jews were forced to contribute not only as a community, but also as individuals. It is recorded that Licoricia, the widow of a rich Oxford financier, had to give more than £2,500, while Moses of Hereford contributed £3,000 (both contributions being listed as 'death duties'). Elias le Eveske was forced to donate a silver-gilt chalice for the new building and others paid for 'internal embellishments'. In fact, in order to pay for some of the Christian religious objects, the Jews had to sell the Hebrew Torah Scrolls used by the Justices of the Jews for administering oaths – a very wry, not to say degrading, operation for Jewish religionists.

The Jew whose fortune was most affected was Aaron of York, the greatest Jewish financier in England in the thirteenth century. It was recorded that, in only seven years, the crown had received from him about 30,000 marks in silver and 200 in gold, in addition to a sum that he had to pay to the queen. Aaron, Archpresbyter for seven years before Elias Le Eveske who was also from York, was the son of Josce of York who was martyred in 1190.

Indeed, although fighting a losing battle, the Jews continued to struggle for justice right up to the end of Henry's long reign and the control of the Jewish Exchequer remained a bone of contention all through the stormy years of the 1230s and beyond. Even though, at one stage, because of the demands of the barons, the king suspended the entire staff of the Exchequer, Christians and Jews alike, in 1249 he again attempted to set up a bureaucracy, and placed the Jewish Exchequer, among other bodies, under the control of Philip Lovel, who had climbed quickly from being a clerk to assuming some of England's highest offices. In 1251, however, he and his clerk, Nicholas of St Albans, were charged with corruption when taxing the Jews in the north and suspended from all their functions. Nevertheless, because he was one of the king's favourites, Lovel was back in office again within six months and continued to serve as before for several years. So the Jews were no better off and, to make matters worse, the Jewish officials at the Exchequer could not help their co-religionists, because, one by one, they were removed from office – Josce fil' Isaac of London, Aaron of York and Elias le Eveske, in particular. The latter, who had been a very unpopular Archpresbyter and who did not scruple to oppress his fellow Jews, in the end became converted to Christianity and tried to get back into the king's good books by making wild accusations against his co-religionists. After this particularly bad example, the Jewish community obtained an undertaking from the king not to make any further such appointment except as a result of election by the Jewish community. For their next Archpresbyter, they chose, on payment of a large sum to His Majesty (for *nothing* came free to England's Jews), Vives (or Hagin), son of Master Moses of Lincoln, who came from a family outstanding for its scholarly reputation.

It was not, however, only the pressure on them to pay unjust taxes that was harassing the Jewish community. During much of the reign – and certainly the second half of it – feelings were running high in eastern counties, where medieval anti-Semitism was always most acute. Norwich Jews were particularly endangered at this time. Because of the expulsions from other areas, there were more Jews in Norwich than ever before and this fed the hatred and racism against them, with the result that, in 1234, certain Norwich Jews were accused of having seized and forcibly circumcised, four years previously, the adored son of a doctor named Benedict, who was probably a converted Jew. Though the alleged offence had happened so long ago, the consequences were no less serious. After a hearing in Norwich, ten people were arrested and sent to London for trial and the case was heard by the king in the presence of the Archbishop of Canterbury and many bishops and barons of the realm. In the end, they decided that it was an offence against the Church and, as such, should be tried by ecclesiastical law and it was then sent back to the Ordinary of Norwich (the clerical court) for a decision. After a long, vain attempt to secure a trial by a mixed jury of Jews and Christians, four of the accused were condemned to be drawn and hanged – in that order, while one, who had fled from England, was outlawed. Following this, repeated rioting against the Norwich Jewish community took place, several Jewish homes were set on fire and there was even a clash between the mob and soldiers who were sent from Norwich Castle to protect the Jews.

The rioting in Norwich was the first of a fresh series of accusations of ritual offences or 'blood libels', but now the accusations were made with the connivance and, possibly the encouragement, of the civil authorities. The feast of St Alban on 22 June 1239, was the backcloth for a very bloody riot in London when a Jew was accused of murder. The king's principal minister, Brother Geoffrey of the Temple, used the incident as an excuse to imprison a number of Jews and put several to death. In addition, a tax of one-third of their property was levied collectively on the entire Jewish community, as a punishment for the crime.

This impression of a prominent Jew, who was born in the latter half of the thirteenth century, was sketched on a deed of the time. The word 'Hake' on the left was a shortened form of the name Isaac.

Five years later, in 1244, another wholly unfounded accusation was made in London. It was alleged that in the churchyard of St Benets, a body of a child was found with a Hebrew inscription cut into the flesh, proving that the child had been killed for ritual purposes. Ridiculous though the story was, the child's body was claimed by the canons of St Paul's Cathedral and buried near the high altar and the country's Jewish community had to pay 60,000 marks to the Treasury to avoid worse consequences. An even more absurd incident took place in 1250 concerning Abraham of Berkhamsted, who made himself so unpopular a year later among his co-religionists by encouraging the commissioners to extort 10,000 marks from the Jews. The wealthy Abraham was arrested on a charge of maltreating an image of the Virgin Mary and murdering his wife for refusing to imitate him! A probable testimony of his innocence was that when his patron, Richard, Earl of Cornwall, intervened, he was released without punishment, although he was made to pay a big fine. The reaction of the Christians to this episode led up to the most famous case of all in the almost unbelievable series of accusations against the Jews.

At the end of August, 1255, large numbers of Jews had assembled in Lincoln, probably to attend the wedding of Belaset, daughter of Magister Moses of Nicole, who lived there with his family. The day after the wedding, the body of a little Christian boy was found in a cesspool near the house of a Jew. Hugh, the son of a widow named Beatrice, had been missing for over three weeks, and there is every reason to believe that, in fact, he fell into the cesspool accidentally while running after a ball. To the local people, however, there could only be one explanation. The boy's body was removed to the cathedral, apparently accompanied with miraculous manifestations, which made it obvious to anyone who wished to believe it, that he was a martyr. Copin, the Jew near whose house the body had been found, was seized and tortured until he 'confessed' that the boy had been put to death for ritual purposes at a Jewish gathering. The king, who happened to be in the neighbourhood, hurried to Lincoln and immediately ordered Copin to be hanged, after being dragged up and down the streets tied to a horse's tail. Nearly a hundred Jews who had been implicated were brought to London, followed by a jury of twenty-four burgesses and twenty-four knights to try the case. Because eighteen of the accused preferred not to submit to the judgement of what was obviously a biased tribunal and demanded a mixed jury of Jews and Christians, this was taken as a confession of their guilt and they were immediately hanged. With the exception of two pardoned and one acquitted before the case, the remainder were convicted and sentenced. Despite the rising anti-Semitism of the people of London, Richard of Cornwall, to whom the Jews had been recently mortgaged by the king, eventually obtained the release of the surviving prisoners.

Little St Hugh of Lincoln (as he came to be called) was buried in an impressive shrine in the city's cathedral, where he was venerated and was said to work miraculous cures right down to the time of the Reformation. His story became an English legend and it was from hearing poetry and songs about it that, for the hundreds of years when there were no Jews in England, British people imagined what the Jews were like.

This and similar episodes, mostly as unfounded as the case of Little St Hugh, made the Jews even more unpopular and many towns sought to exclude them. There was now, indeed, a complete reversal of the tolerant policy of the early years of Henry III's reign, when Jews had been encouraged to settle all over the country and been made quite welcome. One of the leaders of the movement to get rid of the Jews was Simon de Montfort. There were at least three reasons for his attitude. The first was that, in his childhood in Provence, he had seen the Jews persecuted under his parents' influence. The second was that he believed the Jews were, with their wealth, helping to uphold the king's absolutism, of which Simon was a determined opponent. The third was that he was himself heavily in debt to the Jews! In 1231, Simon, (later to become the Earl of Leicester) issued an edict expelling the Jews from the City of Leicester. It was forty-one years since there had been such a Jewish expulsion and that had been from Bury St Edmunds. Simon's example was soon followed by other towns.

In 1233, an enquiry was held in the Lincoln diocese – and perhaps elsewhere – to discover whether any Jews were living in places from which they had previously been absent. This was a prelude to a whole series of expulsions – in 1234, from Newcastle upon Tyne, Wycombe, the county of Warwick and parts of East Anglia; in 1236, from Southampton; in 1237, from Northamptonshire, though not from the town of Northampton itself; in 1242, from Berkhamsted; in 1243, from Newbury with Speenhamland; and there may have been other expulsions. Certainly, *before* the final expulsion in 1290, there were no fewer than twenty-six towns in which the Jews were no longer allowed to live – and, indeed, they were banished from *all* the seven towns in north Wales in which they had previously resided.

In 1253, the year of the king's stringent mandate, an order was issued forbidding Jewish settlement, except by special licence, in any place where no recognised Jewish community was to be found. Previously, Jews had been allowed to live in any city, town or village from which they were not expressly *excluded*. Now, they were *excluded* from all the places in which they were not expressly permitted to live. Consequently more anti-Semitism arose, as many more Jews flooded into the few places in which they *were* permitted to live.

In addition, around, and possibly earlier than, the year 1244, Oxford students had attacked what was then called The Jewry (an area roughly where St Aldgate's now stands) and sacked their solidly-built Jewish houses. In 1261, there was a similar attack in Canterbury, where the people tried to set fire to the Jewish quarter. There were monks and priests among those who had participated in this outrage, despite the fact that, in the previous century, there had been the most cordial relations in Canterbury between the Jews and the monks.

The persecution continued, culminating in 1264, when, after his son was captured by the royalists at Northampton, Simon de Montfort rallied his London supporters. Possibly to divert them, he gave his disappointed followers a free hand and they joined with the City mob, following the circulation of a very odd story that the Jews, as well as providing the king with money, were plotting to betray the City to his forces. The attack on the Jewish community was made on Saturday, 12 April, the eve of the Passover and a classic time for such outrages. It was led by John Fitzjohn, one of the most ruthless of Simon's followers and it is recorded that even contemporaries were horrified at the brutality of this attack, which included an instance of John Fitzjohn himself pillaging the home of the wealthy Isaac fil' Aaron and killing him with his own hands. The synagogues were also looted and defiled, with de Montfort taking a share of the loot.

After London, the massacres spread to Canterbury, (where many Jews were either killed or sent to Dover and deported penniless), to Worcester, Lincoln, Bristol and even to the small town of Kingston in Surrey. The Jewish community in Northampton were forced to take refuge in a castle, while many fled to Oxford in the hope of finding sanctuary. In May, 1264, more persecutions blew up in Winchester, Lincoln and Nottingham and, terrified about their future, many Jewish householders fled to the Continent.

In the final phase of the persecution, the remainder of the anti-royalist party looted Jewish homes in Cambridge and sacked the synagogue in Lincoln, while the surviving members of the capital's Jewish community took refuge in the Tower of London.

Oddly enough, during the sixteen months of his personal control of the government, from 1264 until he was killed at the Battle of Evesham in 1265, Simon de Montfort changed his attitude towards the Jews, obviously because he wanted the use of their money. He attempted to restore their confidence by persuading the London Jews to leave the Tower and be taken under the king's nominal protection, ordering those from Northampton to leave the castle in which they were sheltering and return to their homes and sending the refugees in Oxford back to *their* former homes. In addition, letters patent were sent to the authorities in the principal cities where the persecutions had taken place, ordering proclamations to be issued stating that the Jews might return and resume their lives and occupations peaceably. Twenty-four citizens in each place were named as guarantors responsible for the Jews' protection and, as Cecil Roth tells us, '... The Jewish chirographs were as far as possible re-assembled and the Jewish *archae* renewed; and the instructions were given for those records which were still extant to be consulted to see whether it was feasible to retrieve the heavy losses suffered.'

Nevertheless, the tragic happenings of the past few years were clearly the beginning of the end for Britain's medieval Jewish community, although the official termination was not to come for another twenty-five years.

*   *   *   *   *

Despite the catastrophic downward trend of thirteenth century Jewry in Britain, wherever possible and for as long as possible, they continued their way of life, domestic and communal, as well as commercial.

Whenever possible, the Jews in each city or town built a synagogue for the use of the close community in which they lived. The synagogue would usually be fairly small and would have a cemetery adjacent to it. The site of the pre-expulsion cemetery for London's Jews has been excavated and though Jews were living in London from the time of William I, the earliest reference to the site of this cemetery was 1218. It was situated outside the City by its north-west angle near Cripplegate. The cemetery had several medieval names. Sometimes it was called 'the cemetery of the Jews', sometimes 'the common cemetery of the Jews' or 'the ward of the Jews' or 'leyrestowe' (meaning a religious lying or burial place). It was also erroneously called 'the cemetery of the entire community of the Jews of England', which was most unlikely and which doubt is born out by a later description, 'Jews' Garden', which was also given to other Jewish cemeteries up and down the

The remains of an ancient Jewish cemetery was excavated in York in 1984 when the ground was being dug up for a supermarket to be built on it. The company concerned donated a piece of land in York so that the remains could be reinterred. The Chief Rabbi is seen here with members of the York Jewish community at the consecraton ceremony. Two years later, the plaque pictured here was placed on the original site, which was in the present car park area of the store.

country. Actually, by the time of the expulsion, there were at least ten Jewish cemeteries in England, located from York to Winchester and including Bristol. Cemeteries were, in a way, more necessary than synagogues, because Judaism, as already stated, being a family religion, can always be practised at home, but, aside from the fact that Jews would not have been eligible to have been buried in English churchyards, it would not have been permitted by the *Halachic* (Jewish religious) law.

All Jewish families were *not* wealthy. It would be fair to say that most of them were what today would be called middle class. Their lifestyle was similar to that of Jewish families all over medieval Europe. They dwelt in a close-knit community, living near one another for safety, for religious observance and for social and intellectual companionship. There is a very fair amount of documentary material concerning Anglo-Jewish fiscal and economic activities, but far less on intellectual, social or even religious life. But there is no reason to believe that medieval British Jewry neglected matters either spiritual or intellectual. Despite that, even in large towns, few Jewish communities numbered more than two hundred souls (and (and sometimes fewer), they would have led an active religious life and often an equally active intellectual one. Similar to today, most communities, with or without their own synagogues, would have had both lay and rabbinical leadership. In every town where Jews were settled, there were religious students, and sometimes an academy in which students would study the Talmud (decisions and commentaries of the rabbis of the first to fifth centuries AD). If there was no academy, the groups of students would be presided over by a scholar of special learning, who was recognised as their teacher and mentor. This rabbi (teacher) who might well have been also a wealthy businessman, was called the 'master' (mestre or magister) and the title was often entered in official records. About fifty people are recorded as magister in the records of medieval English administration.

Many of England's most outstanding Jewish scholars, however, came from the Continent. Rabbi Joseph (or Rubi Gotsce), the first Anglo-Jewish scholar whose name is recorded, was one of them. He was a leader of the London community in the time of Henry I. In Henry II's reign, among several foreign scholars visiting Britain, was the Spanish intellectual, Abraham ibn Ezra. He was knowledgeable about many subjects and wrote several books while in London, where he died in 1158. Jacob of Orleans, a renowned Jewish scholar from northern France, was killed in the London massacre of 1189. Yom-Tob of Joigny, a liturgical poet whose hymns are still

sung in synagogues, was the central figure in the Clifford's Tower
episode in York in 1190. There were other visiting Jewish intellectuals, too, but gradually distinguished 'home-grown' scholars began
to emerge, such as Jacob ben Judah who composed a code of relig-
ous law known as 'The Tree of Life' (*Etz Hayyim*) and who was a
reader (*hazan*) in the London synagogue. There were many others,
as time went on, and the most famous was Rabbi Elijah Menahem
(Elias) of London, son of Magister Moses. As well as becoming a
wealthy businessman and an eminent physician, he composed,
among other works, an important commentary on the *Mishnah*, (the
second century code which is the basis of the Talmud), which was
studied by many later scholars. These intellectuals did not only contribute religious writings, they wrote poetry, *belles-lettres* and Hebrew
grammar. The latter was also used by Christian clerics, a number of
whom read Hebrew and often consulted Hebrew sources.

In a land where the status of English women, particularly married
women, was very inferior to men, the position of Jewish women,
whether married, single or widowed, was quite the opposite. As
Michael Adler reports in *The Jews of Medieval England*: 'Again and again
she [the Jewish woman] comes to the front in a way that proves she
occupied a position in the life of Jewry, both within and without
the community, probably unequalled in those days in any other
country. She shared all the vicissitudes of her men-folk, she
engaged in business on equal terms, she paid her tallage to the King,
she claimed her rights without fear, both from her own kinsmen
and from the Royal Exchequer.' Women were not, however,
allowed to sign legal bonds or deeds, but their menfolk signed on
their behalf and legally they had equality with men.

Many cases are recorded which illustrate the important part
Jewish women played both legally and commercially, although, like
their male counterparts, they, too, were charged with such crimes
as defamation of character, coin-clipping, robbery, bodily assault,
even murder and attempted murder. In many cases, however, the
judges before whom they appeared acquitted them, but not always.

Take the case of four married women named Solal, Gente, Gerte-
lote and Prude, who were accused of plotting against an innkeeper
in Stamford in order to charge him with the murder of one of them,
but the man was able to prove his innocence. The women fled,
their husbands were fined heavily and an order was given to arrest
the four women. History does not record whether they were ever
caught.

Four Jewish women were accused of murder between 1278 and
1285, but their fate is not known. Indeed, although there is record

of a number of such accusations against Jewish women around this time, in many cases, there seems to be no record of the subsequent verdicts.

On the normal business side, however, there are many well documented accounts of successful Jewish women. In the middle of the thirteenth century, for instance, Belia, the widow of a Jew called Pictavin, was the most powerful resident of the small Jewish community of Bedford. Aided by her sons, Jacob and Benedict, she managed a loan office on a very large scale. The brothers Isaac and Bonenfant were her deadly business rivals and they appropriated a number of her deeds and other property. She sought legal proceedings against them, with the result that the two brothers and their wives and children were expelled from Bedford for five years.

There were many Jewish capitalists in the thirteenth century, but none could compare with Licoricia of Winchester, who has already been noted as having to contribute a large sum towards the rebuilding of Westminster Abbey. She was indeed probably the most outstanding woman of her time – Jew or gentile. She conducted extensive and successful financial transactions, she co-operated with the chief Jewish bankers of the day and had continuing successful dealings not only with the court, but also with the king himself. One of her commercial associates was none other than Belia, Pictavin's widow.

Licoricia was married twice. By the time she made her second marriage – to David of Oxford – she was already a well known businesswoman and the clergy of Winchester Cathedral were among her clients. Her husband, David, died after only two years of marriage and she had to pay 5,000 marks in death duties. To ensure the payment of the demands of the Royal Exchequer, she was imprisoned in the Tower of London and her bonds and other prop-

This illustration at the head of a 1233 Exchequer document concerning Norwich Jews depicts a great deal of anti-Semitism, as evidenced by the devils shown round the Jewish faces in it. But it also includes the first known drawing of a Jewish woman in medieval England, wearing the English wimple of the period. Licoricia of Winchester, the great female financier, would probably have looked very like the woman in the drawing.

erty was given into the charge of Aaron of York, formerly an Archpresbyter, another of her business associates. At the same time, King Henry ordered the late David's library to be examined. This library included a Bible, a book of Psalms with commentaries and probably several books of Jewish Law – and the king decreed that 'if any book be found that attacks the laws of either Christians or Jews, it should be destroyed.' There is no evidence that any such book was found. Six wealthy Jews were appointed to become securities for the doughty Licoricia and, after she had settled the legacy dues, she was set free to deal with the collection of the many debts owing to her late husband.

Because of her wealth and the various rich Jewish financiers with whom she was associated during her career and also perhaps because of the king's interest and involvement in her business, special arrangements with regard to the payment of the many taxes were made for Licoricia and she was permitted to pay an annual tax of only 25 marks.

Throughout her life, she was in and out of trouble, but always seemed to emerge unscathed – even when she was incarcerated in Winchester Prison, having been accused by a Jewish neighbour called Ivetta of stealing a ring that Belia wanted to present to the king. It was soon discovered, however, that Ivetta herself was the real thief – and Licoricia was free again. Her five sons – Benedict, Cockerel (Isaac) and Lumbard (from her first husband) and Swetman and Asher (from her second) – all became prominent money-lenders; Benedict being the most famous.

A fascinating tale of a very unusual woman, but one with a sad ending – she was murdered in 1277 and was mourned by English Jewry.

Licoricia may well seem a strange name for a Jewess, but, in those days in Britain, it was not all that unusual. Though, on the whole, boys had biblical names, most girls were given Norman-French names, even as late as the thirteenth century. They ranged from Alemandina to Swetecot and included such un-Jewish appellations as Almonda, Antera, Claricia, Columbina, Duzelina, Ermina, Fleur de Lys, Floricote, Glorietta, Iveta, Margalicia, Mirabel, Muriel, Paturella, Popelina, Sapphira, Sigge and many others equally exotic. There is even a record of Alfild, an Anglo-Saxon name, being given to some Jewish girls.

Jewish marriages, of course, were always 'arranged' in this period, planned usually during the infancy of the proposed husbands and wives, with an eye to the suitability, not only of the incomes and possessions of the parents, but of the suitability and compatability of social and family backgrounds – much as many Asian marriages still are today.

The betrothal and marriage contract (*ketuba*) was usually written when the children were betrothed, but not actually signed until they were formally married under a wedding canopy (*chuppah*). It was customary that, following the wedding, the young couple would live in the bride's father's house for at least a year and he would undertake to provide them with food and clothes during that period, to pay any taxes that might be imposed upon them while they lived with him and even to engage a teacher with whom his son-in-law could study.

The bridegroom (or his parents) also had to make a marriage settlement and quite often this would be as much as £100 – a vast sum in those days and a sign of the wealth of at least some members of the Jewish community.

A fascinating picture of Jewish social life was given in a *ketuba* of 1249:

> R. Yom Tob, the son of Moses of Norwich, promises to give his daughter Zeuna to Solomon, son of Eliab, together with a dowry of ten marks, followed by a further five marks in twelve months' time. He undertakes to provide them with clothes and shoes for Sabbaths and weekdays and also with ample board and lodging in his own house for a whole year. He will further pay their taxes, and will engage a teacher for the bridegroom, binding himself under penalty of excommunicaiton to carry out the full terms of the marriage agreement.

Isaac of Warwick, another wealthy man, presented his daughter, Chera, with a wedding gift of a house next to the synagogue in Mancroft Street, Norwich, with the condition that the house must be returned to him if she died childless – and, if so, the father agreed to pay ten marks to her widower as compensation. The bridal couple also agreed to pay fourpence a year towards the funds of the synagogue, sixpence a year to the ground landlord and one halfpenny (the price of a pair of gloves) to the bride's father. The king was permitted to take half of any bride's dowry, but there seems to be only one instance of this being recorded, when £50 was taken by the Exchequer at the marriage of Drua of Winchester to Ursell of Oxford.

If a girl was left an orphan, her brothers had to find her 'a becoming and pleasant spouse' and to give her an adequate dowry. They also had to make proper provision for their widowed mother.

Divorce was and still is allowed under Jewish religious law. Normally, the husband would have to go before the Jewish Court (Bet Din) to obtain it, though sometimes the court, if the husband rebelled against the conditions imposed (such as his providing financial provision for his divorced wife), might well appeal to a more learned body of scholars for a final decision. In 1242, the application for divorce from his wife, Muriell, by David of Oxford (who later married Licoricia), was referred by the Bet Din to Masters Moses of London, Aaron of Canterbury and Jacob of Oxford, the three great minds of contemporary Anglo-Jewry. A woman could sue her husband for divorce, but getting it would not have been easy and there are few recorded cases.

Within their own communities, Jews were free to run their own affairs in thirteenth-century Britain – but the lives of many were often disrupted by persecution and it must have taken oppressed communities a considerable time to return to their normal domestic lives after each outbreak of anti-Semitism.

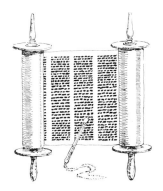

CHAPTER FOUR
The Expulsion and Beyond

At the start of the last seven years of the reign of King Henry III, Britain's Jews were somewhat more secure and settled, but it was not long before complaints against them were again rife, especially in connection with their money-lending, much of which was in the form of mortgages on the land owned by improvident Christian landowners. The easiest way for Jewish money-lenders to recover a debt made on the security of land was to sell the claim to a Christian businessman, who would then foreclose. This soon meant that more and more private estates – and consequently military power – were getting into the the hands of the biggest landowners, a situation very unacceptable to the Crown. Another way for a debtor – or, indeed, a creditor – to proceed was to sell or surrender his title to the land to the Church. Neither was in the best interests of the State and both meant the loss of dues to it and, as has been said, of the military services of the landowners concerned and of their retinues.

Edward, the heir to the throne, who, when he ascended it, was going to find a final solution for the Jews of medieval Britain, was now becoming very powerful in state affairs. It was clear to him that something must be done to curb the increasing power of the wealthy landowners against the Crown. Although the Jews, many of them on the verge of financial ruin, had begged the king to restore their legal claims for debtors to pay interest on loans – and this had been granted, Edward and his brother, Edmund, led a movement which pressed for the reform of land mortgages.

The result of their campaign was the 'Provisions of Jewry', which was issued by the Royal Exchequer in January, 1269. It ordered that no debts whatsoever could be contracted in future with Jews on the security of lands held in fee; all obligations of this kind that were already registered were cancelled forthwith; the transference to a Christian secured in this way was to be treated as a capital offence; and debts of any other sort could in future be disposed of to a third party only by special licence, and on condition that the principal only, without any interest, was repaid.

Now that they could no longer give loans on the security of land, the Jewish financiers attempted to fall back on landowning themselves. Accordingly, they presented a petition to the king requesting the permission 'to hold manors' with all the feudal dues paid to Christian landowners. At the same time, they were granted a reconfirmation of their Charter of Privileges first given to them by Henry I 150 years earlier, in which their right to hold land was guaranteed. However, after a protracted law case involving Cok Hagin fil' Deulecresse of London, with regard to Jewish landowners, (which Cok Hagin, through Christian opposition, eventually lost), the petition of the Jews was rejected and, despite their Charter of Privileges, a new law was made in July, 1271, forbidding Jews to have free holdings henceforth in any manor or lands, whether by charter, by gift or by enfoeffment (the act of giving to someone else the feudal fee of an estate). Even in cities, they were no longer allowed to own houses, except those in which they lived or which they rented to other Jews. Lands already in Jewish occupation were to be vacated immediately on the repayment to the money-lenders concerned of the capital for which the lands had been held as security, without paying any interest.

These stringent measures meant that the financial activities of the Jews were greatly curtailed. In fact, they could no longer carry out any major transactions, because they were no longer allowed to lend money at interest on landed security, whether to the barons or, indeed, to anyone lower down the social scale. Subsequently, a few Jews were allowed to hold property, but even that stopped very soon.

In addition, the king levied on the Jews a comparatively small tax of 6,000 marks towards Edward's 1271 Crusade, towards which they were able to raise only 4,000 marks. The remainder was contributed by Richard, Earl of Cornwall, to whom, once more, the Jews were 'sold' as security.

Richard died shortly before Henry and the king then 'took back' the Jews and demanded a tax from them of 5,000 marks, of which a thousand were earmarked for his 'disbursements for the royal table'. Those who could not pay their share or give security to pay within four months (which, incidentally, included the entire Hereford community) were thrown into prison. When the four months were over, any who owed even part of their dues were held 'at the king's mercy' (a misnomer in every way) with their families and possessions. What this meant was that they were reduced to beggary, even to serfdom. Many were imprisoned in the Tower of London and elsewhere, because it was felt that their sufferings would force them to find the money somehow. Even the Jews' worst enemies are recorded as pitying them in their situation.

As soon as this appalling episode was completed, the king 'transferred' the Jews to Edmund of Almain, Richard of Cornwall's son, so that the remainder of the 2,000 marks due to his father might be extracted from them.

It was the last time Henry could maltreat the Jews, because he died shortly afterwards – in November, 1272, leaving for his son, instead of the prosperous Jewish community that had existed when he took over the reins of government, a ruined group, the condition of which was to cause Edward I much trouble in the first eighteen years of his reign.

At the time of his accession, Edward I was still in the Middle East taking part in the Crusade. He did not return until 1274 and he then found that he was facing many problems, not least of them an almost totally impoverished Jewry, which was of no financial benefit to the Crown – and a very powerful Church, which was loudly clamouring for the end of usury.

It was clear from the start that Edward I was a man who, although he often took the easiest way out of any situation, also often tried well-meaning, if unsuccessful measures to improve the situation of his citizens. This was demonstrated so far as the Jews were concerned, when, a year after he returned to his realm, he issued the *Statum de Judeismo* – the Statutes of Jewry – in which, among a number of other strictures, Jews were forbidden to be money-lenders. Although the debts already owing to them were to be repaid, '.... no Usuries shall run in Time coming from the feast of Saint Edward last past.'

No Jew, therefore, 'shall lend any Thing at Usury, either upon Land, or upon Rent, or upon any other Thing:' and furthermore '... if any Jew shall lend at Usury contrary to this Ordinance, the King will not lend his aid, neither by himself nor his Officers, for the recovering of his Loan; but will punish him at his discretion for the Offence, and will do justice to the Christian that he may obtain his pledge again.' This meant, of course, that *no one* in Britain could now lend money at interest, because Christians had been forbidden to do it long before.

On the face of it, the *Statum de Judeismo* did, however, include many 'plusses' for the Jewish future, because, instead of the forbidden money-lending, the king encouraged the Jews to become merchants, artisans and farmers – and this was the first time in English history that the Jews were allowed to earn their living as merchants and artisans and, for this purpose (though for no other), to enter

When he came to the English throne in 1272, Edward I was still in the Middle East taking part in the Crusade. He returned to Britain in 1274 to face many problems, not least of them an impoverished Jewry. This idealised statue of the king who expelled the Jews is on the south-east corner of the outside of Lincoln Cathedral.

into free intercourse with Christians – providing they were wearing their 'Jew badges'. But right through, it was a case, once again, of the Jews winning on the roundabouts and losing on the swings. For instance, they were allowed to lease or even buy lands for tillage or farming for up to ten years, but were allowed to live only in towns under direct royal authority and only where the chirograph chests (which were now obsolete because of the prohibition on money-lending) had formerly been. The Statutes also emphasised that all Jews from seven years old must 'wear a badge on his outer Garment [this was considerably younger than on the Continent where the age was thirteen for boys and twelve for girls]; that is to say, in the Form of Two Tables joined, of yellow felt, of the Length of Six Inches, and of the Breadth of Three Inches.' And, 'that each one, after he shall be Twelve Years old, pay Three pence yearly at Easter of Tax to the King, whose Bondman he is; and shall hold place as well for a Woman as a Man.'

Except in some small details, the result of the lengthy Statutes of Jewry did much to worsen and little to better the Jews' lot. Although they could now be merchants and could have relations with non-Jews, the Statutes made sure that these contacts were for business communication only and this made both the business and private lives of Jewish traders very difficult. Because they were still officially the king's vassals, they were not allowed to be burgesses, who controlled buying and selling, and, furthermore, they could not join the craft guilds which were mostly of Christian foundation and certainly demonstrated a 'Christian' social sympathy, which was, it was felt by the administrators, impossible between Christian and Jew. In addition, the Jews were deliberately and expressly excluded from a statute given to merchants, both native and foreign, in 1283. Generally, too, normal trading for Jewish merchants would have been very difficult because they could not travel about as freely and as safely as Christians could – and if they gave customers credit, it was seldom repaid.

In farming, of course, these rules did not apply, but living in rural solitude did not attract, indeed, it frightened, many Jewish families, whose lives had been under constant peril in England for so many years. In any case, the permitted period of ten years was, in farming terms, so short as not to offer any security or permanence.

The fact that Jews were forbidden to live in any but the selected urban centres made life difficult enough and this was made considerably harder by orders such as one issued in 1277 for the arrest of people not living in what was now only a handful of authorised Jewries.

The Jew, rich or poor, was henceforth forced to change his way of life drastically, but he was still liable to the same dangers and lack of security as previously. And, needless to say, King Edward I continued to tax Britain's Jews as heavily as his father had. The majority could now no longer manage to pay the Jewish tax, which, in 1275, was 1,000 marks and, a year later, had another 3,000 marks added. Consequently, all those with outstanding debts to the Crown were imprisoned once again, their possessions were sold for the Treasury's benefit and their wives and children were deported overseas. Even the 3d. poll tax, laid down in the Statutes of 1275, was beyond the meagre resources of many really poor Jews.

So what history has always looked on as Edward's well-meaning attempt to re-establish his Jewish community ended in failure, though some of the wealthier Jewish financiers were able to turn to the wholesale corn and wool trades, as well as dealing in trinkets and jewellery. A few, it is true, took over farms, but mainly for the value of the woodcutting on the land, rather than actually farming it.

Many poor Jews, however, were faced with starvation and some, it is believed, were in such straits that they even turned to highway robbery. Some, on the other hand, became Christians, in order to become eligible for church-based charitable grants! Some went on secretly with their old, now forbidden, profession of usury.

Others tried to eke a living by clipping the coinage – filing the edges of coins in circulation and then melting the clippings to make more coins. This was strictly illegal and, if caught, the culprits were savagely punished. There were so many prosecutions of Jews in this connection that the king appointed a special judicial commission to look into coin clipping. On 17 November 1278, Jews throughout the country were arrested and house-to-house searches were made in their quarters in each city and town. Those against whom any evidence was found were arrested and sent for trial. An almost certainly exaggerated report at the time says that 680 Jews were imprisoned in the Tower of London. At any rate, a large number *were* hanged there the following year and some were also executed in other towns – and all the property of the condemned was given to the king. Among the victims were some of the most prominent Jewish men and women in English life, who would hardly have needed to resort to such petty dishonesty and were probably 'framed' as an example, by the planting of coin-clipping tools in their homes by official searchers.

The Jewish community was now in a constant state of alarm and panic, which was added to because anti-Semitism, on Christian religious grounds, was again on the increase. In many towns throughout the country, but particularly in Lincoln and Norwich, the shrines of reputed boy martyrs, who were said to have been put to death by the Jews, were receiving universal veneration. The wearing of the Jew badge, (known as the 'badge of shame') was most rigorously insisted on – even more than in other parts of Europe.

History was repeated when, in 1272, the principal London synagogue was confiscated (as it had been in 1243) with the lame excuse that the chanting disturbed the services in the nearby chapel of the Friars Penitent, to whom the building was then given. Thereafter, Jewish worship had to be carried on in private homes or in chapels which some of the wealthier Jews maintained in their homes – until 1282, when John Peckham, the Archbishop of Canterbury, ordered the confiscation and dismantling of these chapels also, with only one exception. Jews in other towns and cities were treated in the same way. There is, moreover, the strange case of Richard Swinfield, Bishop of Hereford, who having banned all relations between Jews and Christians, handed out wholesale excommunications to those of his flock who, despite his edicts, attended a Jewish wedding!

Then the Holy See took a hand. In November, 1286, a letter addressed to the Archbishops of Canterbury and York from Pope Honorius IV reaffirmed the decisions of the Lateran Councils and pointed out the evil effects of free intercourse between Jews and Christians in England, the pernicious consequences of the study of the Talmud and the continual infringement of the canon law on the subject. He called for counter measures, including sermons and spiritual penalties, to end this improper state of affairs. The Diocesan Synod of Exeter took up his suggestion the following year, reinforcing all the ancient canonical strictures against the Jews with an almost unparalleled severity.

Throughout the years between the late 1270s and the 1280s, all kinds of allegations and subsequent retributions were brought against the Jews, including the old excuse of ritual murder. Even the king joined in the general persecution – he was, in 1276, personally responsible for reviving an allegation of ritual murder that had been hanging over the London Jewish community since the close of Henry III's reign, when a child's body, bearing what were said to be tokens of crucifixion, was discovered in the Thames. This precipitated a massive persecution of the Jews on every side.

The Jews were now fined outrageously, their homes were confiscated, they were accused of blasphemy and sometimes burned and, in addition, great efforts were made to convert them to Christianity, especially because many who had previously converted were quietly returning to Judaism, even though they were threatened with all kinds of penalties for so doing. By 1283, all the London synagogues had been destroyed and, there were, by then, very few in existence in other parts of the country.

The king returned to London in the summer of 1289 direct from Gascony, which was still in the possession of the English monarchy. He had just completed the expulsion of the prosperous Jewish community of Gascony, after arresting them all and seizing their property to swell his ailing royal coffers. On arriving home, he found that many of the wealthier English Jews had already fled to the Continent and he was also faced with the unpleasant and unpalatable fact that his attempt to solve the Jewish problem in Britain had ended in chaos and failure. There and then, it is probable he made the decision to repeat his handling of the Gascon Jews on the considerably larger Jewish community in Britain – to banish them, once and for all. In effect, he was washing his hands – and the hands of Britain – of the Jews. Although, during the first few months after his return to England, he had other domestic matters to deal with, it cannot have been long before his plan for the expulsion was cut and dried. On 18 June 1290, he issued secret instructions to the sheriffs to seal all the *archae* in ten days time. On 18 July, writs were issued to the sheriffs informing them of the expulsion decree.

Was it sheer coincidence that the date chosen was 18 July, on which, that year, the Jewish Fast of the Ninth of Av (Tisha b'Av) was observed? The ninth day of the Jewish month of Av is commemorated each year by Jews fasting, as a sad reminder of all the evils that had befallen the Jews in earlier days – including the destruction of both the Jerusalem Temples. Previous Jewish historians have always seemed to regard the king's choice of this day for his 'final solution' as a great, if tragic, coincidence, but *was* it really a coincidence? The writer believes that it was not. After all, during much of the 200-odd years in which the Jews had lived in England, Christian priests and Jewish rabbis had, as previously stated, been quite often engaged in friendly, and often public, discussion of the merits of both religions. In addition, as has also been stated, Christian theologians are known to have consulted Hebrew sources from time to time. Many of them would, therefore, have had a great deal of knowledge about Judaism and its customs. So is it not likely that, when he was discussing the date of the issue of the writs with them, one of his archbishops or bishops might have advised the king that 18 July would be associated in Jewish minds with this special day of disaster and imprint on them the importance of obeying the royal edict without argument?

The drawing at the foot of this document shows, on the right, a serjeant holding a mace, symbol of royal authority, and three Jews, two of them wearing the 'Jew badge'. The page of text is part of a fourteenth century document, the Rochester annals, which covers the reign on Edward I. The illustration clearly relates to the expulsion of the Jews from England and the relevant part of the text reads: 'About this time, the provoking multitude of the Jews, who had in the past lived on sufferance in various cities and strongholds, were ordered with their wives and children, together with their moveable goods, to leave England around the feast of All Saints, which was given them as a final date which none dared transgress for fear of punishment...'.

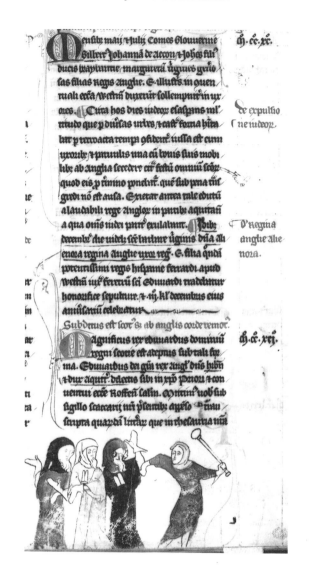

Whether or not the date that was to have such tragic consequences for England's Jews was deliberately planned, there is no doubt that, when they learned what their fate was to be, the effect on them was catastrophic. All Jews, the decree ordered, must leave England's shores before 1 November, 1290, – All Saints Day. Any Jews who were still in England after All Saints Day were liable to receive the death penalty.

Nevertheless, the king made every effort to secure peace and safety for the Jews during the short period (three and a half months) that they were permitted to remain in England. The sheriffs were ordered in the 18 July writs to proclaim publicly that 'no one within the appointed period should injure, harm, damage, or grieve them' and were also to ensure, for those who paid for it, a 'safe-conduct' to London. Furthermore, on 27 July, Edward issued another edict, this time, to all his 'wardens, officers and sailors of the Cinque Ports'. (At this time, the Cinque ports were Hastings, Romney, Hythe, Dover and Sandwich.) It informed them of the time limit fixed for the expulsion and continued:

> As we do not wish that they are harmed at all, whether in person or in possession during this period, we place these Jews in your care when they come to the above-mentioned ports with their wives, children and belongings to cross the sea before the aforementioned limit. You should ensure that their passage is safe and speedy, and that their journey, for which they should pay the expense, is free from danger.

In the same way, he went on, poor Jews were to be treated sparingly (at cheaper rates) and they should be treated with as much consideration as their wealthier co-religionists. In fact, the king also issued special writs of safe-conduct for some individual Jews.

The exiles were allowed to take with them all the property that was in their possession at the time of the expulsion decree, as well as any pledges given them by Christians that had not been redeemed before a fixed date. (It was clear from this that despite the prohibition of 1275, usury had still been allowed to go on.)

There were varying estimates of how many Jews were in England in July, 1290. Matthew Paris of St Albans Cloister, a thirteenth century historian, stated that more than 16,000 Jews left England at the Expulsion. On the other hand, more modern chroniclers put it at between two and four thousand, which seems more likely because so many Jews had left in the fifty years before they were finally banished.

London's poorer Jews started their journey to the coast on 10 October. They and many others did not, however, always meet with the merciful treatment for which the king had asked. The saddest case concerned a quite large group of richer Jews who, with all their property, embarked on a ship in the port of London. When he reached the mouth of the Thames, the rascally master of the vessel dropped his anchor during the ebb-tide, so that the ship grounded on the sands. He then suggested to his passengers that they should walk on the shore until it was refloated. He led them a long way, thus ensuring that they could not get back to the riverside until high tide. When they arrived back at the riverside, he ran into the water,

Bowls similar to this would have been among the possessions that wealthy Jews took with them when they were expelled in 1290. This thirteenth century bronze bowl, however, must have been left behind – it was found by a fisherman in a Suffolk brook in the seventeenth century. The band round the vessel, now known as the Bodleian Bowl, is inscribed in rhyming Hebrew verse: 'The gift of Joseph son of the Holy Rabbi Yechiel who answered and directed the Congregation as he desired, in order to see the face of Ariel [Jerusalem] as it is written in the Law of Jekuthiel [Moses]. "Righteousness delivereth from death".' (Proverbs, X, 2).

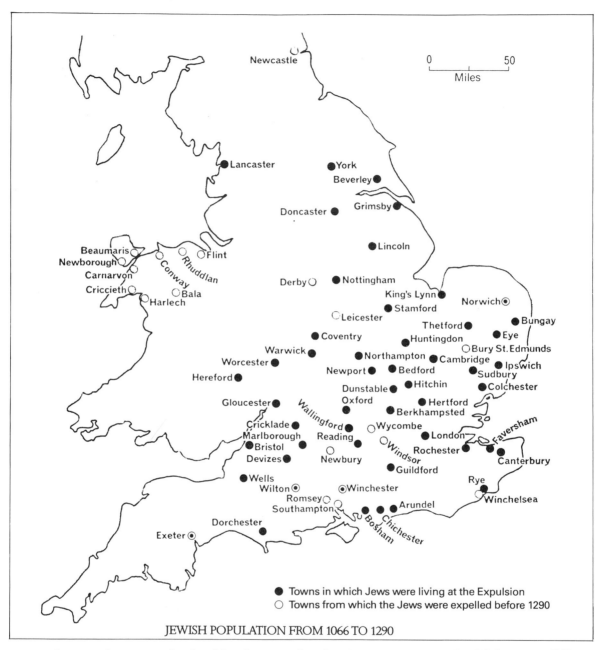

Towns in which Jews were living at the Expulsion
○ Towns from which the Jews were expelled before 1290

JEWISH POPULATION FROM 1066 TO 1290

A map showing where Jews lived in England and Wales up to the Expulsion.

climbed back on to the ship using a rope and told the Jews following that, if they needed help, they should call on their Prophet Moses. Trustingly, they followed him into the water and all of them were drowned and the captain and the crew divided among themselves all that the Jews had left on board. The fact that subsequently the master and his accomplices were arrested, convicted of murder and hanged, was of little consolation to those they had killed so ruthlessly. There were probably other such episodes of piracy against the banished Jews.

Another body of about 1,300 exiles, most of them poor, set sail for Wissant near Calais, at a charge of fourpence per head. During their voyage, fierce storms swept the sea and many were drowned. Most of those that survived were landed destitute on the French coast and were allowed by the French king to live for a short time in Amiens, though, later that year, the Pope censured this merciful action at the Parlement de la Chandeleur and it was decreed that all the Jews from England and Gascony who had taken refuge in the French king's realm should leave the country by the middle of the following Lent. It is believed that another quite large group of less affluent Jews made their way to Flanders (now Belgium).

Little is known of the fate of any of the exiles except that, as B.L. Abrahams tells us in *The Expulsion of the Jews from England in 1290*:

> The only known fact that we have to guide our conjectures as to the ultimate place of settlement of any of those who left England is that, in a list of the inhabitants of the Paris Jewry, made four years after the Expulsion, there appear certain names with the additions of l'Englische or l'Englais. It may well be that many Jews from England, speaking the French language, were able, in spite of the act of the Parlement de la Chandeleur, to become merged in the general body of the Jews of France, who were many times as numerous as those of England had been. Many, too, may have thrown in their lot with their 850,000 coreligionists of Spain.

There is also the possibility that a few may have settled quietly in other parts of France, including Vesoul. A small group certainly settled in Savoy, and, long afterwards, the Jewish Clerli family of Venice apparently traced its descent from the English exiles. Some may even have gone to the little island of Gozzo, near Malta, and at least one family ended up in Cairo! Hebrew manuscripts written in England found their way to Germany, Italy and Spain.

Although a few Jews, who had been in the favour of the king and other royal personages, were allowed before their departure to sell their houses and fees to any Christians who would buy them, most of the property they left behind them fell into the hands of the king. This included dwelling houses (and a few other houses which some Jews had continued to own, despite the Statute of 1275), synagogues and Jewish cemeteries, plus many bonds, partly for the

Boats similar to this one would have carried the Jews expelled from Britain. This type of vessel was used for trading in the North sea during the tenth, eleventh and twelfth centuries. It is called a nef and was a double-ended clinker-built vessel, undecked and steered with an oar over the stern. Details about it are sparse, but remains of earlier vessels that have been found suggest that it would have been 16–20 metres long, 4½–5½ metres beam and 1½–2 metres draught. This picture is after one in an early manuscript in the Bodleian Library. It is possible that it actually depicts the Jews' departure, because the figure on the left is wearing a Jews' hat, although , as it is from a medieval bestiary (a treatise on animals), it is also probable that it illustrates the story of Jonah and the Whale.

repayment of debts and partly for the delivery of wool and corn which had been paid for in advance. The value of the debts was about £9,100, but the king decided not to take the full amount for which the debtors would have been liable to their Jewish creditors, but only the bare principal that had been originally advanced. It seems ironical that even that sum was not fully collected in the king's lifetime, for one reason or another, and some of the debts actually remained outstanding until King Edward III finally gave up the claim to all further payments.

The Jewish community had vanished from Britain and, for nearly four centuries, there were no 'official' Jews living anywhere in the country. In the blood-stained record of Jewish persecution in the Middle Ages, it is a sad fact that what happened in England in 1189 and 1190 surpassed anything done to them in other parts of Europe and the 1290 banishment was the first general expulsion from any country during the medieval period. Edward I's example of expulsion was followed in France sixteen years later and in Spain (and subsequently Portugal) during the Spanish Inquisition in the fifteenth century.

But, nevertheless, there were some 'unofficial' Jews in Britain between the Expulsion and the resettlement in the seventeenth century. Some came by invitation as physicians or advisors, some as royal agents for shipping and finance, quite a few were surreptitious settlers. There is even evidence that there were sufficient Jews in England in 1358 to warrant a second expulsion by King Edward III. And then there were some Spanish and Portuguese (Sephardi) Jews (who had converted to Christianity during the Spanish Inquisition) and were probably doctors, merchants, soldiers and bankers during the reigns of Queen Mary I and Queen Elizabeth, when England's Jewish community was officially a thing of the past.

Nevertheless, the Spanish Jews played an interesting role in the following years. The Jews were expelled from Spain during the Spanish Inquisition in 1492 (and slightly later from Portugal) and the survivors were scattered all over Europe. A few managed to remain in Spain by feigning conversion to Christianity, but practising their Judaism in secret. They were insultingly called Marranos by other Jews (the old Spanish word for pigs or swine). In mortal danger, if their duplicity was discovered by the Inquisition, many of them fled, a few years later, into other parts of Europe. Among them were some forty families who eventually settled in England, still posing as Christians, because entry as Jews was forbidden to them. The way many of them lived was described in a confession of another Marrano, Gaspar Lopes, to the Milan Inquisition in 1540:

Further interrogated he [Gaspar Lopes] said that he knew Alves Lopes in London in whose house he, the deponent, lived for four or five days; and that he, Alves Lopes, holds a Synagogue in his house and lives in the Hebrew manner, though in secret; and that he, the deponent, saw these things and that in this Synagogue they went on one day only, the Sabbath; and that on that day there came to Alves's house other false Christians to the number of about twenty; and that it is true that whenever any refugee false Christians come from Portugal to go to England and Flanders and hence to Turkey or elsewhere, in order to lead the lives of Hebrews, they come to the house of the said Alves, who helps them to go whither they want to go for this purpose.

When Queen Elizabeth I came to the throne in 1558, the 'New Christians' (secret Jews) began to trickle into the country again, especially because the queen encouraged foreign merchants to settle and carry on their business in England. At the start of her long reign, there were only three thousand foreigners in the City of London; by the end of it, there were about ten thousand, among them quite a number of Spanish and Portuguese Marranos.

However, these secret Jewish communities, as such, did not survive long, not because they were Jewish, but because they were regarded as Protestant refugees. After Henry VIII's death, when his daughter, Mary I, came to the throne of England, her campaign of persecution against Protestants, including torture and burning at the stake, made life very dangerous indeed for anyone professing to be Protestant. Quite soon after her accession, therefore, the community leader, Henrique Nunes, and his family (and undoubtedly other families in the London community) went hastily to France and settled there, leaving, it is believed, very few of his group in England.

When Queen Elizabeth I came to the throne in 1558 with a totally opposite view of Protestants and Roman Catholics from her half-sister, the 'New Christian' Marranos began to trickle into the country again. The queen encouraged foreign merchants to settle and carry on their business in England. Indeed, at the start of her long reign, there were only three thousand foreigners in the City of London; by the end of it, there were about ten thousand. Among them, inevitably, were quite a number of Spanish and Portuguese Marrano 'New Christians', who found new opportunities of trade in England and, during the war with Spain, were used by London merchants as a cover for trade with Spain and Portugal. Jews were once more being 'used' by the English, but it enabled the Marrano community to reform and to become relatively well established. It was not long before another 'secret' Marrano Jewish community, led by a young unmarried doctor and international businessman named Heitor Nunes (or Dr Hectour, as he was generally known), was quite well established in London, as reported by Thomas Fernandos, a Marrano who was forced to give evidence to the Lisbon Inquisition.

And says, that eleven years ago, or thereabouts, finding himself orphaned of both father and mother, he left this city and went to an uncle named Anrique Nunes, physician, who at that time was living in Bristol, in the Kingdom of England, and about a year and a half ago he left Bristol, and has gone, as he is told, to Alvao [?] in France. And upon reaching his said uncle's house, he stayed with him about a year, and did what his uncle told him to do and after being a year in his house, his said uncle and his wife, who is called Beatriz Fernandes – began to speak to confessant upon certain matters of the old law, previous to which he remembers that both one and the other had said to him that the law of the Jews was good.

.... and he observed Saturdays, doing no work on that day, and he likewise observed the fast of Kippur every year while he was in that country, with his said uncle and aunt.

.... and so they kept the feast of unleavened bread, eating it on six or seven days. And he remembers that when he, this confessant, was going a sea journey his said aunt put unleavened bread in his provision bag, and told him if there was a storm to throw it into the sea, and the storm would cease; but confessant did not throw it into the sea, only before he was leaving the ship he threw it into the sea so it might not be seen on shore. And upon some of these festivals they did not work; and his said aunt made the said unleavened bread at home.

And he further remembers that a licentiate named Heitor Nunes, physician, a young unmarried man living in London, sent word every year to his uncle of the days on which Jewish festivals would fall.

.... he had worn clean shirts on Saturdays in honour of the Sabbath, and he also remembers that in the house of his uncle as aforesaid they observed other festivals besides that of unleavened bread.

.... his aunt, Beatriz Fernandes, of whom he has spoken, was reciting certain Jewish prayers, which she knew by heart, and one Jorge Dias, of whom he has spoken in one of his previous confessions, was writing down the said prayers on paper, and deponent believes that the said Jorge Dias was writing them down in order to say them, and deponent cannot say which prayers they were, because he was never able to learn Jewish prayers, for which reason his said aunt complained of him.

And deponent thinks, but he is not certain of this, that the said Rodrigo da Veiga said to him in London, about three years ago, that he was hoping that tables of the festivals and fasts of the Jews would come from Italy.

.... says: that when he was in Bristol, about three years ago, there came there one, Anrique Gonsalves, new Christian, who told this deponent several times that he came from London to Bristol with an aunt of deponent's named Beatriz Fernandes, and deponent's sisters, of whom he has spoken in his confessions, and that he had trouble to find clean things for them to eat in the inns, things which had not been in pans used by Christians, and he gave deponent to understand that they would not eat anything, but what Jews were accustomed to eat according to their rites.

Much of Hector Nunes' freedom in England was clearly due to the fact that he was able, with his widespread business contacts, to obtain valuable information for the English government in its struggle against Spain.

Though it is not believed that Shakespeare based his Shylock in *The Merchant of Venice* on any real Jew – and, indeeed, it is doubtful if he ever met one, it is possible that the other great Elizabethan dramatist, Christopher Marlowe, *did* base the character of Barabas in *The Jew Of Malta* on Dr Roderigo Lopez, a Portuguese Marrano, who became a medical attendant to Queen Elizabeth I in 1586. As a result of a court intrigue, Lopez was falsely accused of plotting against the queen's life and was executed in 1594. In the play, Barabas is also put

Despite his creation of Shylock (seen here in a scene from *The Merchant of Venice*), it is doubtful if Shakespeare ever met a Jew.

The Famous
TRAGEDY
OF
THE RICH IEVV
OF *MALTA*.

AS IT WAS PLAYD
BEFORE THE KING AND
QVEENE, IN HIS MAJESTIES
Theatre at *White-Hall*, by her Majesties
Servants at the *Cock-pit*.

Written by CHRISTOPHER MARLO.

LONDON,
Printed by I. B. for *Nicholas Vavasour*, and are to be sold
at his Shop in the Inner-Temple, neare the
Church. 1 6 3 3.

Lopez compounding to poyson the Queene.

Christopher Marlowe possibly based the character of Barabas in *The Jew of Malta* on Dr Roderigo Lopez, a Portuguese Marrano, who became one of Queen Elizabeth's doctors in 1586. The contemporary cartoon wrongly accuses Lopez of plotting against the queen's life, for which, as a result of a court intrigue, he was executed in 1594. In Marlowe's play, Barabas is also put to death, but Marlowe could only have guessed at the real life execution when he completed his play in 1590.

to death, but Marlowe could surely not have guessed at this when he completed his play in 1590.

The Marrano community in England did not start to decline until almost the end of the sixteenth century. One of the main reasons was the virtual close of trade relations between Britain and Spain and many Marranos were by then attracted to the newly established and very prosperous Jewish community in Amsterdam. Some of those who remained in England became totally assimilated with the Christian community. Some of the leaders, including Hector Nunes, had died. Others went to the Levant.

The positive end of the Marrano community, however, did not come until 1609, six years after King James VI of Scotland became King James I of England. At this time, a quarrel blew up among the now reduced community. One faction avenged itself on the other by denouncing its opponents as Judaisers (secret Jews) and the authorities had no alternative but, once again, to banish them, with the result that all Portuguese merchants living in London who were suspected of Judaising were expelled from the country.

It was in no way the same as the great expulsion of 1290, because, during the years that these people had resided in England, they had never publicly admitted their Jewishness, although many English people may have suspected that, underneath their Christian façade, they were still Jews.

It was to be another fifty years before the start of the great Resettlement.

CHAPTER FIVE
The Return

After the expulsion of the Portuguese Marranos in 1609, there was a break of some twenty years, during which there were neither Marrano secret (Crypto) Jews nor, of course, professing Jews in Britain. But, in about 1630, another small Marrano community entered the country. Its most distinguished member – and probably its leader – was Antonio Fernandez (otherwise Abraham Israel) Carvajal. A man of considerable wealth, it is believed that Carvajal was either born in the Canary Islands or that he was originally a native of Portugal and had settled in the Canaries. He had widespread commercial connections and, when he settled in England (coming from Rouen in France, where he had lived for a time in a small Marrano community), he naturally transferred his commercial activities to his new country and, in so doing, made a valuable contribution to the English economy. The group in which he was prominent formed the basis of what was later to be Britain's resettled Jewry. Carvajal became very prosperous and was soon known as 'the Great Jew'. He is said to have ridden fine horses, collected armour and imported £100,000-worth of bullion each year.

While most Marranos worshipped in their homes, there is good reason to believe that there was at least one secret synagogue in existence from sometime in the 1630s. It was in Creechurch Lane, between Houndsditch and Leadenhall Street in the City of London, and was in a property owned and lived in by a Jew named Moses Athias, who may well have been a clerk employed by Carvajal and, it is believed, was also a rabbi. It was, reports Lucien Wolf in his paper *Crypto-Jews Under the Commonwealth*,

> ... a large and mysterious-looking gabled house, which differed from its fellows chiefly in respect that the local gossips could make neither head nor tail of it ... Over a glass of canary in the Jeames Tavern hard by, garrulous busy-bodies would ask one another what use old Athias could have for so large a house, with its basements so strongly barred and its upper

windows so impenetrably curtained; and strange tales would
sometimes be told of papistical mysteries enacted within its
walls by the swarthy strangers and their mincing and bejewel-
led spouses who flocked thither at frequent but regular intervals. Muffled melodies and nasal recitatives were heard in the
still morning proceeding from the upper storeys ...

If, indeed, it *was* being used as a synagogue, there is no doubt that
what non-Jews heard as they passed the building was cantorial
music being sung and Hebrew prayers being said in unison. It is
probable that the secret synagogue in Creechurch Lane was not the
only one of its kind in London at that time. A baptised Jew, Paul
Isaiah, who wished to convert all Jews to Christianity, published a
brochure on the subject early in 1655, in which he stated that he
knew for certain that the Jews living in England at that time 'have
their Synagogues and there exercise Judaism.' Another manuscript
in existence mentions that, as well as the Creechurch Lane
synagogue, there was another Jewish house of worship in St
Helen's, of which one David Mier was 'priest'.

At the beginning of the seventeenth century, the subject of religion in Britain became not only very important, but also controversial and complicated, culminating in the Civil War between King
Charles I and his Royalists and Oliver Cromwell and his Parliamen-
tarians, which had religion as its root and perhaps its strongest *raison
d'être*, though not its whole cause.

As part of this coming upheaval, Puritanism was rising and, as its
fundamental creed was basically a return to the Bible, this automatically fostered greater Puritan tolerance towards the Jews, who
were, after all, the 'people of the Old Testament'. There was even
hope, among some Puritans, that Jews would become so interested
in the pure, fundamentalist Puritan doctrine that they would be willing to convert to it. At this time, Puritanism was naturally deemed
a danger towards the established Church and, coupled with it, was
fear and hostility towards the Jews or those who were tolerant of
them. As early as 1600, the Bishop of Exeter complained of the pre-
valence of 'Jewism' in his diocese and, in fact, numerous people
were prosecuted in London and England's eastern counties at that
time for holding what were termed 'Judaistic opinions' based on lit-
eral interpretation of the Old Testament. In 1612, two 'Arians' were
burned at the stake for teachings regarding the nature of God which
were similar to those of Judaism. (The Arians were a sect which
denied that the actual blood and body of Jesus were present in the
bread and wine of the Eucharist.) These two unfortunates were,

incidentally, the last two people in England to suffer capital punishment purely for their religion.

The disciples of John Traske, an extreme Puritan, so firmly followed the way of literalism that they were imprisoned on a charge of Judaising between 1618 and 1620. Probably the accusation was not far from the truth, because, shortly afterwards, a number of Traskites emigrated to Amsterdam and formally joined the synagogue there.

There was a growing movement for religious toleration during Oliver Cromwell's Commonwealth – and he was to be the instigator of bringing the Jews back to Britain.

Despite all this, the group of London Marrano Jews in the earlier part of the seventeenth century stayed relatively secure and, it is certain, continued to practise Judaism behind closed doors. One of the group, however, was not a Marrano. Simon (or Jacob) de Caceres was born in Amsterdam, where all Jews could practise Judaism freely and publicly. He settled in London because he had considerable business interests in the City and not only openly boasted of his Judaism, but did his best to persuade his secret co-religionists in the group to follow his example and proclaim their Judaism. How many of them did, however, is not clear, but his forthrightness certainly did not seem to do Simon de Caceres any harm, probably because he gave considerable service to his adopted home.

All Christians were not anti-Semitic, however. There was a growing movement for religious toleration and among the Baptists, one of the few sects to survive Oliver Cromwell's Commonwealth, it was urged that religious tolerance should be extended to all people without exception. In 1614, a member of this body, Leonard Busher, presented to King James I a tract entitled *Religious Peace or a Plea for Liberty of Conscience* and in this, the earliest English publication in which religious liberty, in its fullest sense, was urged, the point was made for the first time that by excluding the Jews, their conversion was impeded. Consequently, the writer suggested that not only should they be readmitted to Britain forthwith, but also that they should be allowed to take part in religious disputations without hindrance. This tract was reprinted in 1646, while the Civil War was still raging. Indeed, as the years passed, there was more and more controversy, not only on the subject of religion generally, but also as to whether or not the Jews should be readmitted and allowed to practise their religion. Many people *were* in favour of both, providing that Jews made no attempt to convert Christians.

The war was really 'all over bar the shouting' after the Battle of Naseby on 14 June 1645, but the Commonwealth (or Interregnum) did not officially start until after a second Civil War, followed by the execution of King Charles I on 30 January, 1649. In the winter of

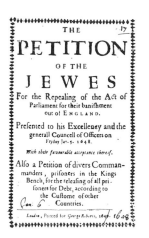

THE
PETITION
OF THE
JEWES
For the Repealing of the Act of
Parliament for their banifhment
out of ENGLAND.

Prefented to his Excelleney and the
generall Councell of Officers on
Fryday Jan. 5. 1648.

With their favourable acceptance thereof.

Alfo a Petition of divers Comman-
ders, prifoners in the Kings
Bench, for the releafing of all prifoners for Debt, according to
the Cuftome of other
Countries.

London, Printed for George Roberts, 1648. 1648

By the middle of the seventeenth century, there were strong feelings that Jews should be readmitted to Britain. In 1648/9 Joanna Cartwright and her son, Ebenezer, two Baptists from Amsterdam, presented a petition requesting the readmission.

1648–49, immediately after Pride's Purge, which had swept away the dominance of the Presbyterians in Parliament, the Council of Officers started to discuss the formation of a new constitution based upon what was called the Agreement of the People. One of its basic principles, it was suggested, should be a wide measure of liberty for all men to preach and advance their opinions in a peaceable manner. Furthermore, a group known as the Mechanic Council (possibly members of various trade guilds), meeting at Whitehall, passed what was, for those days, a very bold resolution in favour of universal tolerance of all religions 'not excepting Turkes, nor Papists, nor Jewes'. This policy was endorsed by the Council of War when it met on Christmas Day, 1648, and it is believed that it was suggested that a clause to this effect should be included in the new constitution.

The feeling that the Jews should be readmitted to the country was clearly growing stronger. Indeed, the Council of Officers actually petitioned Parliament to consider the repeal of the banishment of the Jews. Then, in January, 1649, Joanna Cartwright and her son, Ebenezer, two Baptists from Amsterdam, presented, through Lord Fairfax, the Commander-in-Chief, a petition requesting the readmission of the Jews 'to trade and dwell in this land, as they now do in the Netherlands'. It was agreed that this should be considered immediately the present urgent public affairs were dwelt with (not least of them the king's execution the same month).

But the time was not yet ripe for the Jews' readmittance. There were still many Dissenters, mainly on religious grounds, despite a plea at the time in the public press by Edward Nicholas entitled *An Apology for the honourable nation of the Jews, and all the sons of Israel*, which described the troubles England had suffered as a punishment for her past maltreatment of the people of God, and stressed that it was only by making amends that she could hope to enjoy the Divine blessing again, as she had done in former times.

Though it would probably have accepted the re-entry of the Jews, the Establishment could still not accept the possibility of religious toleration for a 'non-Christian' religion and this feeling led one William Erbury, the chaplain of Skippon's regiment, to ask 'To what purpose will you give that liberty to the Jews and others to come in, unless you grant them the exercise of their religion?' Subsequently, on 20 January, 1649, the modified Agreement of the People was presented to Parliament, allowing religious freedom for only those who would 'profess faith in God by Jesus Christ'.

This set-back for religious toleration made it clear that, if and when the Jews were readmitted, it would not be on idealistic grounds.

It is the opinion of Antonia Fraser, in her biography, *Cromwell – Our Chief of Men*, that Oliver Cromwell himself had, by the early 1650s come to the conclusion that the Jews should certainly be readmitted to Britain, not from the standpoint of religious tolerance or missionary zeal to convert them to Christianity (the reason that many Christian sects would have welcomed them back), or even, primarily as successful financiers and businessmen (and here she differs from the views of some other historians). Cromwell, as Protector,

> ... had begun to have an extremely pragmatic respect for the activities of their people as a whole, not so much theological... as in their role as skilled purveyors of foreign intelligence. The Protector of the 1650s was no longer the straightforward soldier of the the 1640s: the resettlement of Jews, their employment in his world-wide activities fitted well into the dreams of imperial expansion which from 1654 onwards were beginning to occupy the most grandiose mansion of his mind.

There are many references in letters written by John Thurlow, Secretary to the Council of State, to Jews being used as intelligence agents for England, and, some indeed, in other contemporary documents. As Antonia Fraser further explains:

> The Jews then were rapidly establishing themselves in Oliver's mind as people willing and anxious to share in his vision of an expanding and successful England; as with some Catholics, he was increasingly willing to overlook their religious proclivities in favour of their peaceful and profitable intentions. And from every point of view he was surely right; the first Jews were said to have brought one and a half million in cash into England.

If Antonia Fraser's contention is correct, the Lord Protector was seeking the best of two worlds.

In Amsterdam, the Jewish religious and intellectual leader was Rabbi Manasseh ben Israel; born Manuel Dias Soeiro in Madeira in 1604, but brought by his family to the Netherlands when he was very young. His parents were probably Marranos, which would account for his original name, which he or they changed when they settled in Holland where, as has been said, Jews were allowed total religious freedom.

Manasseh ben Israel wrote many books and sermons and, in 1650, he produced a treatise in Latin, which dealt with recent discoveries of Jewish settlements all over the world except in England.

Rabbi Manasseh ben Israel, Amsterdam's Jewish leader, who was to be the architect of the Resettlement of the Jews in Britain, is seen here in an etching by the great Dutch artist, Rembrandt, whose friend he was.

Manasseh ben Israel wrote many books in different languages, including Dutch, Hebrew, Latin, Spanish and English. Illustrated here are two of his works; (left) one in Spanish called *Piedra Gloriosa*, written in 1655, about the book of Daniel, with special reference to Nebuchadnezzar and (right) *Nishmat Hayyim*, written in 1651, a treatise in Hebrew on the nature of the soul.

His treatise, called *The Hope of Israel*, was an instant success. During the same year, it was published in English and he dedicated this edition to the English Parliament whose 'favour and goodwill' were respectfully solicited for the scattered Jewish nation. It ran into three editions in as many years and many theologians discussed and answered it. The most memorable contribution to the discussion was written by Sir Edward Spenser of Middlesex who, as a member of the body to whom the work had been directed in the first instance, composed a formal answer, *An Epistle to the Learned Manasseh ben Israel, in answer to his, dedicated to the Parliament.* This work discussed seriously the conditions upon which the resettlement of the Jews in England might be allowed. Some of those conditions were quite ludicrously severe but it was nevertheless clear that the writer – and other leading English figures – were quite sincere about the possiblity of the Jews' return.

In 1651, an English mission, headed by Chief Justice Oliver St John, arrived in the Hague to negotiate an alliance between England and the United Provinces. While the mission was in Holland, its secretary, Secretary of State John Thurlow, visited Amsterdam and sought out Manasseh ben Israel. In the light of the strong possibility that Oliver Cromwell now wanted the Jews to return, it is very likely that Thurlow was acting to further Cromwell's plans when, as is believed, he advised Manasseh ben Israel to make formal application to the English government for the readmission of the Jews. Unfortunately, before Manasseh could set out for London to put this plan into operation, war broke out between England and Holland and he had to turn back. He did not give up hope, however, and, when, in 1654, illness prevented him from making the journey himself, he sent his son, Samuel Soeiro, and a Marrano merchant named Manuel Martinez Dormido to London to see Oliver Cromwell, who had been ruling England as Lord Protector since December, 1653.

On 3 November 1654, Dormido and Soeiro presented two petitions to Oliver Cromwell. One recounted Dormido's' personal history (he had been ruined by the recent Portuguese reconquest of Brazil) and requested that diplomatic representations should be made to assist him to recover his fortune. The other pleaded that the Jews should be readmitted to England 'graunting them libertie to come with their families and estates, to bee dwellers here with the same eaquallnese and conveniences which your inland subjects doe enjoy', with Dormido as their consul.

There is no doubt that Cromwell was very favourably disposed to Dormido's second request and, perhaps to demonstrate his goodwill, early the following year, he wrote to the king of Portugal requesting compensation for the losses that Dormido had suffered in Brazil. Since Dormido was not only a Jew, but a foreigner who had been in England only a few months, this was a very considerable concession on the part of the Protector, who, it is believed, at the same time, told Dormido that he approved of the idea of readmitting the Jews. However, he also made it clear that he felt it was important that Manasseh ben Israel should come to England, as soon as possible, to deal with the matter personally.

Accordingly, some time in the middle of 1655, Samuel Soeiro returned to Amsterdam to report to his father and although Manasseh was not fully recovered from his illness, he insisted on setting out for England without delay. He arrived in the middle of September, just before Rosh Hashanah, the Jewish New Year, which was, in fact, because of his presence, celebrated publicly in London probably for the first time for 365 years.

It is interesting to note that Manasseh's lodging, where he was to stay for his two-year sojourn in England, was in the Strand in London, near the New Exchange (a kind of seventeenth century Burlington Arcade) which was situated where the Adelphi now stands. Most Jews who came to visit London lodged somewhere in the City, near the Marrano community in and around Creechurch Lane, and it may seem surprising that Manasseh ben Israel did not do the same, particularly since he had at least one cousin living in the community. The reason for staying where he did may well have been

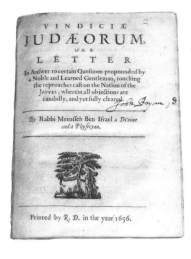

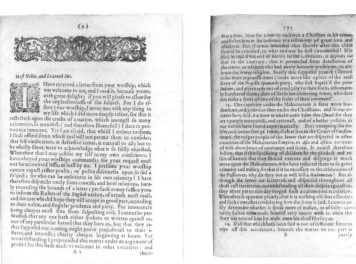

Manasseh ben Israel lived in London for two years and, in 1656, during his stay, he wrote *Vindiciae Judaeorum*, to defend the Jews against attacks and accusations which were being made on them at the time. Pictured here are the title page of this work, the first page of the text and page 7, on which he discusses a blood libel accusation.

because he had been, officially or unofficially, invited to come by Oliver Cromwell and so his lodgings may have been provided by the government, which would have found it more convenient for him to be nearer the seat of government.

Manasseh brought with him a short pamphlet which he had prepared in English some time previously. It was addressed *To His Highness the Lord Protector of the Common-wealth of England, Scotland, and Ireland. The Humble Addresses of Manasseh ben Israel, a Divine, and Doctor of Physick, in behalfe of the Jewish Nation.* It stated the following:

Three things if it please your Highnesse, there are that make a strange Nation well-beloved amongst the Natives of a land where they dwell: (as the defect of those three things make them hatefull) viz. Profit, they may receive from them; Fidelity they hold towards their Princes; and the Noblenes and purity of their blood. Now when I shall have made good, that all these three things have been found in the Jewish Nation, I shall certainly persuade your Highnesse, that with a favourable eye (Monarchy being changed into a Republicq), you shall be pleased to receive again the Nation of the Jews, who in time past lived in that Island: but, I know not by what false informations, were cruelly handled and banished.

Profit is a most powerful motive, and which all the World prefers before all other things and therefore we shall handle that point first. It is a thing confirmed, that merchandizing is, as it were, the proper profession of the Nation of the Jews. I attribute this in the first place, to the particular Providence and mercy of God towards his people: for having banished them from their own Country, yet not from his Protection, he hath given them, as it were, a naturall instinct, by which they might not only gain what is necessary for their need, but that they should also thrive in Riches and possessions; whereby they should not onely become gracious to their Princes and Lords, but that they should be invited by others to come and dwell in their Lands.

... As for Fidelity, this same affection is confirmed by the inviolable custom of all the Jews wheresoever they live: for on every Sabbath or festivall Day, they every where are used to pray for the safety of all Kings, Princes and Common-wealths, under whose jurisdiction they live, of what profession-soever: unto which duty they are bound by the Prophets and the Talmudists; from the Law, as by Jeremie chap 29 verse 7. 'Seek the peace of the City unto which I have made you to wander: and pray for her unto the Lord, for in her Peace you shall enjoy peace.' He speaks of Babylon, where the Jews at that time were captives. From the Talmud ord. 4. tract. 4. Abodazara pereq. 1. 'Pray for the peace of the Kingdome, for unless there were feare of the Kingdome, men would swallow one the other alive, &c.'

... Now, I will not conceale to say, but that alwayes there have bene found some calumniators, that endevouring to make the Nation infamous, laid upon them three most false reports, as if they were dangerous to the Goods, the Lives, and withall to the very souls of the Natives. They urge against them their usuries, the slaying of infants to celebrate their Passe-over, and the inducing Christians to become Jews. To all which I shall answer briefly.

1. As for usury, such dealing is not the essential property of the Jews, for though in Germany there be some indeed that practise usury; yet the most part of them that live in Turkey, Italy, Holland, and Hamburg, being come out of Spaigne, they hold it infamous to use it; and so with a very small profit of 4. or 5. per Cent, as Christians themselves do, they put their money ordinarily in Banco: for to lay out their money without any profit, was commanded only towards their brethren of the same Nation of the Jews, but not to any other Nation.

...Our Religion forbids absolutely the robbing of all men, whatsoever Religion they be of. In our Law it is a greater sinne to rob or defraud a stranger, than if I did it to one of my own

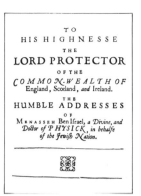

When he first came to stay in London, Manasseh ben Israel brought with him a short pamphlet he had previously prepared in English, the title page of which is reproduced here.

profession: because a Jew is bound to shew his charity to all men: for he hath a precept, not to abhorre an Idumean, nor an Egyptian; and that he shall love and protect a stranger that come to live in his land. If notwithstanding there be some that do contrary to this, they do it not as a Jewes simply, but as wicked Jewes, as amongst all nations there are found generally some Usurers.

2. As for the killing of young children of Christians; Whereas the whole world may easily perceive, it is but a mere slander, seeing it is known that at this day, out of Jerusalem, no sacrifice nor blood is in any use by them, even that blood which is found in an Egg is forbidden them, how much more mans blood? But I must not be too prolix; it may suffice to say, that by the Pope himself it was defined in full Counsell the accusation to be false;

3. As for the third Point, it may happen, that some of the Sect of the Papists, of a better mind, embrace the Jewish Religion; it cannot therefore be presumed, that they were induced thereunto by the Jews; seeing the Jews do not entice any man to profess their law: But if any man of his own free-will come to them, they by their rites & Ceremonies are obliged to make proof of them, whether they come for any temporall interest, and to persuade them to look well to themselves what they do: that the Law unto which they are to submit themselves, is of many precepts; and doth oblige the transgressor to many sore punishments. And so we follow the example of Nahomi, cited in the Sacred Scripture, who did not persuade Ruth to go along with her, but said first to her: Orpa thy sister returned to her Nation and her Gods; go thou and follow her, But Ruth continuing constant, then at length she received her.

Besides this, the Jews indeed have reason to take care for their own preservation; and therefore will not go about by such wayes to make themselves odious to Princes and common-wealths, under whose Dominions they live.

Cromwell wasted no time. He took Manasseh's petition to a meeting of the Council of State on 12 November 1655, determined to have it accepted as quickly as possible. He further tabled a motion that 'the Jews deservinge it may be admitted into this nation to trade and trafficke and dwel amongst us as providence shall give occasion'.

But, as is the habit of councils and committees, they did not pass it immediately. Instead, they set up a sub-committee to consider the matter and this body promptly recommended that outside opinion should be consulted. For just under a month, the matter was debated and written about in and out of Parliament. Judges were asked for their opinions and high ranking members of the Church contributed theirs, mostly opining that to bring people into Britain, otherwise than as Christians in a Christian country, was nothing short of blasphemous.

On Tuesday, 4 December, a representative conference, including some of the leading political, legal, theological and business men in the country, met in the Council Chamber in Whitehall. The meeting was presided over by the Lord Protector, who with his usual direct-ness and good sense, declared that there were only two questions for the conference to debate; namely, whether (a) it was lawful to admit the Jews and (b) if it were lawful, on what terms it was proper to receive them. Sir John Glynne, Chief Justice of the Upper Bench, and William Steele, Chief Baron of the Exchequer, declared forth-with that, despite the general belief, there was no law which for-bade the return of the Jews to England – the Expulsion of 1290, they explained, had been an act of royal prerogative and applied only to the persons immediately concerned. (A wry pronouncement, which meant, in essence, that the Jews could have come back at any time *after* the Expulsion without breaking the law.)

The second question was not so easily or quickly answered. Dur-ing the first and four further sessions of the conference (on 7, 12, 14 and 18 December) the argument continued. The 'motion' was mainly contested by the theologians, who contended that for the Jewish religion to be followed 'publicly' was totally blasphemous and expressed their fears that there would be attempts by Jews to proselytise Christians. Only a few agreed with the political rep-resentatives who were for unconditional readmission.

The final meeting was thrown open to the public and this evoked much controversy raised by members of the not-very-orderly mob who attended, including many merchants protesting that the admission of the Jews would enrich foreigners at the expense of the natives and thus cause the decline of English trade. Even those who agreed with readmission said that it should be permitted only under most stringent conditions – mostly following the medieval codes which precluded Jews from holding legal positions or public office, speaking or acting against Christianity, profaning the Christ-ian Sabbath, employing Christian servants, printing anti-Christian literature, converting Christians to Judaism or discouraging people who attempted to propagate the Christian gospel among the Jews.

They argued well into the night and did not come to a decision and, at last, Cromwell intervened, saying that it was clear that no help was to be expected from the conference and that he and the Council would have to take their own course. He therefore asked those present to give him the benefit of their prayers and that he might be directed to act for the glory of God and the good of the nation. So saying, he stepped down from the daïs and abruptly closed the conference.

The Council of State came to no firm decision either. Christmas came and went and, by the time the year 1656 was three months old, it seemed doubtful if a definite ruling on the subject of the Jews' readmission would ever be given.

It is likely that Cromwell decided that at that time, public opinion was too strong to go the whole way and he compromised by maintaining the *status quo* – the present state of affairs which permitted those Marrano Jews living mainly in London to observe their ancestral rights undisturbed. There were, however, one or two unpleasant incidents at this time involving members of the London Marrano group, because of the war that broke out in the autumn of 1655 between England and Spain. The following March, the Council of State proclaimed that all Spanish monies, merchandise and shipping would be lawfully confiscated by the State. This meant that the Marranos, almost all of whom had been born in Spain, were under threat, because, despite fleeing that country to avoid persecution or death, they were still Spanish subjects in the eyes of the English law. One of their wealthiest members, Antonio Rodrigues Robles, who lived in Duke's Place, London, nearly lost all his property and ships when he was denounced by a jealous scrivener and a compatriot. Eventually, however, the matter was straightened out and Robles and other Jews in the same situation were safe from molestation while living in England.

Shortly after this, Manasseh ben Israel and some other London Jews sent another petition to 'His Highness Oliver Lord Protector of the Commonwealth of England, Scotland & Ireland & the Dominions thereof'. It stated:

> The Humble Petition of the Hebrews at present Residing in this city of London whose names are underwritten Humbly showeth:
>
> That acknowledging the manyfold favours and Protection your Highness hath been pleased to grant us in order that we may with security meet privately in our particular houses to our Devotions, and being desirous to be favoured more by your Highness we pray with Humbleness that by the best

meanes which may be such Protection may be granted us in writing as that we may therewith meet at our private devotions in our particular houses without feare of molestations either to our persons, families or estates, our desires being to live peaceably under your Highness' Government. And being we all mortal, we also humbly pray your Highness to grant us license that those which may die of our nation may be buried in such a place out of this city as we shall think convenient with the proprietor's leave in whose land this place shall be, and so we shall as well in our lifetime, as at our death be highly favoured by Your Highness for whose long life and prosperity we shall continually pray to the almighty God.

The petition was signed by Manasseh ben Israel, David Abrabanel, Abraham Israel Carvajal, Abraham Coen Gonzales, Jahacob de Caceres, Abraham Israel De Brito and Isak Lopez Chillon.

The Jews were now safe to live in Britain openly, but they had not been formally readmitted. It was to be eight years before their presence was made official and, by then, Oliver Cromwell, the man who was undoubtedly their champion, had been dead for six years.

Part of the unofficial recognition by the State which the Jewish community now enjoyed was freedom to cease worshipping secretly and to bury their dead in a public Jewish cemetery. The first move was to open a synagogue. Accordingly, in December, 1656, the upper floor of a house in Creechurch Lane in the City of London was rented on a 21-year lease for £40 per annum from William Whitby, who then owned the property. Could it have been the same building in which the secret synagogue had been housed over twenty years earlier? It seems quite likely. Work was begun immediately to adapt it for religious use and the synagogue was opened for worship at the beginning of 1657. The lease had been acquired by Antonio Carvajal and, in February, 1657, he and his equally wealthy colleague, Simon da Caceres, leased land in Mile End, London, to be used as a Jewish cemetery.

Perhaps even a more positive sign, in English eyes, of the legitimacy of the Jewish community in England was that, fairly early in 1657, Samuel Dormido became the first Jewish member of the Royal Exchange, ultimately to become the Stock Exchange, and, furthermore, he was not required to take the prescribed Christian oath.

Nevertheless, readmission, as such, had still not been ratified and the feeling of disappointment and failure felt by Manasseh ben Israel, was very acute, especially since he was still living in England

and, by the end of 1656, was in considerable financial straits. So short of money was he that he was forced to appeal to Cromwell for help. The Lord Protector granted him first £25 and then a pension of £100 per annum. But, alas, the Treasury would not or could not pay. Then in September, 1657, his only surviving son, Samuel, who had come from Holland with Manuel Dormido, died. Manasseh was again forced to plead for financial help – enough to take the body of his son home to Amsterdam for burial. In return for surrendering his pension rights, he was granted £200, but it is believed that, in the end, the money came from a private source and not from the Treasury. It was probably a loan from Antonio Carvajal and other members of the Marrano community. Manasseh outlived his son by only a few weeks. On his way home from England, he died, on 20 November, in his brother's house in Middleburg in Holland. His body was taken to Amsterdam to be buried there by the Amsterdam Jewish community which he had served for nearly forty of his fifty-three years.

Some historians have claimed that Manasseh ben Israel died from a broken heart because of his failure to obtain official readmission to England for the Jews. It is possible that whatever terminal illness he had was hastened by the worry, harassment, shortage of money and the travelling that his endeavours had involved, but it is unlikely that his state of mind alone was the cause of his death. He had not, in any case, really failed in his mission and a man of his perception must surely have realised that. While he had not completed his plan, he had set the scene for the successful re-establishment of Britain's Jewish community.

The debate about the Jewish question was still going on when Oliver Cromwell died on 3 September, 1658. He was reluctantly succeeded by his gentle and ineffectual son, Richard, who remained Protector for just over a year.

Very soon, a petition was sent to the new Protector by a group of London merchants who saw a chance to rid themselves of their Jewish competitors. The petition demanded the expulsion of those Jews who were back in England and that their property should be confiscated before they left. Fortunately for the Jews, Richard who had a lot else on his mind, ducked the issue and deferred dealing with it. Richard withdrew from public life in June, 1659. Six months later a merchant of questionable character, named Thomas Violet, made an application before the courts for the law to be set in motion against the Jews, but the courts also deferred dealing with the matter, telling Violet that '... in the present delicate state of political affairs, consideration had better be postponed'.

It was again a providential decision so far as the Jewish community was concerned. On 16 May 1660, King Charles II, son of the beheaded King Charles I, returned to England, after fifteen years in exile, to ascend the throne from which his father has been ousted. Though it might have been expected that all Oliver Cromwell's decisions would be reversed, one, at any rate, was not – indeed, it was helped, at last, to come to fruition.

Charles had nothing against the Jews as citizens – and religion, at least at this stage of his life, did not interest him. Besides, he realised with a shrewdness that would stand him in good stead in his royal career, that he might well find the Jews useful in the future – certainly financially. The readmission of the Jews to Britain must clearly have been in his mind when, still in exile, he had attempted to raise a loan from the Jews of Amsterdam, assuring them that, if they were amenable, 'they shall find that when God shall restore us to the possession of our rights and to that power which of right doth belonge to us we shall extend that protection to them which they can reasonable expecte and abate that rigour of the Lawes which is against them in our several dominions'. Even so, he failed to raise the loan he sought, though among those who were seriously helping to restore him to the throne were members of the wealthy Jewish da Costa family and Augustine Coronel, who was also a personal friend of General Monk, the 'King Maker'. The king's future behaviour seems to have confirmed his tolerance and, indeed, kindness towards the Jewish community, which was now growing steadily, if still surreptitiously, as a steady trickle of Jewish families arrived on Britain's shores from several parts of Europe.

The king himself, there is no doubt, would have been perfectly willing to legalise the Jews' position in his realm very early in his reign, but it was not to be. The Lord Mayor and the Corporation of the City of London, which included many prominent merchants, began immediately to intercede with the new king to turn back the clock so far as his Jewish subjects were concerned. They protested, with considerable exaggeration, about the great increase of Jews in the country. They complained that the Jews interfered with the trade of the citizens. They stressed that the Jews' correspondence with their co-religionists in other countries was treasonable. *And* they beseeched the King:

> to cause the former laws made against the Jews to be put into execution, and to recommend to your two Houses of Parliament to enact such new ones for the expulsion of all professed Jews out of your Majesty's dominions, and to bar the door

On 16 May 1660, King Charles II, son of the beheaded King Charles I, ascended the throne from which his father had been ousted. One of Oliver Cromwell's decisions which he did *not* reverse was the readmittance of the Jews; indeed, he helped it, at last, to receive official recognition.

The Right Hon.ble
Denzil Baron Holles of Ifield.

Denzil Holles, the Privy Council spokesman, who presented a petition from the Jewish community to the House of Commons on 17 December 1660 to counter several petitions from non-Jews, including City merchants, to have Jews expelled from the country again.

after them with such provisions and penalties, as in your Majesty's wisdom shall be found most agreeable to the safety of religion, the honour of your Majesty, and the good and welfare of all your subjects.

In addition, the reprehensible Thomas Violet (who had also tried, without success, to discredit the Jewish community by planting a collection of counterfeit foreign coins on its newly appointed rabbi) renewed his previous application in the courts, which advised him to lay the matter before the Privy Council. He did so most virulently, in common with several other bigots, who also presented vitriolic petitions against the Jews. The small London Jewish community were naturally terrified at all this and quickly prepared a counter-petition, but they need not have worried – or hurried. The king had obviously made it clear to the Privy Council that the Jews were not to be proceeded against or harassed in any way, because when the city merchants' and others' petitions and the Jews' counter-petition were put before it on 7 December, no order was made. Instead the various documents were referred to Parliament, not for adjudication but, as Cecil Roth puts it in *A History of the Jews of England*, '... so that measures might be taken into consideration for safeguarding those concerned, the desirability of whose presence in the country was assumed to be beyond discussion.'

Denzil Holles, the Privy Council spokesman, presented the documents to the House of Commons on 17 December 'as specially recommended to them for their advice therein, touching protection for the Jews'. The House promised to consider the matter 'at an early opportunity', but the Convention of Parliament was dissolved a week later and it is more than possible that the City of London and the others who petitioned never received any reply. Nevertheless, it was clear to all that the attitude of Charles II towards the Jews was very much the same as that of Oliver Cromwell, however much they may have differed on other aspects of government.

But nothing official had yet emerged from Parliament when, on 26 February 1663, a vote was passed in the House of Commons 'that a Committee be appointed to prepare and bring in laws to prevent encroachments in trade by the Jews or French or any other Foreigners'. Probably because of the royal protection, nothing came of that either. On I July 1664, however, the Conventicle Act came into force. This act, actually aimed only at Christian non-conformists, prohibited assemblies for prayer except in accordance with the liturgy of the Church of England. Once again, the Jewish community panicked, especially when, almost immediately, the Earl of

Berkshire told them that he had been instructed by the king to protect them, but he would only do so if they 'came to an arrangement' with him. If they did not, he said, he would confiscate their property. It is interesting to note that the Earl of Berkshire was a son of the Earl of Suffolk, the man who had been responsible for the expulsion of the Marranos from England in 1609. Fortunately, however, the Jews suspected the Earl and sent an address to the king himself, pleading to be allowed to remain in his kingdom under the same protection as the rest of his subjects. The king referred this petition to the Privy Council with, obviously, the instruction that something official was to be done. The result, on 22 August 1664, was a written document which assured the Jews that no instructions had been given for disturbing them and, further, that they might 'promise themselves the effects of the same favour as formerly they have had, soe long as they demeane themselves peaceably & quietly with due obedience to his Mat^{ies} Lawes & without scandall to his Government.' Although it was not until 1673 that the *religious* status of Britain's Jews was made legal, the authorisation for Jews to live in Britain had been given in writing for the first time.

* * * * *

The religious life of the Spanish and Portuguese Jewish congregation was now carried on openly in the synagogue in Creechurch Lane. The congregation welcomed two special Christian visitors in 1662 and 1663 and their detailed descriptions of their visits paint a fascinating picture of Jewish worship, as seen through seventeenth-century Christian eyes.

The first visit was recorded in a letter from John Greenhalgh to his friend Thomas Crompton on 22 April 1662.

> ... lately having a desire to spend some of my time here in learning the Hebrew tongue, and inquiring of some one that professed to teach it, I lighted upon a learned Jew with a mighty bush beard, a great Rabbi as I found him afterward to be, with whom after once or twice being together, I fell into conference and acquaintance; for he could speak Latin, and some little broken English, having as he told been two years in London. He said he was an Hebrew of the Hebrews of the Tribe of Levi, and his name (I had like to have said his Christian name) Samuel Levi.... He said he was brought up, and was a student eleven years, in the Jews College in Cracovia the chief city of Poland ... and that himself had formerly been Priest to a Synagogue of his own nation in Poland ... he told me that he had special relation

as Scribe and Rabbi to a private Synagogue of his nation in London, and that if I had a desire to see their manner of worship, though they did scarce admit of any, their Synagogue being strictly kept with three doors one beyond another, yet he would give me such a ticket, as, upon sight thereof, their porter would let me in upon their next Sabbath Day in the morning being Saturday. I made show as though I were indifferent, but inwardly hugged the good hap.

When Saturday came I rose very early, the place being far from my lodging; and in a private corner of the City, with much ado, following my directions, I found it at the point of nine o'clock, and was let come in at the first door, but there being no Englishmen but myself, and my Rabbi not being there then (for they were but just beginning the service) I was at first a little abashed to venture alone amongst all them Jews; but my innate curiosity to see things strange spurring me on, made me confident even to impudence. I rubbed my forehead, opened the inmost door, and taking off my hat (as instructed) I went in and sate me down amongst them; but Lord (Thoma frater) what a strange, uncouth, foreign, and to me barbarous sight was there, I could have wished Thoma that you had then sate next me, for I saw no living soul, but all covered, hooded, guized, veiled Jews, and my own plain bare self amongst them. The sight would have frightened a novice, and made him to have run out again.

Every man had a large white vest, covering, or veil cast over the high crown of his hat, which from thence hung down on all sides, covering the whole hat, the shoulders, arms, sides, and back to the girdle place, nothing to be seen but a little of the face; this, my Rabbi told me, was their ancient garb, used in Divine Worship in their Synagogues in Jerusalem and in all the Holy Land before the destruction of their City: and though to me at first, it made altogether a strange and barbarous show, yet me thought it had in its kind, I know not how, a face and aspect of venerable antiquity. Their veils were all pure white, made of taffeta or silk, though some few were of a stuff coarser than silk; the veil at each of its four corners had a broad badge; some had red badges, some green, some blue, some wrought with gold, or silver, which my Rabbi told me were to distinguish the tribes of which each was common....

Their Synagogue is like a Chapel, high built; for after the first door they go upstairs into it, and the floor is boarded; the seats are not as ours, but two long running seats on either side, as in school: at the west end of it there is a seat as high as a pulpit, but made deskwise, wherein the two members of the Synagogue did sit veiled, as were all both priest and people. The chief Ruler was a very rich merchant, a big, black, fierce, and stern man to whom I perceive they stand in as reverential an awe as boys to a master; for when any left singing upon books and talked, or that some were out of tune, he did call aloud with a barbarous thundering voice, and knocked upon the high desk with his fist, that all sounded again. Straight before them, at some distance but upon a seat much lower, sate the Priest. Two yards before him, on midst of the floor, stood that whereon the Service and Law were read, being like to an high short table, with steps to it on one side as an altar, covered with a green carpet, and upon that another shorter one of blue silk; two brass candlesticks standing at either end of it; before that on the floor were three low seats whereon some boys sat, their sons, richly veiled, as gentle comely youths as one should see; who had each his Service Book in hand in Hebrew without points, and were as ready and as nimble in it, and all their postures as the men.

There was brought in a pretty Boy at four years old, a child of some chief Jew, in rich coats, with black feathers in his hat, the priest himself arose and put a veil over the child's hat of pure white silk, fastening it under the hat and that he should not shake it off, and set him upon a seat among the boys; but he soon leaped off, and ran with his veil dangling up and down; once he came and looked at me, wondering perhaps that I had no veil; at length he got the inner door open and went to his mother; for they do not suffer the Women to come into the same room or into the sight of the men; but on the one side of the Synagogue there is a low, long, and narrow latticed window, through which the women sitting in the next room, do hear; as the boy opened it, I saw some of their wives in their rich silks bedaubed with broad gold lace, with muffs in one hand and books in the other.

At the east end of the Synagogue standeth a closet like a very high cupboard, which they all call the Ark, covered below with one large hanging of blue silk; its upper half covered with several drawing curtains of blue silk; in it are the Books of the Law kept. Before it, upon the floor, stand two mighty brass candlesticks, with lighted tapers in them; from the roof, above the hangings, two great lamps of christal glass, holding each about a pottle filled up to the brim with purest oil, set within a case of four little brass pillars guilded. In the wall at either end of the Synagogue are very many draw boxes, with rings at them like those in a Grocers Shop; and in it (as I came sooner in the morning than many or most of them) I saw that each Jew at his first entrance into the place did first bow down towards the Ark wherein the Law was kept, but with his hat on, which they never do put off in this place; but a stranger must; for after a good while two Englishmen were brought in, at which I was glad, being alone before, and they were bareheaded until they sat down amongst them, which then put on their hats ... Each Jew after he had bowed went straight to his box, took a little key out of his pocket, unlocked it, took out his veil and books, then threw his veil over his hat and fitted it on all sides, and so went to his place and fell a tuning it upon his Hebrew Service Book as hard and loud as he could; for all is sung with a mighty noise from first to last, both of priest and people, saying some prayers; and all was done in the right true Hebrew tongue, as my Rabbi affirmed to me afterwards; which, to this end, they do industriously teach all their children from infancy, having their schoolmistress on purpose, especially their Service books, which they have at their finger's end. There was none but had a book open in their hand, about the bigness of our hand Bibles. I looked upon several of their books as they sate by me and before me, yea I could plainly see both lines and letters in the Priest's book wherein he read, I sate so nigh him, and all were the true Hebrew letters, but in all the books without any points. The Priest's son, a comely youth standing at the Table or Altar alone, sung all the former part of the service which was a full hour long, all the rest singing with him, with a great and barbarous noise; this consisted mostly of the Psalms of David with some prayers intermixed, which they sung standing up looking East, and with a lower noise and tune not unlike to that when the reading Psalms are sung in our quires; but their reading Psalms they sung much like as we do sing ballads; and I observed that when mention was made of the Edomites, Philistines, or any enemies of David, or Israel's, they stamped strongly with their feet, that all the Synagogue sounded again. There were two or three composed Hymns, which they, all standing up and looking towards Jerusalem, sang very melodiously. After this former part of the Service finished, the Priest's son, officiating hitherto, which was about an hour, there was deep silence for a pretty while; then the Priest arose and some of the chief Jews with him, and they went with a grave, slow pace, up the Synagogue, to fetch the Law of Moses, and when they came to the Ark wherein it was kept, the priest drew the curtain, and opening the double door of it, the Law appeared, then the whole assembley stood up and bowed down just toward it, and the priest and those chief ones with him, stood singing a song to it a little while. The Law was written on two great rolls of very broad parchment (as my Rabbi told me afterwards, and he told me the meaning of each thing that I desired, to which you must impute all that I here interpret) .... Then there arose one out of the assembly and came unto the priest, making low reverence: when the priest asked aloud whether he desired to hear the Law read, who saying 'yes' the priest bade him pray then, and he looked upon his Hebrew Service Book which he had in his hand, and read over a short prayer very fast; then the priest read a few lines of the Law with a loud voice in a thundering barbarous tone, as fast as his tongue could run, for a form only; then asked the man whether he had heard the Law, who saying 'Yes' he bade him give thanks then, and he read a short prayer out of his book as before: so, bowing himself to the Law and the Priest, he went to his place, and another came, and did in like manner until five or six had thus heard the Law read to them; which they count a special piece of honour to them....

I confess that looking earnestly upon them in this, and thoughts coming into my mind of the Wonders which God wrought for their fathers in Egypt, and who heard the Voice of God speak to them out of the midst of the fire on Sinai, and seed of Abraham the friend of God, I was strangely, uncouthly, unaccustomedly moved, and deeply affected; tears stood in my eyes the while, to see those banished sons of Israel standing in their ancient garb (veiled) but in a strange land, solemnly and carefully looking East toward their own Country.... After this, for a conclusion of all, the Priest read certain select promises of their restoration, at which they showed great rejoicing, by strutting up, so that some of their veils flew about like morris dancers, only they wanted bells. This forenoon service continued about three hours, from nine to twelve, which being ended, they all put off their veils, and each man wrapping his veil up, went and put it and his Hebrew Book into his box, and locking it departed.

My Rabbi invited me afterwards to come and see the feast of Purim, which they kept he said for the deliverance from Haman's Conspiracy, mentioned in the Book of Esther; in which they use great knocking and stamping when Haman is named. Also he desired me to come and see them at the Passover .... afterwards I understood that several had been there to see them eat it, who brought away some of their unleavened bread with them, and showed to some who told me, one year in Oliver's time, they did build booths on the other side of the Thames, and kept the Feast of Tabernacles in them, as some told me who saw them; but since the King's coming in, they are very close, nor do admit any to see them but very privately.

When I was in the Synagogue I counted about or above a hundred right Jews, one proselite amongst them, they were all gentlemen (merchants) I saw not one mechanic person of them; most of them rich in apparel, divers with jewels glittering (for they are the richest jewellers of any) they are all generally black so as they may be distinguished from Spaniards or native Greeks, for the Jews hair hath a deeper tincture of a more perfect raven black, they have a quick piercing eye, and look as if of strong intellectuals; several of them are comely, gallant, proper gentlemen. I knew many of them when I saw them daily upon the Exchange and the Priest there too, who was also a merchant.....

The other account was by Britain's greatest diarist, Samuel Pepys, who visited the synagogue on 14 October 1663, on the occasion of the Jewish festival of Simchat Torah – the Rejoicing of the Law, when Jews give thanks to God for the great gift of the Jewish Law contained in the first five books of the Bible and handwritten on the sacred Torah Scrolls, which people are honoured to carry round the synagogue during the service. This service is usually a very joyous and demonstrative occasion on which much of the solemn decorum of Jewish worship is omitted.

...after dinner, my wife and I, by Mr. Rawlinsons conduct to the Jewish Synagogue – where the men and the boys in their Vayles, and the women behind a lettice out of sight; and some things stand up, which I believe is their Law, in a press, to which all coming in do bow; and at the putting on their veils do say something, to which others that hear him do cry Amen, and the party doth kiss his veil. Their service all in a singing way, and in Hebrew. And anon their Laws, that they take out of the press, is carried by several men, four or five, several burthens in all, and they do relieve one another, or whether it is that everyone desires to have the carrying of it, I cannot tell. Thus

they carried [it] round, round about the room while such a service is singing. And in the end they had a prayer for the King,
which they pronounced his name in Portugall; but the prayer,
like the rest, in Hebrew. But Lord, to see the disorder, laughing,
sporting, and no attention, but confusion in all their service,
more like Brutes than people knowing the true God, would
make a man foreswear ever seeing them more; and endeed, I
never did see so much, or could have imagined there could
have been any religion in the whole world so absurdly performed as this. Away thence, with my mind strangely
disturbed with them, by coach, and set down my wife in
Westminster-hall...

This was, in fact, Pepys' second visit to the synagogue. His first was
in 1659, when he attended a memorial service for Antonio Fernandez Carvajal, one of the distinguished founders of the congregation.

These graphic descriptions of what went on in England's first
public synagogue since the resettlement establish that, though
Judaism as a religion had not yet been officially recognised in Britain, it was certainly 'alive and well' and the building in which it was
followed had become an established part of the London scene.

CHAPTER SIX
The Stuarts and the Jews

Most Jews now felt they could at last look forward to a peaceful, secure and even prosperous life in Britain. There were, of course, still only small numbers of Jews in England just after the Restoration and they were allowed to live and carry on their businesses or professions without interference from the authorities. In addition, some of the more distinguished and wealthy members of the community were being singled out for royal favour.

Augustine Coronel (or Coronel-Chacon, as he later became known), one of those Marranos who had worked hard to restore the king and who had first settled in England early in the 1650s, was a case in point. Before the Restoration, ostensibly a merchant, but also a Royalist secret agent, he had been involved with his cousins, the Mendes, and also with the da Costas, in receiving and distributing funds for the exiled Charles II. By then, he was already known on the Royal Exchange as 'the littell Jue'. After the fall of the Commonwealth, Coronel was made consular and financial agent for Portugal in London and it was he who, in 1660, suggested to General Monk that the perennially hard-up king should marry the wealthy princess, the Infanta Catherine of Braganza. This advice, which was promptly followed, greatly increased his standing at court; so much so, that he was knighted by the king for his services. Presumably because he knew the knighthood was coming to him and was also aware that a Jew could not, in seventeenth century England, be so honoured, he left the synagogue and converted to Christianity shortly before the great event.

Sir Augustine Coronel (or Collonel, as he was also sometimes called) was the first Jew to be knighted in Britain. Neither his conversion nor his knighthood did him much good, however, because eventually he got into financial difficulties, was prosecuted by the Portuguese ambassador, was expelled from the Royal Exchange and, for a time, was thrown into the Fleet prison. After unsuccessfully informing against some of his former co-religionists, he left England and, it is believed, ended his days living on his rich Jewish relatives on the Continent. It is also possible that, with 'an eye to the main chance', he returned to Judaism later in life, in order to obtain family help. Nevertheless, all this did not affect his knighthood or even possibly his popularity with the king, who was always loyal to his friends. Coronel's desertion of the Jewish community in 1660 did not change the king's tolerant attitude towards the Jews either. Charles II granted the Jews many small favours and he was also most generous with the granting of denizations (a limited form of naturalization). Before the end of 1661, nineteen Jews had been made English citizens in this way. When the king married Catherine of Braganza in 1662, incidentally, two members of the Portuguese entourage were Marrano brothers, Duarte and Francisco Da Silva, both 'New Christians'. Duarte had been deputed to administer the queen's dowry (and he spent more than one period in the Tower of London, when the payments were too slow in arriving to suit the king!).

When King Charles II married the Portuguese princess, Catherine of Braganza, in 1662, two members of her entourage were Marrano brothers, Duarte and Francisco Da Silva. Duarte's main task was to administer the queen's enormous dowry.

The king's Portuguese marriage also helped to increase the London Jewish community. At the beginning of 1661, there were only thirty-five heads of families listed in the London synagogue's records. By the end of 1663, fifty-seven new names were added to the list of well-to-do Jews in London – and there were probably a number of poorer immigrant Jews from Portugal, though their names were not recorded. As it increased in numbers, the community also greatly increased in prosperity, since more than a few of the new immigrants were already successful financiers and businessmen.

A number of these wealthy Portuguese Marranos came to England to assist Duarte Da Silva administer the queen's enormous dowry, which actually meant that they would have loaned the Treasury considerable amounts, obviously at interest, because the king always needed the next instalment of the dowry before it was due. Another much less happy cause of the influx of immigrants was the terrible persecution to which Portuguese Marranos were being subjected at this time. Indeed because of this, Fernando Mendes (also known as Fernando Mendes da Costa), who had settled in London some years earlier, organised an emigration of Marranos, which would have included many of his own relatives, from Spain and Portugal into England and Italy.

After official permission for Jews to settle in Britain was granted in 1664, the influx of immigrant Jews increased from a trickle to a fairly steady stream. Among them were fugitive Marranos from the Peninsula and the Canary Islands and enterprising merchants from Amsterdam, Hamburg, Leghorn and the south of France – most of them Sephardi families – with such names as Aboab, de Vega, Dazevedo, Francia, Rodrigues, Berahel, Serra, Brauo, de Chaues, Sasportas, Nunes, Gonsales, Netto, Vega, Pardo, Mussaphia and many more, including, of course, da Silva and Mendes da Costa. In 1664, too, the London Sephardi congregation felt itself secure enough to draw up its first Code of Ascamot (regulations) modelled on those of the Amsterdam synagogue, which had, in its turn, modelled its regulations on the Ponentine synagogue in Venice.

Although it is very likely that the 'secret' rabbi, Moses Athias, may not have served the community much beyond 1658, the Sephardi synagogue did not bring over its first official rabbi until 1664. He was the learned Rabbi Jacob Sasportas of Amsterdam, who, at one time, had been a Moroccan envoy to Spain. The now official Jewish community of London called itself the Holy Congregation of the Gate of Heaven (in Hebrew: *Kahal Kados Sahar Asamaim*).

Outside London, however, there was as yet barely any trace of Jewish settlement, though, as early as 1661, there *was* a tiny Jewish community in Dublin. Its leading member was Manuel Lopes Pereira, alias Jaques Vanderpeere, whose family had played an important part in Crypto-Jewish life in Rouen, London and elsewhere. What is known of the earlier history of the Jews of Ireland is sparse. The earliest documentary reference to them is an edict from King Henry III on 28 July, 1232, which said '...with the provision that all Jews in Ireland shall be intentive and respondent to Peter [des Rivall or des Rivaulx] in all things touching the King'. On the same day, letters were sent from the king to Irish Jews instructing them 'to be intentive to Peter des Rivall'. The only named Irish Jew in the thirteenth century was Aaron, son of Benjamin, who was born in Colchester, gaoled in Bristol Castle and put on trial in 1283 for 'selling plate made of parings from coin of the realm'. The last thirteenth century citation of Jews in Ireland is in the Calendar of Documents in about 1286, but this could have referred to English Jews involved in Irish affairs. Irish Jews were probably expelled with the rest of those in Britain in 1290 and there were very few Jews noted during the next two hundred years. Some Spanish and Portuguese refugees from the Inquisition may have gone to Ireland after 1492, but they probably did not stay there for very long.

The Great Plague devastated London in 1665 and the Jewish community suffered heavily, though not perhaps in the same proportion as its non-Jewish neighbours, either because of its strict health and dietary laws or because, on the whole, Jews mixed very seldom with their Christian neighbours and the 'contact' spread of infec-

The learned Rabbi Jacob Sasportas from Amsterdam was the first official minister of the London Sephardi Synagogue in 1664. His stay was short, however; he fled back to Amsterdam to avoid the Great Plague a year later, leaving the synagogue without a rabbi for five years.

tion would have been less. Certainly, six victims of the plague were buried in the new cemetery in Mile End, the details being noted on their tombstones. In addition, between these graves was a space that would – and probably did – accommodate fifteen other interments, but these were unmarked. Jacob Sasportas, the newly appointed rabbi, fled back to Amsterdam to avoid the plague, of which it is possible his predecessor, Rabbi Athias, had died.

In 1666, the synagogue area luckily escaped the ravages of the Great Fire of London and it was a sign that the Jews were fast becoming accepted as 'English people' that they were left unmolested when violence was shown to Roman Catholics and foreigners in general, who were hysterically accused by some people of having started the fire in order to destroy the City.

But the defection of Jacob Sasportas, the Sephardi Haham (Chief Rabbi), from the London synagogue during the Great Plague left a vacancy that took five years to be filled. It was not until 1670, that Joshua da Silva of Amsterdam, a friend of Sasportas, was appointed. He received a salary of £50 a year (about £3,000 today), with free residence in the synagogue building. This was on the same terms on which Sasportas had been employed, but Sasportas had demanded and got an increase of £20 a year early in his short term of office. Rabbi da Silva, who was the synagogue's Haham for seven years, received no rise in all that time. It is more than possible, however, that during the time he ministered to the congregation, Rabbi da Silva and his family would have received many gifts from members of the congregation, ranging from quite substantial sums of money to food and clothing.

Clarification of the legal position of the Jews in Britain now commenced in a series of judicial decisions. In 1667, the Court of the King's Bench pronounced that Jews might give evidence in a court of law and be sworn in on the Old Testament, in accordance with their own practices, instead of on the Old and New Testaments combined, as was normal. In 1667, the venue in which a case was held was altered, in order to save a Jewish witness appearing on a Saturday, the Jewish Sabbath. In 1684, there was a much more important and very significant decision when Judge Jeffreys – Britain's notorious 'hanging judge' – refused to entertain the plea that, as the Jews were 'perpetual enemies' in law, the religion of a Jewish plaintiff made it impossible for him to bring an action for the recovery of a debt.

Nevertheless, the period also had its worries for the Jewish population. In Feburary, 1670, for instance, when the anti-popery movement was at its height, a select committee of the House of Commons was appointed to investigate the causes of the growth of papistry, with instructions also 'to enquire touching the number of Jews and their synagogues, and upon what terms they are permitted to have their residence here'. Fortunately, the pressure of public business was too great to allow too much time to be spent on this side of the investigations and, in the end, the report dealt only with Roman Catholicism. Later on, the second Conventicle Act was passed. This prohibited assemblies for prayer, unless the liturgy of the Church of England was strictly followed. However, this measure was directed only against native Dissenters and, because they were still considered aliens, the Jews were not involved. Here, at any rate, was one instance in which their *not* having attained full citizenship was in the Jews' favour.

Then came a more serious threat. In 1672, Charles II issued his Declaration of Indulgence, by which the right of public worship was conferred on Papists and Dissenters. The king's promise to the Jews eight years previously had guaranteed their position over this, so they were not directly affected. The following year, however, the Declaration was withdrawn, because of the public agitation it had caused and it was at this point that people turned on the Jews who were, of course, still allowed to worship publicly. During the winter of 1673, at the Quarter Sessions at Guildhall, the leaders of the Jewish community were indicted for causing a riot, because they had 'met together for the exercise of their religion', and a true bill was found against them by the Grand Jury. The leaders of the synagogue petitioned the king in great consternation, with the result that on 11 February 1674, he issued an Order in Council that 'Mr Atturney Generall doe stop all proceedings at Law against the Petitioners'.

There were smaller irritations, including a written plea from the Bishop of London and an eminent lawyer, Sir Peter Pett, suggesting that the Jews should be segregated on pre-Expulsion lines, under the control of a justiciar (the first to be Pett himself), but though the king allowed this to go before the Privy Council, it was dropped completely, probably on Charles's instructions. No such suggestion was ever again seriously considered.

A Jew who earned himself a small, if notorious, place in British history was an adventurer named Francisco da Faria, who, born in Brazil, later lived in Antwerp posing as an artist, in Holland as an 'army officer' and in England as an interpreter to the Portuguese Embassy, which apparently believed in his probity. In 1680, at the time of the uproar over the Popish Plot, he came forward with some startling disclosures and accused the Portuguese ambassador of having attempted to bribe him to murder the Earl of Shaftesbury and others. In return for these spectacular revelations, the Privy Council, which was also taken in by him, granted him a government allowance. When the Popish Plot frenzy died down, da Faria tactfully disappeared.

If he was not precisely the Jews' champion, King Charles II certainly supported them and kept his promises to them throughout his twenty-five year reign, during which the Jewish community lived happily and relatively freely. It was a sad day for them when he died in 1685 and was succeeded by his Roman Catholic brother, James II. This ill-fated king occupied the British throne for only three fraught years, but, because of his determination to secure the position of Roman Catholicism in England, the Jews again came under direct fire.

Almost as soon as the reign began, a publicist named Haynes issued a pamphlet which included an abstract of the various statutes concerning aliens in the realm, plus his own observations proving that the Jews broke them all. The main cause of resentment was the fact that Jews were exempted from alien duties, which enabled them to compete, on equal terms, with native-born merchants. Charles II had granted many Jews denization and this included that exemption, the abolishing of which had been the unsuccessful subject of many petitions to him from merchants. Now, a customs officer named Pennington came up with the idea that the denizations had become void at the king's death and that therefore Jewish merchants, all of them born abroad, should now be liable to pay aliens' custom dues. At the same time, he entered action against twenty Jewish merchants for non-payment of alien customs. To make matters worse, the Corporation of London, which had not been blameless in the past over anti-Semitic attacks, backed Pennington up and sent a petition to the king which stated that, in any case, the exemptions violated the ancient privileges of the City. The Court of Aldermen accordingly instructed Sir Robert Jeffrey and the town clerk to wait on the Lord Chancellor and intercede with the king 'against the remission of the alien duties'.

At that time, perhaps surprisingly, this representation was unsuccessful, but it encouraged further attacks against the Jews, this time on religious grounds. In the autumn of 1685, thirty-seven London Jews (nearly half the Jewish community) were arrested while carrying on their business on the Royal Exchange. Thomas Beaumont and his brother, Carleton, a lawyer, had applied for a writ against them and another eleven who actually escaped arrest, under an anti-Catholic law of Queen Elizabeth I which levied a penalty of £20 a month for each non-attendance at church! The wardens of the congregation immediately petitioned King James II to allow them to 'abide here free in ye Exercise of their Religion as heretofore'. What can only be described as a bribe of £300 from the Jewish community to the Earl of Peterborough persuaded that gentleman to sponsor the application at court. This resulted in the king following the example of his late brother and issuing an Order in Council on 13 November 1685, instructing the Attorney-General to stop all proceedings against the Jews: 'His Majesty's intention being that they should not be troubled upon this account, but quietly enjoy the free exercise of their Religion, whilst they behave themselves dutifully and obediently to his Government'.

A new chapter in the history of Britain's Jews opened with the success of the bloodless (or glorious) revolution in 1688, which quickly led to the abdication of King James II. It is interesting to note that the expedition which launched the revolution and the official placing of William of Orange and his wife, Mary Stuart, on the English throne in 1689, was, to a large extent, financed by Dutch Jews. Francisco Lopez Suasso of the Hague, who was later to be made Baron d'Avernas le Gras, advanced Prince William the enormous sum of two million crowns, free of interest, for his expedition to England. Furthermore, the commissariat of the campaign was supervised by Francisco de Cordova, acting on behalf of Isaac Pereira, who provided bread and forage for the troops. So it was not surprising that, as relations between England and Holland became closer, more and more Jewish immigrants from Amsterdam came to England to swell the Jewish community and increase its prosperity.

By this time, Ashkenazi Jews, mainly from Eastern Europe, were beginning to arrive in England. Indeed, by 1690, there were enough of them – including a German-Polish group from Hamburg – to establish a separate congregation from the Sephardis in Creechurch Lane. They worshipped somewhere in the same area, however, probably in Duke's Place, but until the first official Ashkenazi synagogue was built there in 1722, there is no official record of the actual building that was used as a synagogue in the preceding thirty-two years. Some Ashkenazis came from Holland, where they had previously settled as refugees from eastern Europe, in the wake of William and Mary and these, too, helped to swell London's second Jewish community. The first minister of this community is believed to have been Rabbi Juda ben Ephraim Cohen. This community also acquired its own cemetery, not far from the Sephardi cemetery in Mile End. An interesting statistic is that in 1695, in East London

A new chapter in the history of Britain's Jews opened when King William III came to the throne with his wife, Mary, after the Glorious Revolution of 1688. Because he was Dutch, relations between England and Holland became closer and more and more Jewish immigrants came from Amsterdam to enlarge Britain's Jewish community and increase its prosperity.

parishes, there were 853 Jews, one quarter of them, Ashkenazis.

There were occasional disturbances for the Jews under the new king, some affecting them incidentally and not because they were Jews. But soon the vexed question of their being liable to pay aliens' custom dues again reared its head, piloted by the same customs officer, Pennington, who had raised the matter with James II. This time, Pennington entered actions against the twenty Jewish merchants he had previously cited, for arrears amounting to £58,000. King William upheld him, but when the Privy Council was petitioned by the London Jewish community, it ordered proceedings to be stopped. The English merchants, of course, supported Pennington. After much argument and accusations from the merchants that the Jews had used bribery to get the matter stopped and that the Treasury stood to lose £10,000 annually, plus the arrears, as a result, the Commissioners of Customs were brought in. On 14 October 1690, the Privy Council issued instructions for the duties payable by aliens on exported commodities to be levied, notwithstanding previous decisions to the contrary. No mention, however, was made of the arrears and, the following December, the increased duties were abolished by Parliament. It seems to have been a storm in a teacup.

By now, the Jews were not the only 'aliens' in the country and the others would have been treated similarly, if similar conditions arose, but this was not the case in another episode in the financial history of this reign, the outcome of which was of decisive importance in establishing the legal status of British Jews.

As has been recounted, throughout the medieval period, the Jews in England had been subjected to extra special taxation of a disproportionate severity. During Charles II's reign and his brother's, happily this had not recurred. Unfortunately, the financial troubles of the country after the so-called Glorious Revolution, and the wars which followed, brought the idea forward once more, particularly since this sort of taxation was still being levied on Jews living in many other parts of Europe, including, surprisingly, Amsterdam. In the autumn of 1689, the House of Commons passed a resolution ordering a bill to be introduced which would levy £100,000 on the Jews, in addition to their ordinary contributions to taxation and their quota of £10 each, rich or poor, for the newly instituted poll tax, for which all Jews were assessed as 'merchant strangers'.

Horrified, and probably seeing before them a repeat of the events of the thirteenth century, the Jewish community prepared a petition indicating how the country's commerce benefited from their presence and also pleading their inability to support any new burden. Nevertheless, the Commons refused to countenance any petition against a financial measure and the bill was introduced and read for the first time on 30 December. The Jews, however, continued to fight strenuously against it, and, in the end, the unfairness or, more likely, the impracticability of the proposals was realised and the bill was dropped.

The measure of giving the Jews different treatment in the matter of taxation drifted on a little longer, because, in an Act in the same session which fixed the poll tax for the following year, Jewish merchants were placed in a separate category and assessed at £20 each – twice the rate that had to be paid by other merchant strangers. But fortunately this discrimination disappeared when the new Poll Tax Act of 1691 did not make any special provision for the Jews – a precedent which was from then on strictly observed.

Finally, in 1698, Parliament passed a bill, after some objections, 'for the more effective suppressing of Blasphemy and Prophaneness', which was phrased so that its provisions did not apply to people of Jewish birth. So, at last, the practice of Judaism in Britain received parliamentary sanction, as well as royal protection and recognition which dated from an act of 1695 'for granting to His Majesty certaine rates and duties upon Marriages'.

The London Sephardi community, the Holy Congregation of the Gate of Heaven, was now flourishing. Its congregation was growing steadily and, though the synagogue in Creechurch Lane had been considerably enlarged and redeveloped in 1674, by the turn of the eighteenth century, it was bursting at the seams. The community ran its own affairs, paying special attention to the education of its children, had its own physician and its own 'treasury'. The members of the community piously preserved the culture of the countries into which they or their fathers had been born and thus the Sephardi synagogue had a great deal in it of Iberian tradition. Indeed, they often spoke to each other in 'Ladino' – a mixture of Hebrew and Spanish or Portuguese. In 1685, the synagogue was honoured during Passover by a visit from King James II's daughter, Princess Anne, who was later to become queen of England.

It was clear that the community had outgrown the building in Creechurch Lane and, at the end of the seventeenth century, the synagogue council (the Mahamad) took steps to obtain permission to be allowed to build a larger synagogue.

Accordingly, on 12 February 1699, four members of the Mahamad, Antonio Gomes Serra, Menasseh Mendes, Affonso Rodriguez and Manuel Nunes Miranda, made a contract with a

The London Sephardi Synagogue was now flourishing and, in 1685, it was honoured during the Festival of Passover by a visit from King James II's daughter, Princess Anne, who was later to become Queen of England.

By the beginning of the eighteenth century, the London Sephardi Synagogue was bursting at the seams and a new building in Bevis Marks, a small street near Creechurch Lane where the community had their original building, was opened in 1701 and the interior remains unaltered today.

builder named Joseph Avis for the erection of a new synagogue building in Bevis Marks, a small street very near Creechurch Lane, at a cost of £2,650, to be paid in instalments. It later transpired that Mr Avis was a Quaker and when he realised that this was a building which would be devoted to the worship of God, his conscience would not allow him to accept the whole sum agreed upon. Though there is no documentary evidence to prove it, it is believed that on the day of the opening of the new building in September, 1701, the pious and extremely generous Mr Avis went to the wardens of the synagogue and returned to them the profit that he had made on the building work. Another 'tradition' (though again not substantiated in writing) is that Princess Anne presented the synagogue with an oak beam from one of the Royal Navy's ships to be incorporated in the roof of the building.

Many people have mistakenly thought that the name Bevis Marks is of Jewish origin, because the synagogue was built there. Nothing could be farther from the truth. As early as 1407 (when officially there were no Jews in England), the little street was recorded as Bewesmerkes; by 1450, it had become Bevys Marke. Later it was known as Buries Markes, Bevers Market, and Beavis Markes. The name was probably derived from the Abbey of Bury St Edmunds which owned the land before 1156. On the dissolution of the Abbey by Henry VIII, the king gave the land and the buildings on it to Thomas Heneage. The derivation seems likely because, as can be seen today, adjacent to Bevis Marks is Heneage Lane.

The new synagogue could accommodate about 400 men, plus 160 women in the strictly segregated women's gallery which was built round three sides of the synagogue. Except for an annexe with a hall and other rooms on a lower level, it has remained unchanged up to the present day.

The interior of the synagogue, which primarily derives its beauty from its proportions, is of severely simple architecture; it has, indeed, been likened to a contemporary Dissenters' chapel. Its high, rounded windows and general arrangement of ladies' gallery, Ark, seats, reader's desk and great brass hanging candelabra are very obviously influenced by its impressive – and much larger – sister synagogue in Amsterdam, which was opened in 1675. Members of the Amsterdam Mahamad donated four of the six great brass candlesticks which stand before the Ark and one of the candelabra.

It is traditionally held that there was a deliberate symbolism in the accoutrements of the synagogue. The seven many-branched candelabra represent the seven days of the week. The ten brass candlesticks (four more stand on the reading desk in the centre of the synagogue) symbolise the Ten Commandments, while the twelve columns supporting the gallery signify the twelve Tribes of Israel.

The congregation still owned the lease of the building in Creechurch Lane and continued to do so until 1723. It was used as a school for the children of congregants and, in part, as residences for the haham and other officials.

Though many members of the Bevis Marks Synagogue were wealthy, many more were much humbler and a number lived on the poverty line. A very large proportion of the synagogue's annual income was used for charitable work among its needy members.

Although anti-Semitism in Britain was not dead, the lives of the Jews there were fast becoming more settled and subject to less interference than was the case in other countries. By the end of the seventeenth century, Britain's (or rather, London's Jews, because there were still few to be found outside the capital) had built up their economic position and gone far to establish themselves securely in British commercial life. They were still, however, prevented from opening retail shops in the City of London, because this privilege was confined to Freemen of the City of London, which, with one or two exceptions, they were not allowed to become. Consequently, they were driven into wholesale commerce and they carried on extensive trade with overseas countries – in the New World, as well as the old, and even with Spain and Portugal.

These Jewish wholesalers dealt in all kinds of commodities – from salt fish, which they exported from England to Venice, to diamonds. And two members of the Francia family were among the earliest contractors for the lighting of London's streets.

Several pillars of the Jewish community were sworn brokers on the Royal Exchange, to which the first Jew, Samuel Dormido, had been admitted in 1657, but from which the Jews had been eventually excluded in 1680. It was after a considerable struggle by the Jews in 1697 that the Corporation of the Royal Exchange agreed to admit twelve Jews, among a total of 124 sworn brokers, to the privilege of the Exchange. This was proportionately far higher than the actual number of Jews then in the country warranted. The figure equalled the number of all the other alien brokers together and while the number of Christian brokers was at this time reduced by one-half, the Jews were only reduced by one-third and they were, moreover, the only category of people who could be admitted without being Freemen of the City of London.

Queen Anne came to the throne of England in 1702 and it was during her reign that many more Ashkenazi Jews came to Britain. Most of them came from Germany, which could trace its Jewish settlement back to the Roman occupation of the Rhineland, although many had been swept away during the severe German persecution of the Middle Ages. Germany's Jewish population had been swelled, however, during the late 1650s when there had been terrible Jewish massacres in Poland, in which, during the previous two hundred years, the world's largest Jewish population had been established.

These people were quite different from the Sephardi Jews, with whom, by now, English people had become more or less familiar. Their pronunciation of Hebrew was different, as well as their synagogue customs, their liturgical melodies, their cantillation (the chanting of prayers) and the details of their prayer rituals. But, more important to their non-Jewish neighbours, many of them would have looked different – in their features, in their dress and particularly in the strange language in which they spoke to each other. The language was Yiddish – or what was called in those days, Judao-German. It was written in Hebrew characters, with a very strong percentage of Hebrew in its vocabulary and, depending where the immigrants came from, an overlay of either German or Polish.

Socially and economically, these new settlers came generally from a much lower social stratum than the earlier, or, indeed, the later, Sephardi immigrants who, probably without exception, refused to intermarry with them. At the 'top end' of the Ashkenazi community, it is true, there were a few brokers, jewellers and wholesale merchants of much the same kind as those already in Britain, but they were only a small fraction of the whole. The bulk were what might be described as a complete proletariat, composed, to a large extent, of the most recent arrivals, whose occupations ranged from acting as servants (including footmen) in the houses of their wealthy co-religionists to making small handicrafts and carrying on retail trade.

Although the majority of the immigrants were from the old-established Jewish communities of Germany, they came not only from the great centres, such as Frankfurt and Hamburg, but also from smaller towns in the central and southern parts of the country – mainly from Bavaria and Franconia. There were also a few from Alsace and a proportion from eastern Europe – Silesia, Moravia, Bohemia and Poland, though, as yet, despite the persecution, Poland contributed in only a small degree to British emigration.

During this time, too, Sephardi Jews were still emigrating to Britain from Amsterdam and other Dutch cities and another influx of Marranos came direct from Spain and Portugal because of the continuing Inquisitions in both countries. Composed, as the new Ashkenazi immigrant wave was, of people of widely different status, occupations and antecedents, it was bound to lack the peaceful spirit and cohesion of the Sephardi congregation. Because of this, it grew in a series of groups, each of which ultimately resulted in the formation of another congregation. The first split from the original Ashkenazi synagogue took place as early as 1706 when, because of a dispute between its rabbi, Aaron Hart, and a wealthy layman, Marcus Moses, another congregation, the Hambro Synagogue, was formed. After worshipping privately for a little while, the new group purchased a burial ground and started to erect a synagogue in St Mary Axe. The leaders of both the Sephardi and Ashkenazi communities were very worried that a new congregation, over which neither had any control, might jeopardise the position and reputation of all London's Jews. So, surprisingly enough, in March, 1704, they protested jointly against the opening of the new synagogue to the City's Court of Aldermen (which had the power to close a synagogue if it was erected without the permission of the Corporation). After an enquiry, the court ordered that the new building should not be used as a synagogue. It is an interesting point that the sole occasion on which the Court of Aldermen exercised its power to close a synagogue was at the request of some of the Jews. Nevertheless, when, twenty-one years later, Marcus Moses started to build another Hambro Synagogue, this time in his own garden in Magpie Alley, despite similar 'official' protests from the main Ashkenazi Synagogue, it appears that he was allowed to proceed.

In 1714, the last year of Queen Anne's reign, John Toland, a radical free thinking Christian, made a very serious plea that, instead of mere denization, Jews in Britain should be eligible for full naturalization, in the following passionate terms:

Tis manifest almost at first sight, the common reasons for a GENERAL NATURALIZATION, are as strong in behalf of the Jews, as of any other people whatsoever. They increase the number of hands for labor and defence, bellies and backs for consumption of food and raiment, and of brains for invention and contrivance, no less than any other nation. We all know that numbers of people are the true riches and power of any country.

My Purpose at present then, is to prove, that the Jews are so farr from being an Excresence or Spunge (as some wou'd have it) and a useless member of the Commonwealth, or being ill subjects, and a dangerous people on any account, that they are obedient, peaceable, useful, and advantageous as any; and even more so than many others: for being excluded every where in Europe, from publick Employment in the State, as they are from following Handicraft-trades in most places, and in almost all, from purchasing immovable Inheritances, this does no less naturally, than necessarily, force 'em to Trade and Usury, since otherwise they cou'd not possibly live. Yet let them once be put upon an equal foot with others, not only for buying and selling, for security and protection to their Goods and Persons; but likewise for Arts and Handycraft-trades, for purchasing and inheriting of estates in Lands and Houses (with which they may as well be trusted as with Shares in the publick Funds) and then I doubt not, but they'll insensibly betake themselves to Building, Farming, and all sorts of improvement like other people.

We deny not that there will thus be more taylors and shoomakers; but there will also be more suits and shoos made than before. If there be more weavers, watchmakers, and other artificers, we can for this reason export more cloth, watches and more of all other commodities than formerly: and not only have 'em better made by the emulation of so many workmen, of such different Nations; but likewise have 'em quicker sold off, for being cheaper wrought than those of others, who come to the same market. This one Rule of

MORE, and BETTER, and CHEAPER, will ever carry the market against all expedients and devices.

This pamphlet, which Toland called *Reasons for naturalizing the Jews in Great Britain and Ireland, on the same footing with all other nations* was widely circulated, but it was a voice in the wilderness which had, at the time, little or no effect. It was to be nearly forty years before a Jewish naturalization act was passed and even that was very selective and did not go anything like the whole way to give Britian's Jews full citizenship.

But, as Lucien Wolf opines in *Essays in Jewish History*, long before this, 'The Jewish merchants had become indispensable to the City by reason of the great volume of trade they controlled, and the City had acknowledged its obligation to them in this respect.' For while Jews were still debarred from becoming freemen of the City of London, despite this, as has been said, their admission to the Royal Exchange was allowed. In fact, when, in 1708, the Ministers, elders and deacons of the Dutch and French Churches protested against the preferences shown to the Jews over the other alien brokers and asked that they too, might be admitted to the Royal Exchange without having to be freemen, the Court of Aldermen announced their adhesion to the rules their committee had drawn up in 1697 in the following resolution: 'That no person whatsoever (except Jews) shall be admitted a broker upon this Royal Exchange that is not a freeman of this City.'

The position of the Jews in the commercial life of the City was in this way officially recognised at last and, implicitly with it, their position in the country as a whole. This was the first real step in Anglo-Jewish emancipation, but, as Lucien Wolf comments dryly: '... the Jews won their first victory over the invidious laws which excluded them from the privilege of English citizenship; and won it, be it observed, not through the force of abstract principle, but by sheer weight of civic merit and commercial utility.'

The next step was to consolidate their position, but a century-and-a-half was to pass before Britain's Jewish community became a free and undifferentiated body.

CHAPTER SEVEN
The Upward Climb

When Queen Anne died in 1714 without heirs, George, the Elector of Hanover, who was the son of James I's granddaughter, Sophia, was invited by Parliament to ascend the British throne. His accession, which naturally brought Britain and Germany into a closer relationship, was also an encouragement to many Ashkenazi Jews from Germany to follow the new king to his new country. Consequently, although there were still a number of Sephardi immigrants, mostly fleeing from the continuing Spanish and Portuguese Inquisitions, the vast majority of Jews entering and proposing to settle in Britain were Ashkenazi. The latter, at this time, did not come to England because they were particularly under stress in Germany, but because they saw a chance of a freer and more prosperous future in a new land.

From the beginning of the Resettlement of the Jews in Britain, they were better treated there than in any other European country. In Germany and Italy, for instance, they still had to live in ghettos. Even in the Netherlands, the historic bastian of free worship and speech, they were not allowed to reside in some towns and provinces, while in Muslim Turkey, at the other end of the scale, they were allowed only the very restricted rights of unbelievers. Jews were excluded from Spain and Portugal and, surprisingly, much of France. In Poland, the large Jewish community was both terrorised and persecuted. In eighteenth century Britain, however, the law now protected its Jewish citizens, they could live wherever they chose and they enjoyed an increasing social equality with non-Jews. It is true that there was still a degree of anti-Semitism, but it seldom got out of hand and was never sanctioned by the government of the day.

During the thirteen years that George I was on the throne, Britain's Jewish community greatly increased and, towards the end of his reign, new congregations were already springing up, including the Hambro Synagogue, the establishment of which had been prevented in 1704 by its fellow Jews, but which was built in the City gar-

The rich Jewish merchant and stockbroker, Moses Hart (left) built Britain's most important Ashkenazi place of worship, the Great Synagogue in Duke's Place, in 1722. In 1705, he had brought his brother, Rabbi Aaron Hart (right), over from Germany to be the congregation's first minister.

den of the home of Marcus (Mordecai) Moses, its lay leader, in 1725. Three years earlier, in 1722, the most important Ashkenazi place of worship, the Great Synagogue, was built in Duke's Place by Moses Hart, a rich Jewish merchant and stockbroker. Moses Hart, one of the sons of Hartwig Moses, was born in Breslau in Germany in 1675. He emigrated to England in about 1697 and was helped to establish himself in business by his cousin, Benjamin Levy, who had settled in England nearly thirty years earlier, and was admitted as one of the twelve Jewish members of the Royal Exchange in 1697 and became very wealthy and influential. When Levy retired from business, his cousin Moses took over as a broker on the Royal Exchange in his place and was soon equally wealthy. He also, it is believed, obtained a lucrative government appointment under Godolphin, the High Treasurer. In 1705, he had brought his brother, Rabbi Aaron Hart, five years his senior, over from Germany to be the first Ashkenazi congregation's minister, a position Aaron held until his death in 1756. Described as the High Priest of the Ashkenazis, Aaron Hart is always regarded as the first Chief Rabbi. But Moses Hart's philanthropy was not only directed at his co-religionists. In Richmond, Surrey, he is looked on with affection as one of the town's earliest philanthropists, because of his generosity to non-Jewish causes in the area.

The Great Synagogue was rebuilt in 1790. Alongside the new synagogues, various voluntary bodies were established, such as burial societies, help organisations and societies for educating children, for sick visiting and for aid to imprisoned debtors.

It was at this time that the first provincial congregations were becoming established. They were almost exclusively Ashkenazi. Many of these immigrants, as has been said, were extremely poor and they were happy – and grateful – to settle anywhere, so long as there was a chance of earning enough to sustain their families. Almost at the beginning of the eighteenth century, a small number of Jewish settlers were entering and settling in the chief ports, including Portsmouth, Liverpool, Falmouth, Bristol and Plymouth in the south and west of England and Hull and Yarmouth in the east. Those who had brought a little capital with them soon set up shops for trading with the seafaring people in the ports. Many more, who were literally destitute, became pedlars, mostly financed by the Jewish shopkeepers, who sent them inland to sell to farmers and their families such goods as trinkets, laces, pocket watches and chains, shoe buckles, cigars and other portable and attractive trifles.

In a preface to his *History and Genealogy of the Jewish Families of Yates and Samuel of Liverpool*, Lucien Wolf tells us: 'Accounts were settled at the ports once a week on Friday afternoons, after which the shopkeepers and their dependent hawkers would assemble for the inauguration of the Sabbath, either in the shop or a hired room. On the Sunday the wallet would be replenished, and the following day the pedlars would trudge off again on their weekly circuits.'

Jewish pedlars became a familiar sight in the English countryside

The Great Synagogue was rebuilt much more lavishly in 1790, as this view of the impressive interior shows.

Jewish pedlars became a familiar sight in both town and country from early in the eighteenth century. This detail from an engraving by William Hogarth clearly shows a Jewish pedlar with his box of wares.

from early in the eighteenth century. Soon their activities also extended to the towns, selling, besides beguiling trifles, old clothes, fruit, dried herbs and so on. They were not all Ashkenazi Jews. Many of the Sephardi refugees from the Inquisition who entered Britain from about 1720 to 1735 were also extremely poor and they, too, had perforce to become itinerant traders. It is believed that, during those years, no fewer than 1,500 Marranos arrived directly from Spain and Portugal, more than doubling Britain's Sephardi community at that time. That total, added to the large numbers of Ashkenazi Jews, many of them very poor, who flooded into Britain in the eighteenth century, posed great problems for both Jewish communities, because so many of them needed financial aid if they and their families were to survive.

The Sephardi synagogue had, from its inception, offered financial help to its own poor members as well as to some of the early Ashkenazi settlers. In addition, as has been stated, with the establishment of a growing number of Ashkenazi congregations, related help societies were also formed. As the eighteenth century proceeded, however, the influx of needy Jews into Britain was so great that the charitable resources of the Jewish communities were almost used up and their wealthy members were repeatedly asked for donations to help their poorer brethren.

The majority of the poorer immigrants were still in London and few of them were able to enter into the 'working' trades because restrictions in the countries from which they had come had prohibited them from learning the normal 'useful' trades. Consequently, peddling was the only occupation open to them and, for many, this led to begging. Indeed, Lucien Wolf reports that the London streets, in the middle of the eighteenth century '... became dotted thickly with Jewish beggars and worse, and the East End was choked with a Jewish population without resources of any kind, and unable to take up any handicrafts.'

This situation led to another development. Rich London merchants gave many of the poverty-stricken Jews the chance to earn a living – and, at the same time, reduced the number of destitute immigrants whose survival was dependent on the charity of the congregations of the two main synagogues. They equipped their unemployed co-religionists with small amounts of merchandise and sent them off to other towns to peddle their wares. During this period Jewish hawkers appeared in Lancashire and other northern counties. This inevitably led to Jewish settlements in those towns, as the pedlars and their families settled in the places in which they could not only earn a living, but also found congenial.

Not long after George II followed his father to the throne in 1727, the number of Jews in Britain had increased to approximately eight thousand and, at the end of the eighteenth century, this number had risen to about twenty thousand. They were not, however, all either very poor or very rich. There was now developing a Jewish middle class, many, indeed most of them, merchants and therefore city dwellers. They were what today would be termed 'comfortably off' and they fitted into the middle strata of British people who, as Jane Austen termed it, were 'in trade'.

Nevertheless, there were a surprisingly large number of really wealthy Jewish families who were ambitious not only to fit into the 'landed gentry' pattern of the eighteenth century, but were also anxious to acquire its culture and its way of life. And this many of them did. As early as 1709, a writer called John Macky noted somewhat angrily that the area around the fashionable village of Hampstead, then just outside London, was 'overstock'd with Jews'.

The Mendes and the da Costas (who often intermarried) were among the wealthiest Sephardi families. Traditionally accepted as the earliest surviving 'country' house in Jewish ownership was Cromwell House, which stood on ground that is now 104 Highgate Hill. The copyhold of the house was purchased in 1675 by Alvaro da Costa, who had come from Portugal as part of Catherine of Braganza's entourage and was granted denization in 1667. Alvaro da Costa and his brother-in-law, Fernando Mendes, and their large families shared the house, probably adding a south wing in about 1685 and a north wing some twenty-five years later. A number of other Jewish families lived in Hampstead and Highgate houses, including Moreton (now 14 South Grove, Highgate), which was bought by Anthony Mendes in 1715, and The Grove in Highgate, which another of the family, Jacob Mendes da Costa, acquired in 1733. James Mendes, a stockbroker, leased Eagle House in the Surrey village of Mitcham in 1724 and his brother-in-law, John Mendes da Costa, purchased the freehold of another property at Mitcham, known probably as Baron House, in 1721. Another member of the da Costa family bought Copped Hall at Totteridge in Hertfordshire in 1721 and remained there until 1758.

But not only the Sephardis acquired distinguished and expensive properties. The leading Ashkenazi families of the eighteenth century were the Harts and the Franks. Moses Hart, the wealthy benefactor of the Great Synagogue, bought Gordon House, in the Isleworth-Twickenham area, in 1718 and rebuilt it lavishly several

Moses Hart purchased Gordon House at Isleworth in 1718 and rebuilt it more impressively in 1750, as in this engraving. It was altered and enlarged in the nineteenth century and is now the headquarters of the West London Institute of Higher Education, which has a modern building on its campus called Moses Hart House.

Moses Hart's daughter, Judith (Mrs Judith Levy), became as wealthy as her father. She lived at Richmond for many years at 4 Maids of Honour Row and was nicknamed 'The Queen of Richmond Green'.

years later. It is today the headquarters of the West London Institute of Higher Education in St Margaret's Road, Twickenham. (Indeed, one of the other buildings on the Institute's campus is called Moses Hart House.) In about 1750, Moses Hart 'crossed the river' to Richmond and acquired another house – Asgill House in Old Palace Lane, where he entertained on a grand scale. His daughter, Judith, who married her wealthy cousin, Elias Levy, Benjamin's only surviving son, when she was twenty, proved to be a very good businesswoman. When her husband died at forty-eight in 1750, he left his large fortune to his wife and she launched herself into English society. All her children died in infancy or in youth and, in the 1750s, she left London and purchased a house on Richmond Green – number 4 Maids of Honour Row, where she spent the remainder of her long life. She, too, was a local benefactor and it was said that she distributed more than a thousand pounds a year (a huge sum in those days) in charity. By the time she died in 1803, at the venerable age of ninety-seven she had become known as the Queen of Richmond Green!

Isaac Franks probably had a house nearby Moses Hart in the 1730s and his brother, Aaron, purchased the Simplemarsh estate at Chertsey in 1738 and, in 1753, acquired Misterton Hall in Leicestershire, in which another member of the family, Naphtali Franks, quite often stayed, though his main home outside London was The Limes, which still stands at Mortlake by the River Thames. Naphtali lived at The Limes for over fifty years and the house was the subject of a famous painting by Turner in 1826.

There were Jewish 'stately homes' in Wimbledon, near London, and Teddington, Isleworth and Stanmore in Middlesex, in

Loughton in Essex, at Richmond and Epsom in Surrey, in Barnet in Hertfordshire, Wargrave in Berkshire and Sidmouth in Devon.

While the top echelon of British Jewry was establishing itself in 'the country', another phenomenon, so far as Britain's Jews were concerned, was developing in some of the ports in which so many of the immigrants of the merchant and pedlar classes had entered from eastern and western Europe and then settled.

Most of the merchants had first established small businesses selling general goods, but, very shortly, in at least six principal ports which served the Royal Navy, they began to stock merchandise specifically for clothing and equipping naval ratings and officers. They became, in fact, mercers and sea drapers or, as the Royal Navy put it, slopsellers, offering, as Geoffrey L. Green describes in *The Royal Navy & Anglo-Jewry: 1740–1820*: clothing which '... did not confirm with any laid down regulations but was usually much more colourful and distinctive than that issued by the purser aboard ship. For example, trim straw hats with ribbons and the ship's name printed on, glazed tarpaulin hats, gaudy waistcoats and neckerchiefs, baggy blue and white striped trousers and seamen's gear such as knives and hammock stretchers.' Seamen could also buy from the Jewish merchants second-hand clothes in great variety, ranging from blue baize eight-buttoned jackets to smart metal-buckled shoes.

By the start of the 1750s, Jewish slopsellers were well established certainly in Bristol, Chatham, Liverpool, Plymouth, Portsmouth and Sheerness and in these towns there were also Jewish congrega-

One of Moses Hart's sons-in-law, Aaron Franks, lived for some time at Isleworth House by the River Thames. Today, his former home houses a convent, Nazareth House.

tions of varying sizes. There was to be a further development of the Jewish slopsellers' role in the nineteenth century.

Although there were still anti-Semitic pinpricks, including mob violence against Jews in the City as a result of allegations that Portuguese Jews had murdered a woman and her baby because the father had been a Christian, and sustained prohibition on Jews becoming Freemen of the City, the Jewish community became much more securely established under the Hanoverian kings. As has been said, by then, they were more strongly beset by their own 'internal' problems caused by the waves of destitute Jews now regularly arriving from abroad.

A way out of this problem seemed possible in 1732, when Colonel James Oglethorpe, a Member of Parliament, obtained a charter to establish a settlement in Georgia in the New World, as a refuge for paupers and persecuted Dissenters, which would also act as a barrier for the British colonies against Spanish aggression. Among the agents appointed to solicit public subscriptions in aid of the scheme were a number of leading members of the Bevis Marks Synagogue. Instead of handing over to the authorities concerned the sums they collected, they tried to utilise them to finance the emigration of some of England's destitute Jews, who were becoming an endless financial embarrassment to them. However logical a move it may have seemed to them, this was in excess of their powers and, as a result, the gentlemen of Bevis Marks were compelled to surrender their commissions. Nevertheless, their efforts resulted in 1733 in the dispatch to the new colony of two small batches of Jewish immigrants, coming from both sections of the Jewish community. Then, in 1734, the Bevis Marks Synagogue set up a special committee to apply for lands for an exclusively Jewish settlement in Georgia, but the application was not granted. Three years later, however, a tract of land for the same purpose in Carolina was offered to the Jewish community, but the conditions for settlement were unacceptable. Undaunted, the committee continued its work and, in 1745, it received an extension both of its powers and its income. In 1748, negotiations were started to establish a settlement in South Carolina, but this scheme also fell through, though some Jewish families did emigrate to the colony shortly afterwards.

In 1749, when Nova Scotia in Canada was colonised after the Peace of Aix-la-Chappelle, an attempt was made to encourage poor Jews to settle there, with a promise from the London Jewish communities of a charitable allowance for three years, to get them started. This scheme also failed. It seems that, impoverished though they were, the immigrants preferred 'the devil they knew to the devil they did not' and few took up the offer to leave Britain. There was, however, a steady stream of emigration from England to the American colonies and, by the end of George II's reign, there were, as well as the older settlements in the West Indies, half-a-dozen Jewish communities, largely of Sephardi origin, though no longer exclusively so, stretching from Georgia to Rhode Island. In this new country, Jews were able to enjoy a very free way of life and, indeed, a greater measure of tolerance than had been shown to them even in Britain.

Nevertheless, throughout King George II's reign, Jewish life became richer and freer in Britain, especially in London where most Jews still resided. Possibly the most important step for Jews in this reign was the introduction into the House of Lords on 3 April 1753 of what came to be known as the Jew Bill. This was the first bill to make naturalization possible for Jews and it passed through the Lords without a division. The Jewish Naturalization Act, as it was properly called, was, however, very selective. Although it simplified the procedure for permitting foreign Jews to be naturalized after three years' residence in Britain and did not insist on them taking the Sacrament (communion) as it did non-Jews, it limited the right of naturalization to persons of property and the richer classes. It also prohibited purchases that gave Jews (whether native-born or foreign) control over any ecclesiastical office or property. Oddly enough, this reservation implicitly confirmed, for the first time, the right of Jews generally to hold land, other than that which included the right of presentation of any ecclesiastical office.

Despite its limitations on Jews, the bill aroused widespread protests, even at its first reading in the House of Commons on 7 May. The protests were led by a former Lord Mayor, Sir John Barnard, one of the Freemen of the City of London who opposed all naturalization measures. Religious reasons were put forward against the bill, but one suspects that trading jealousy and fear were at the root of the matter. Nevertheless, the second reading was passed by 95 votes to 16 and, after another furore in the House set up by the Lord Mayor of London himself (Sir Crisp Gascoigne), the bill was passed at its third reading on 22 May by 96 votes to 55.

The Jewish Naturalization Act accordingly received the royal assent and became law, but the struggle was by no means over. Over a period of six months, public agitation against the Jew Bill was manifested everywhere and the Jewish population were attacked verbally and with printed matter by every side of public opinion. For instance, *The London Magazine* published a satire on the subject which suggested that Sir John Bernard's statue was to be taken down and a statue of Pontius Pilate was to be put in its place; that the Jews had now taken over the running of the country and refused to naturalize Christians; that the new Attorney-General was to be Moses da Costa; and that 'Jewish services are daily held at the London synagogue, formerly St. Paul's...' and so on, in the same vein. Petitions against the bill also poured in, mainly from stock-jobbers and so-called patriotic merchants who, if the bill survived, would have to meet formidable Jewish competition. Walls were plastered with the slogan: 'No Jews, no Wooden Shoes' (wooden shoes were thought to be the characteristic footwear of religious refugees from France, so this slogan had a double meaning). The Member of Parliament for Exeter even distributed papers to prove that he observed his Sabbath with other Englishmen and therefore could not seriously be suspected of clandestine adherence to Judaism. The spiritual peers who had supported the bill were accused of delivering the 'keys of the Church' to those who had murdered their Saviour, while grand juries and pocket boroughs presented extravagantly phrased petitions imploring that the bill should be withdrawn. All the old anti-Jewish libels were revived, including that of ritual murder. The attacks were endless. Most of them were spurious and even ludicrous, but they had the desired effect. When the bill had been only eight months on the Statute Book, the government of the Duke of Newcastle proposed on 15 November, the opening day of the new session, a new bill in the House of Lords

When the Jewish Naturalization Act was passed, it aroused a storm of anti-Semitic protest. All the old libels were brought up, such as the image of the grasping Jewish money lender, as shown in this cartoon by Thomas Rowlandson.

which would repeal the Jew Bill. Despite some opposition from those who were in favour of keeping the Jewish Naturalization Bill, the rescinding bill went through the Lords and, after some debate in the Commons, it was passed unanimously and received the royal assent on 20 December 1753.

In a way, Jewish equality with other Britons had taken a step backwards and it was to be seventy years before the Jews of Britain again received specific mention in any Act of Parliament.

King George III – Farmer George, as he was soon nicknamed – succeeded his grandfather, George II, in 1760. He occupied the throne (though, for the last nine years, his son, also George, was Regent) until 1820. During his long reign, Anglo-Jewry was to witness the dawn, though not the complete fulfilment, of a new era.

It was now that a Jewish institution, which had been operated more or less internally by the Bevis Marks Synagogue from the early part of the eighteenth century, came into official being. In somewhat similar mode to the group of Deputies appointed to protect the civil rights of the Protestant Dissenters which first met in 1737, a committee within the synagogue had nominated their own *deputados* (deputies), from time to time, to deal with national – and particularly political – matters that concerned Jews. These deputies would approach the government on the Jew's behalf, when they considered it necessary. The deputies had already made one previous representation as a body before the new king came to the throne. On his accession, seven deputies were appointed to represent the Sephardi community and they presented the following Loyal Address to the king:

> The Portuguese Jews most humbly beg leave to condole with his Majesty on the demise of the late king, whose sacred memory will ever be revered, and to congratulate his Majesty on his accession to the throne of these kingdoms; humbly craving the continuance of his Majesty's favour and protection, which they hope to merit by an unalterable zeal for his Majesty's most sacred person and service, and by promoting to the utmost of their abilities the benefit of his Majesty's realms.

When, a week or so later, the Ashkenazi community heard that a Loyal Address had been presented to the king without recourse to them, they formally protested to Bevis Marks that they had been ignored on such an important national occasion and nominated their own 'German Secret Committee for Public Affairs' to present a Loyal Address to His Majesty on their behalf. It became clear to the leaders of both communities that it was ridiculous for two such bodies to act independently of one another and towards the end of 1760, a motion was passed by the Sephardi *deputados* that, in future, in any public affair that would interest the two Jewish 'nations', they would act together. This was the start of the London Committee of Deputies of British Jews (known today as the Board of Deputies of British Jews), the functions of which, intermittent until the end of George III's reign, were to be of considerable importance and gain statutory recognition during the nineteenth century.

Britain's Jews were by now much more integrated with their non-Jewish neighbours, but few of them assimilated to the extent of losing their Jewish identity. There were, of course, exceptions, such as an immigrant from Silesia, for example, who when he first arrived in England as a youth, wrote to his parents in Yiddish and certainly knew no English. Within twenty years, the same man had turned into a staid British merchant, with one of his sons (who both married non-Jewish girls) becoming a sea captain and the other, who was later buried in Bath Abbey, entering the colonial service. Then there were a number of foreign-born sons of London synagogue members who soon lost touch with their co-religionists and entered English life as playwrights, authors, doctors and even naval officers. Some of these gave up their religion in order to be eligible for positions in public life. One such was Alexander Schomberg, the son of a German-Jewish doctor, who became a captain in the Royal Navy and was later knighted. Others stopped professing Judaism because of a desire to be seen to be 'British'. On the other hand, there were now a number of conversions in the other direction – often when a non-Jewish girl or man changed before marriage with a Jew. However, this did not particularly please the Jewish authorities, because of the promise made at the time of the Resettlement that Jews would never attempt to convert Christians.

Like any other group, the Jewish community had its miscreants, too. Many destitute Jews took to petty crime in order to survive. As Todd M. Endelman reports in *The Jews of Georgian England: 1714–1830*: 'The Jewish poor in Georgian England were in many respects very similar to the non-Jewish poor. They lived in accordance with a system of values and priorities that often clashed with the morals and manners of polite society.' Many adapted to the rough-and-tumble ways of English street life with speed and enthusiasm, including a taste for the rougher English amusements, which often disregarded Jewish ethical conduct, and even included violence. More well-to-do Jews were sometimes convicted of crimes associated with the trades in which they worked – as dealers of second-hand goods of every kind, for instance, they often purchased stolen goods. For the most part, however, as a direct result of the abject poverty in which so many of them lived, Jews engaged in petty crime such as picking pockets, shoplifting, breaking and entering, forgery, swindling and, surprisingly, brothel keeping.

There was little recorded Jewish criminal activity before the 1760s, possibly because there were fewer poor Jews in England in the early part of the eighteenth century. In the 1730s, there were, in fact, only four Jews convicted at the Old Bailey – two for stealing from their masters, one for burglary and the fourth for forging an acceptance to a bill of exchange; while, in the 1740s, there were eighteen convictions (including one for stealing some of the ritual silver from the Great Synagogue in Duke's Place). Even in the 1750s, there was not a great increase in Jewish crime. From the 1760s until the end of the century, however, the Jewish crime rate rose steadily, mostly perpetrated by the very poor. So much so, that, in 1795, Patrick Colquhoun, a well-known London magistrate, claimed that of the 20,000 Jews in London, some 2,000 of them were 'engaged in nefarious practices because they were not trained for useful employment.' He also declared that if the 'leading and respectable characters' of the Jewish community did not take steps to train their children in 'useful and productive labour' and save them from careers of crime, special legislation would be necessary to deal with them.

The British attitude towards the Jews changed very much for the better during the eighteenth century. One reason may have been that more and more Jews were speaking English, not only in their relationships with non-Jews, but also in their communal life, rather than Ladino or Portuguese, if they were Sephardi, or Yiddish or German, if they were Ashkenazi. As early as 1735, English was included in the curriculum of the Sephardi community's public school and, from the end of the reign of George II, synagogue sermons and special orders of Jewish services frequently appeared in English translation, though the originals were in Hebrew. For a long time, the Jewish authorities opposed the publication of the Siddur (the prayer book) in English, but, in 1770, it was at last allowed, though it would, of course, have also included all the prayers in Hebrew.

Increased toleration towards the Jews was furthered by the spread of Freemasonry, which implicitly inculcated a high degree of tolerance among its members. Indeed, some Sephardi Jews had held high office in the English lodges as early as 1723. Freemasonry's mystical content was particularly attractive to Jewish exponents of the occult, which was included in Jewish Cabbalism, but many wealthy and not-so-wealthy Jews were much more attracted to it because it held out the possibility of close companionship with respectable Christians on an equal basis. By the middle of the century, so many Sephardi and Ashkenazi Jews wanted to become Freemasons that all-Jewish lodges began to appear, which, in a way, must have defeated the original reason for entering Freemasonry. The élite Jewish strata still joined the mixed lodges whenever they could, however, and the Jewish lodges catered mainly for shopkeepers and artisans. In these, the ritual was adapted to Jewish usage, the dietary laws were observed and meetings were so arranged as not to conflict with Jewish festivals. The establishment of Jewish lodges had the effect of encouraging some of the earlier mixed lodges to prohibit Jews joining them. This kind of discrimination also encouraged the creation of more Jewish lodges and, by the beginning of the nineteenth century, there were at least six in London alone, with their members drawn entirely from the lower end of the Jewish commercial world.

By 1790, the minutes of most Jewish communal organisations were recorded in English, but though the community itself was becoming more and more anglicised, its foreign character was maintained by the now constant stream of Jews from abroad.

At the end of the eighteenth century, a spirit of restlessness was pervading the Jewish world because of the uncomfortable conditions in Germany, wars in central Europe, Jewish expulsion from Bohemia, continuing massacres in Poland and smaller persecutions elsewhere. All this, combined with the lure of freedom and opportunity in Britain, fostered immigration and many came across the North Sea to try their luck in a new land. Like all immigrants, once a settler had established himself, he sent for his younger brothers or other relations to join him – or, even if he did not send for them, they came to join him willy-nilly. The number of extra synagogues which were built – and filled – during the second half of the eighteenth century confirmed that London was still the principal, though, by now, not the sole, Jewish centre. There were still restrictions on Jews living in the City of London, so many settled just outside the City boundaries – in the East End near the original settlement and a few in the West End beyond Temple Bar.

While the well-to-do Jews were now mainly engaged in wholesale commerce, brokerage, jobbing on the Royal Exchange and trading in precious stones, a different pattern was emerging for the middle class and the artisans, of which there were a great many. Members of the middle class mostly carried on business as shopkeepers, silversmiths and watchmakers, while those who were primarily craftsmen and women became pencil makers, tailors, hatters, embroiderers, glass engravers, diamond polishers, necklace makers, feather curlers (usually a women's occupation) and so on. Nevertheless, a number of the unskilled, and especially those living close to the poverty line, continued with the only trade they had been allowed in the countries from which they had come – buying and selling old clothes. These last were, in fact, offering a service of some importance to their non-Jewish fellow citizens. In the days before cheap tailoring (which was introduced by Jews in the nineteenth century), it was almost impossible for the labouring classes to buy any new clothes and they had to make do with the cast-offs of wealthier people. Certainly in London, and probably in other towns where Jewish communities were now getting established, Jewish hawkers would patrol the streets, lanes and alleys, offering to purchase second-hand clothes, hats, hare and rabbit skins, old glass, broken metal – in fact, any item of personal or household merchandise that would otherwise have been discarded by the owners. It is estimated that, by the end of the eighteenth century, there were no fewer than 1,500 Jewish old-clothes men in London alone.

Jews were to take an increasing part in Britain's sport as the years

Daniel Mendoza was one of the outstanding prize fighters of the later eighteenth century, mostly due to the fact that he introduced the scientific form of boxing. He was born in 1763 and died in 1836, but his boxing career spanned only about ten years. This etching of Mendoza is by the famous nineteenth century cartoonist, James Gillray.

went on and one of the first was Daniel Mendoza, the prize fighter. Although there had been 'prize fighters', both Jewish and non-Jewish, before him, Daniel Mendoza has always been considered the founder of tactical or scientific boxing – boxing in which finesse and agility are emphasised instead of brute strength – and this method included defensive moves that enabled him to fight against much heavier opponents.

Born in Aldgate, London in 1764, Mendoza learned to defend himself with his fists at an early age. His parents were believed to be middle class, though, as Mendoza stated in his memoirs, they were 'by no means in affluent circumstances'. He was educated at a Jewish school, which he left when he was twelve and he worked for several shopkeepers until he was seventeen, but was never indentured or apprenticed to learn a trade. He was attracted to the boxing ring after he had collected £14 from spectators who saw him defend himself from two street attacks. A natural middleweight, his first professional fights in 1780 were backed for no more than five or six guineas a side and, for his next two matches, he was able to raise the 20-guinea stake himself. He always proudly billed himself as 'Mendoza the Jew'. In 1785, he defeated 'Martin the Butcher', having, it is said, been backed by 'a great personage' who was believed to be the Prince of Wales himself. Whether this was true or not, the great personage presented the young boxer, who was still only about 20, with £550 and the same sum was contributed by grateful punters. During the same year, Mendoza collected £200 for a sparring display and a further 150 guineas from some Lloyds underwriters to express their indignation against 'a gentleman who had cheated him'! He opened his own boxing academy in Capel Court in the City shortly afterwards, but closed it in about 1790.

Probably his greatest rival was Dick Humphries, who had become the national boxing champion in 1786. Mendoza became the acknowledged champion during the years 1788 to 1790, during which he beat Humphries three times. Neither combatant made much money out of the three epic fights. Indeed, within three years, Mendoza was in a debtors' prison!

Though he is usually best remembered as a great prize fighter, Mendoza was a man of other talents, not least of them as a showman, which was demonstrated by the sparring exhibitions he put on at Covent Garden Opera House and in theatres in Edinburgh, the Midlands and Dublin. In 1791, he leased the Lyceum Theatre in the Strand for regular exhibitions which could be attended by both sexes. 'The ladies are respectfully informed that there is neither violence nor indecency in this spectacle that can offend the most delicate of their sex' he announced in an advertisement. It may well have been the money lost on this venture which steered him into the King's Bench debtors' prison in 1793. When Britain went to war with France in 1795, he obtained his release and became a recruiting sergeant for the Fifeshire Fencibles and later a sergeant-major in the Aberdeenshire Fencibles. A year later, he left his post and returned to boxing, but his greatness was gone. He wrote two books, *The Art of Boxing* in 1789 and *The Memoirs of the Life of Daniel Mendoza* in 1816. He and his wife had eleven children.

By the close of the century, many more immigrants had arrived from western Europe – from Amsterdam, Leghorn in Italy (many of them straw bonnet makers), Venice and other Italian cities and towns. Some had also come from Gibraltar as a direct result of the Treaty of Utrecht in 1714, which ceded it to Great Britain. One of the conditions was that Jews and Moors were forbidden to set foot on the Rock. In 1729, however, a treaty was signed with the Emperor of Morocco (who was represented by a Jew, Moses ben Attar) which empowered his subjects of whatever religion to visit the fortress for business reasons for a period of not more than thirty days. This limitation was soon ignored and, by 1749, a Jewish community was established in Gibraltar. Indeed, by 1776, a third of Gibraltar's civil population of 3,000 people were Jewish and they were in almost complete control of its trade. Despite this, in June, 1781, a number of destitute Jewish families arrived in England from Gibraltar, bringing with them their Chief Rabbi and their Torah Scrolls, which they had managed to rescue during the third siege of Gibraltar by the Spanish, which lasted from 1779 until 1783. Another 160 Gibraltarian Jews set sail for England on the Royal Naval frigate, *Tisiphone*, on 31 October 1782, a few months before the end of the siege. When peace was restored to Gibraltar by the British, many of the immigrants opted to remain in England. Around this time, a trickle of Jews from Morocco had come to settle in England, as a result of being sent to the Court of St James on missions from the Sultan of Morocco.

During the French Revolution, there was no normal immigration from the Continent and, thereafter, British Jewry became more or less self-contained. Despite the tolerant attitude now prevailing in England, there were occasions when anti-Semitism, or even persecution, reared its head, such as when Jews were suspected of Jacobite sympathies or they were accused of treasonable correspondence with their co-religionists in Venice when it was occupied by the French. Nevertheless, on the whole, British Jewry lived in peaceful co-existence with their fellow non-Jewish citizens.

The reactions of Jews at times of crisis was much the same as other Englishmen, though during the eighteenth century (and considerably later), they were usually debarred from holding commissions and, as has been said, it was necessary for them to become Christian in order to be eligible. One who did go to these lengths to further his naval ambitions was a young Sephardi, Donald Fernandez, who joined as a midshipman in 1790, when he was nineteen. He served on several ships and was promoted lieutenant in 1797, a few days before the Battle of St Vincent. He commanded the 14-gun brig, *Speedwell*, for a few months in 1803 on the home station (his only command), saw no more active service afterwards and was on half-pay when he was made a commander in 1838. He died, aged eighty, in 1851. From the middle of the eighteenth century, quite a few Jewish naval ratings served before the mast and Jews were also to be found in small numbers in the British army. On the renewal of the war with France, hundreds of Jews enlisted in the Volunteer Corps.

Many of the Jewish merchants and slopsellers who had established themselves in ports serving the Royal Navy had changed or added to their role by the early 1800s. They had become prize or navy agents appointed by the Admiralty for a period of three years. The agents' main terms of reference were the handling of the sailors' share of the prize or booty which they were legally awarded after capturing foreign ships and their contents during battles or other sea encounters. The Royal Navy's system for rewarding crews was very involved and took a long time, frequently years, to complete and the members of the crews concerned might very well be on the other side of the world by the time they were paid. In order to avoid this delay, sailors gave the licensed agents power of attorney to negotiate with the Admiralty on their behalf or alternatively to sell the prize, depending on the circumstances of the capture. In either case, the crews received their payments promptly, in either cash or goods, on the estimated value of the prize and subsequently the agent made his profit on whatever sum he could obtain from either the Admiralty or an independent purchaser. In the early years of this system, very few of the licensed naval agents were Jewish. Indeed, the first Jewish London agent, Isaac Levy of Whitechapel, was appointed in May, 1808, during the Napoleonic Wars and he was the only Jew among the thirty or so prize agents in the capital.

In the ports outside London, however, Jewish agents were probably in the majority and the earliest, Solomon Alexander of Broad Street, Plymouth, a watchmaker, silversmith and slopseller, was appointed in March, 1795. The official published lists of licensed navy agents for 'inferior petty officers, seamen and marines' covering the towns of London, Chatham, Sheerness, Portsmouth, Portsea, Gosport, Plymouth, Plymouth Dock, Hull, Leeds, Southampton, Liverpool, Wolverhampton, Manchester, Edinburgh, Guernsey, Canterbury, Nottingham, Exeter, Bath, Cowes (Isle of Wight), Birmingham, Dover, Falmouth, Penzance and some other locations, between the years 1795 and 1863, listed no fewer than 285 Jewish agents – and there may have been more. Not only does that indicate a high percentage of specialists in a minority group, but it gives a good idea of the very rapid spread of Jews and their families up and down the country during some seventy years – and the foregoing list was only of those who made their homes in *naval*-orientated towns.

Many more, as has been said, were settling in other towns in Britain during this period. Jewish settlements of varying sizes were often formed as a direct result of the travels of the Jewish pedlars. A pedlar would probably, for a time, make an inn in a large town his headquarters and, from there, travel around the nearby countryside, selling his wares from door to door in the villages and even going to the remotest cottages and farmhouses. There was danger in this, because pedlars were often attacked by footpads and baited by rural tearaways. In addition, communication was still very slow

Jewish settlements outside London were often formed as a direct result of the travels of the Jewish pedlars, like this one in an anonymous engraving of 1824. The lad on the far left of the picture is picking the pocket of the pedlar's customer, but it is not clear whether the artist intended to imply that the pickpocket and the pedlar were working as a team!

and, quite soon, many of the Jewish pedlars settled with their families in proven centres of trade, instead of constantly travelling from place to place. It would not have been long before other Jewish families, particularly the relatives of the original settlers, joined them and thus new congregations were born.

Exact dates are not available for the establishment of Jewish communities in every town, but by the time of the Battle of Waterloo in 1815, the following English and Welsh towns had settled Jewish congregations: Birmingham (from 1730), Falmouth (from 1740), Plymouth (also from 1740, though the first synagogue was not opened until 1754), Portsmouth and King's Lynn (both from 1747), Liverpool and Chatham (both from 1750), Bristol (from 1754), Exeter (from 1757), Canterbury (from 1763, with a burial ground dating from three years earlier), Sunderland (from 1768), Ipswich (from 1792) and Bedford (from 1803). Norwich, Sheerness, Swansea, Gloucester, Bath, Coventry, Brighton, Penzance, Dover, Hull and Yarmouth also had Jewish communities by 1815 and, at least in the south of England, Jewish families or individuals were to be found in almost every other town of importance.

There are records of Jews in Edinburgh as early as 1691 and, from time to time in the following years, other Jews certainly lived in the city. There is also reason to believe that there was an organised community there as early as 1780, but it was not until 1816 that twenty Jewish families living in Edinburgh established a synagogue in a lane off Nicholson Street. Its first minister was probably Moses Joel, who died in 1862. Little is known, however, about the early history of the Jewish community of Glasgow. It is thought, though no precise date is confirmed, that a Jewish congregation was set up about 1830 and that the first synagogue was opened in Post Office Court about 1840. There is conflicting evidence even about these dates and it is certainly possible that there was some sort of Jewish organisation in the city as early as 1823, with Moses Lisenheim as the minister.

Jews were now becoming prominent in banking. Among the earliest and most distinguished bankers were two brothers, Benjamin and Abraham Goldsmid, of a long-established Anglo-Dutch family. Indeed, the Goldsmids were the first Jews since the Middle Ages whose place in British financial history was of real significance. They also played a prominent part in the realm of charity, in both the Jewish and the secular communities. Both entertained widely and had many famous friends, among them Admiral Lord Nelson, who lived at Merton and was a neighbour of Abraham Goldsmid, who had a country seat at Morden Hall in Surrey. His brother, Ben-

This caricature is of Abraham Goldsmid, who, with his brother, Benjamin, was among Britain's earliest and most distinguished bankers. Though they owned valuable homes and mixed with both the nobility and the aristocracy, both brothers eventually committed suicide. Abraham and Benjamin had a sister, Polly, who became the wife of a diamond broker, Lyon de Symons. This unflattering caricature of her by James Gillray was obviously intended to show how Jews had risen in society.

Welcome, three Welcome, Bretheren to the Synagogue

CUMBERLAND LEAD
CAMBRIDGE BUTTUR
SUFFOLK CHEESE

It is recorded that so friendly were they with King George III's sons, that the Goldsmid brothers took them to synagogue one Friday evening. This contemporary cartoon of 1809 clearly mocks the visit.

jamin, took up residence in a smaller house, called The Rookery, at Roehampton, near Putney. The brothers were also on friendly terms with George III's sons, whom they often entertained in their own homes. It is recorded that the Goldsmid brothers even took some of the royal dukes to a service at their synagogue one Friday evening. Sadly, Benjamin committed suicide at his Roehampton home during a fit of acute depression on 15 April 1808, and his brother, who also suffered from bouts of depression, could not face the possibility of a financial crash as a result of the failure of a government loan two years later. He, too, took his own life – on 28 September 1810.

By this time, a member of the greatest European banking family had begun to make his mark in Britain. Nathan Meyer Rothschild was born in Frankfurt in Germany in 1777 and came to London when he was only thirteen. In 1797, he established himself in Brown Street, Manchester, as a manufacturer of cotton goods, exporting to his father, Mayer Amschel Rothschild (the founder of the great international banking firm) in Frankfurt. In 1802, having made a fortune of £200,000, Nathan went to London and founded a financial house in St Helen's Place in connection with his father's business, which was gradually increasing. While living there, he married Hannah Barent Cohen and their oldest son, Lionel, was born in that house. Later, they moved to New Court in St Swithin's Lane. From 1808 to 1812, Nathan Rothschild received large sums from his father for investment in England. The money had been entrusted to him by members of the continental nobility who were terrified at what might happen to their fortunes in a Europe being ripped apart by war. The enormous sum of £600,000 was handed over for investment, for instance, by no less a personage than the Elector of Hesse-Cassel. One of the factors that established Nathan Rothschild as Britain's first great merchant banker was the fact that he accounted punctually for the money invested and repaid it with interest after the fall of Napoleon. The Rothschilds' great honesty in business was, indeed, a topic of astonished conversation at the Congress of Vienna, which commenced in 1814 after the defeat of Napoleon, to settle the boundaries of the various European nations.

Nathan and Hannah had four sons. Two of them, Lionel and Mayer, were later created barons, the third, Anthony, was knighted and the fourth, Nathaniel, married a cousin, the daughter of Baron James de Rothschild of Paris, who ran the French side of the Rothschilds' merchant banking firm. The three sons who stayed in England further established the great banking company founded by their father.

Nathan Rothschild was closely involved in British government circles because of his helpful activities to the government during the closing stages of the war with France. It was, in fact, Nathan Rothschild, with his great international connections, who brought the news of the Battle of Waterloo to the anxious British Prime Minister, William Pitt, and this naturally greatly increased his prestige. Nathan was also friendly with the royal dukes, who encouraged their Jewish friends in every way. There were Jewish musicians in their households, they gave patronage to Jewish charities and they often presided at Jewish public dinners. The Duke of Sussex, George III's sixth son, in particular, had many Jewish friends. He also studied Hebrew and built up a superb Hebrew library.

Royal patronage went a long way towards completing the social emancipation of the Jews in Britain and was the prelude to the removal of political disabilities, because even though the Jewish community was now equal with its fellow citizens in most things, its members were still not allowed to hold any political office.

In the meantime, British Jewry was putting its own house in order. Because of the growing numbers of Jewish poor now in the country, it had been obvious for many years – as early as the 1750s – that general Jewish institutions of one kind or another would have to be established to look after those in need. Much discussion – including argument and some dissension – had gone on over the years between the Askhenazi community and the Sephardi community, which already had its own hospital, asylum and school and saw no advantage to itself of the proposed amalgamation.

Eventually, however, on 28 June 1807, a 'Jews' Hospital for the reception and support of the aged poor and the education and industrial employment of the youth of both sexes' was opened in the Mile End Road. This institution was entirely dependent on voluntary subscriptions and was established by the dedication of Abraham Goldsmid, whose brother, Benjamin, had founded the Royal Naval Asylum. Some years previously, Goldsmid had set up an appeal for this cause and had raised £20,000 from both Jews and non-Jews (contributing undoubtedly a substantial sum himself) and this money was used to set up the Jews' Hospital.

For its day, Jews' Hospital was very extensive, containing, according to the records, a boys' bedroom, a men's bedroom, a dining-room, a 'counting room', a matron's bedroom, a master's bedroom, two store-rooms, a male sick room, an aged person's room, a shoemakers' room, a basket-makers' shop, a shoe workshop, a basket workshop, a mahogany chair manufactory, a kitchen, a female sick room, a girls' bedchamber, a women's bedchamber, a schoolroom, a mistress's bedchamber, a girls' workroom and a matron's parlour. This first building was created by the reconstruction and adaptation of a number of houses that the management had purchased. In 1811, a contemporary periodical described the building as 'an elegant modern edifice in Mile End Road on the south side between Globe Fields and Bancroft's Almshouses'. The building was designed to house five aged men and five aged women, ten boys and eight girls. Three years later, it was enlarged to accommodate twelve aged people, twenty-three boys and eighteen girls and, in 1821, there were, as well as the twelve old people, forty-seven boys and twenty-nine girls in the hospital. Neither of the Goldsmid brothers, alas, lived to see the development of the institution.

King George IV came to the throne in 1820, having been Regent for his father since 1811, because of George III's mental illness, porphyria. By then, Jews were prominent in every walk of life except politics. They were also respected by many believing Christians as 'the ancient people of God', although there were movements to convert them, such as the London Society for the Promotion of Christianity among the Jews, which was established in 1795, but which had little success despite quite a lot of money being poured into it by rich, dedicated missionary souls. The horror of the French Revolution had further encouraged the millennium theorists (those who believed in the second coming of Jesus) and many felt that the Jews should be restored to their own land. They were, in fact, foretelling, more than a hundred years too early, the formation of a Jewish state – and they even urged the British government to take steps to further the project.

Nevertheless, throughout all the years leading up to and during the beginning of the emancipation of Britain's Jews, they were still described on the Statute Book as 'aliens' and, as late as 1818, Lord Coke stated that the Jews in law were perpetual enemies 'for between them, as with the devils, whose subjects they are, and the Christians there can be no peace.' So public life was, in law, still barred to Jews. They were excluded from any office under the Crown, any part in civic government or any employment, however modest, in connection either with education or the administration of justice.

On 14 July 1820, however, a young Whig, John Cam Hobhouse (later Lord Broughton de Gyffard) gave notice to the House of Commons of his intention to move a resolution that the conditions of the Jews and the disabilities under which they laboured (which, he pointed out, would hardly be believed to exist in such an age as this) should be taken into immediate consideration. Although this was but a small blow for Jewish political and civic freedom, it was the beginning. Thenceforward, over some years, many other Members of Parliament and other prominent people, pushed and encouraged by the Jewish Board of Deputies, fought for Jews to be given the same rights as everyone else – in law, in politics, in teaching and so on. The gaining of those rights took a long time and actually developed piecemeal. For instance, in 1830, the last year of the reign of George IV, the Common Council of the City of London passed an act that henceforth any person who took up the Freedom of the City of London could make the necessary oath in a form agreeable to his religious convictions, and this meant that Jews could, at last, become Freemen, could join Livery Companies and trade in the City.

It was a significant step towards complete emancipation.

CHAPTER EIGHT
Emancipation

In 1833, during the short reign of King William IV, the first Jewish barrister, Francis Goldsmid, was called to the Bar and, in the same year, the first Jewish jury man was sworn in on the Pentateuch (the Torah), instead of the combined Old and New Testaments, as a member of the Grand Jury at the Kirkdale Quarter Sessions.

Born in Leghorn in 1784 while his parents were there on a visit, but brought up in London, was a man who was destined to be the most famous Jew – revered by Jews and gentiles alike – of the nineteenth century. His name was Moses Montefiore and, when he had completed his education, he was apprenticed to a firm of wholesale grocers and tea merchants, which he left to become one of the Royal Exchange's twelve Jewish brokers. Later, he went into partnership with his brother, Abraham, and their firm acquired a

In this picture of the Montefiore family, painted by R. Jelgerhuis in 1797, Moses Montefiore, who was to have so important a part in the life of British Jewry, is seen on the right standing beside his father, Joseph Elias Montefiore, On the left are his mother, Rachel, two of his sisters and his brother, Abraham (centre).

Sir Moses Montefiore,
when he was in his
nineties, painted by
Henry Weigall.

high reputation. In 1812, he married the daughter of Levi Barent Cohen, Judith, who was always to have a great influence on him. He retired from regular business in 1824, when he was only forty, though retaining various commercial directorships, and devoted the rest of his life – and much of his money – to the welfare of Jews in Britain and throughout the world and his impact on the development of British Jewry was tremendous.

At a time when globetrotting was not only a slow, but also a fairly hazardous undertaking, Montefiore travelled round the world with the sole purpose of improving the quality of life of oppressed Jews in different countries, including Russia, Morocco and Rumania, and, although he was not always successful, his influence was very great. He made his first of many visits to Palestine in 1827 and is particularly remembered in Israel today for his encouragement of the early Jewish settlers to become self-supporting through agriculture and industry, both of which he supported financially.

At first, he was not a particularly religious Jew, but after his first visit to Palestine, he became strictly observant and, from 1833, even maintained his own synagogue on his estate at Ramsgate in Kent.

He was Sheriff of London in 1837 and 1838 and was knighted by Queen Victoria on her first visit to the City. She further honoured him with a baronetcy in 1846, in recognition of his humanitarian efforts on behalf of his fellow Jews. He was literally a prominent figure, being six feet three inches tall and, both in his own lifetime and since, enjoyed enormous prestige; his great philanthropy and general behaviour making him highly respected in Britain and overseas. The support for his activities given him by the British government – consonant with its overseas policies – and the personal regard shown him by Queen Victoria, added to his reputation. His one hundredth birthday was celebrated as a public holiday by Jews all over the world and there was great sadness when he died a year later. He and his wife had no children. Dr Claude Montefiore, one of the founders of the Liberal Jewish movement, was his great nephew – ironic, because Moses had been totally and determinedly against *any* Jewish reform movement. Bishop Hugh Montefiore, who converted to Christianity while at university, is his great-great-great-nephew.

But it was Moses Montefiore's work for the Jewish Board of Deputies which was undoubtedly his greatest contribution to the welfare and furtherment of the Jews of Britain. During the seventy-five years since its foundation, the deputies had met infrequently, despite the fact that they were still endeavouring to form an official constitution for the organisation., It is true that, in 1817, an attempt had been made to improve upon the informality of the rules when it was founded, but no meeting had been called by the president, Raphael Brendon, during the previous five years. When the deputies met, they agreed that 'independent of the established right of the president to call a meeting of the United Deputies of the four City Congregations at any time he should think proper', any five members could call a meeting themselves. Alas, despite this attempt to progress, it was about eleven years before the group met again to transact any important business – and this was only as a result of an initiative taken by a non-committee member, who wanted to secure relief from parliament from the various civil disabilities which applied to Jews. As a result of this, the deputies met in 1828 (the first meeting of any kind for eight years) to draw up a petition to the House of Lords on the subject of the relief of Jewish disabilities. The House of Lords did nothing about the petition and almost another year was to elapse before the deputies met again to discuss the subject. After considerable controversy, and at the initiative of members of the Rothschild family who had already been in touch with leading members of the government, it was agreed to present a further petition to the House of Lords, but the government refused to give any support and, once again, the matter was dropped. As Aubrey Newman explains in *The Board of Deputies of British Jews: 1760–1985*, 'In practice the four parent synagogues were unwilling to incur expense on a topic in which it is clear they had little direct interest, and the only move towards the future was an agreement that a small committee should be set up to assist the President [then Moses Mocatta], and that there should be on it a representative from each congregation.' This, then, was the very passive situation of the only official 'Jewish watchdog' in Britain when Moses Montefiore was invited to become president in 1835.

From the time he took office as President of the committee and for the following forty years, Montefiore was the dominating influence on the Board of Deputies. At various times during this period, there *were* other Presidents – usually standing in during his absences overseas – but he virtually personified the institution until he finally retired from office in 1884 when he was ninety years old.

It was Montefiore who was mainly instrumental in drawing up the Board's first constitution in 1836. This established its title – Deputies of the British Jews; its content – seven deputies from the Portuguese Synagogue (Bevis Marks), seven from the Great Synagogue, four from the Hambro synagogue and four from the New Synagogue; and it set out (among its various terms of reference) that 'in all cases which may tend to protect and promote the

An anonymous cartoon of the early nineteenth century showing a service in the Great Synagogue, suggesting that prayers were being said by Jewish financiers in thanks for repayment of a loan.

'Rag Fair' was an open air market in Rosemary Lane, Houndsditch, for the purchase and sale of old clothes. In this anonymous sketch, all the signboards above the stalls have Jewish surnames and the Jewish old clothes men wear piles of hats on their heads and some of them are bearded and wear long coats.

welfare of the Jews, the Deputies shall be authorised to adopt such measures as they may deem proper, in order to obtain such objects.'

In the same year, probably the first official recognition of the board – and one which was to give it widespread authority – came as a result of two acts of parliament: the Marriage and Registration Acts. Under these, British law recognised the rights of Jewish congregations to conduct lawful marriages and to register them, provided that each synagogue appointed a duly recognised and registered 'marriage secretary'.

Although today the board operates only in Britain, under Montefiore's leadership, its activities were enlarged to defend Jewish rights throughout the world.

In 1837, the non-sectarian University College of London, in the foundation of which Isaac Lyon Goldsmid, father of the first barrister, had been one of the most active and generous workers, was incorporated and this enabled Jews to gain the degrees from which they were still excluded by the older universities. The queen rewarded Goldsmid for his outstanding charitable service by creating him a baronet – the first Jew to receive a hereditary British title.

In 1845, the Jewish Disabilities Removal Act was passed, which allowed any person of the Jewish faith who was admitted to municipal office to substitute for the declaration laid down by law, one in a form acceptable to his conscience. Thus, municipal offices of every description, including even that of Recorder with its judicial functions, were at last thrown open to Jews.

It was not until 1847, however, that Baron Lionel de Rothschild became the first Jew to be elected to the House of Commons, representing the City of London as a Liberal. Though he was re-elected year after year, he could not take his seat for eleven years, because, as a Jew, he refused to take the Christian oath. From Rothschild's first election, his right to be admitted without taking the Christian oath was strongly supported by Benjamin Disraeli. Disraeli, later to be twice Britain's Prime Minister, who had been born a Jew, but, at thirteen, was baptised a Christian, cited, during his recommendation on Rothschild's behalf, the debt which Europe – and especially Britain – owed Jewry from whom Jesus had come.

Despite being baptised, Disraeli, who was also a distinguished and quite prolific novelist, was intensely proud of his Jewish background. His father, Isaac d'Israeli, a Sephardi Jew of Italian origin, was a member of the Bevis Marks Synagogue, though in no sense ardently religious. Benjamin's mother, Maria, was the sister of George Basevi, a well known English Jewish architect. Isaac d'Israeli was a minor poet and literary critic who refused to follow his family into commerce. He quarrelled with the Bevis Marks Synagogue when he was chosen to be a warden of the congregation in 1813, declining the office and refusing to pay the statutory fine of £40 for so doing, and, for this reason, he left the synagogue. He had his children baptised Christians a few years later – Benjamin in St Andrew's Church, Holborn, when he was about thirteen and

A sketch of Benjamin Disraeli when he was a young man.

Isaac d'Israeli, father of Benjamin Disraeli, who left the Bevis Marks Synagogue when his son was about thirteen and had him baptised a Christian. Around this time, he also removed the apostrophe from his surname.

would normally have been barmitzvah (read a portion of the Torah in the synagogue). Isaac's quarrel with the synagogue is often given as his reason for changing his children's faith. It is just as likely, however, that in a country where, at that time, Jews were not allowed to hold most public offices, including political posts, Isaac, ambitious for them, decided that they would have more chance as Christians to become prominent. He also removed the apostrophe from his name, though for what reason is not clear.

Benjamin Disraeli entered English society in 1826 and in 1837, the year of Queen Victoria's accession, was elected to Parliament as a Tory. He always regarded the farmer as the backbone of British society and this led him, in 1848, to oppose the repeal of the Corn Laws which protected farmers. This controversy split the Conservative Party, Sir Robert Peel, the Prime Minister, resigned and Disraeli became one of the acknowledged leaders of the party. In 1852, Disraeli became Chancellor of the Exchequer and leader of the House of Commons under Lord Derby's premiership. In 1868, Lord Derby resigned and Disraeli became Prime Minister. It was at this time that he became particularly friendly with Queen Victoria, with whom he already had a cordial relationship. The Conservatives were defeated in a General Election after Disraeli had been only a few months in office, but, in 1874, they were returned to power after a decisive victory over the Liberals led by William Gladstone.

On the party's re-election, Benjamin Disraeli again became Prime Minister, an office he was to hold for six years. He applied the social principals for which he had always stood – and with which several of his novels were concerned – and, in a paternalistic, rather than a modern way, bridged the gap between capital and labour by social and factory legislation. He also worked to establish the British Empire as a stronghold of culture, peace and liberty. He concentrated particularly on India and his acquisition of shares in the Suez Canal ensured Britain's control over the vital route to the sub-continent. In 1876, as a result of this, Queen Victoria was proclaimed Empress of India and she rewarded Disraeli – her favourite statesman – by creating him the Earl of Beaconsfield. It is believed that Victoria was also the one who gave Disraeli the affectionate nickname of 'Dizzy'.

In 1839, Disraeli married Mary Anne Lewis, widow of Wyndham Lewis who, when he was Member of Parliament for Maidstone, Kent, helped Disraeli get his seat in Parliament. Mary Anne was twelve years Benjamin's senior, but they had a completely happy, though childless, marriage of thirty years until Mary Anne died in 1872. Because of his devotion to his wife, Disraeli asked the queen

A satirical Punch cartoon showing Queen Victoria creating her Prime Minister, Benjamin Disraeli, the Earl of Beaconsfield, as a reward for making her Empress of India in 1876.

to honour her, rather than him, after his first, brief premiership – and she was created Viscountess Beaconsfield in her own right in 1868. They lived at Hughenden Manor, near High Wycombe in Buckinghamshire, and also in London, but they preferred Hughenden and Disraeli spent as much of his time there as his Parliamentary duties permitted.

In 1851, Sir David Salomons, an Alderman of the City of London who had been elected MP for Greenwich, entered the House of Commons for the first time and took his seat without uttering the full Christian oath. He then stood up and delivered his maiden speech; the relevant portions were as follows:

> Sir ... I trust the House will make some allowance for the novelty of my position, and the responsibility I feel for the unusual course which it may be thought I had adopted. But having been returned to this House by a large majority ... I thought I should not be doing justice to my position as an Englishman and a gentleman did I not adopt the course which I thought right and proper of maintaining my right to appear on the floor ... and stating before the House and the country what I believe to be my rights and privileges ... I hope this house will not refuse what I believe no court in the country refuses the meanest subject of the realm – that it will not refuse to hear me before it comes to a final decision.

He was cheered by members and complimented on his speech by Lord John Russell and later he voted in three divisions, but nevertheless he was removed from the House by the sergeant-at-arms as a trespasser.

Two years later, Lord John Russell, now Foreign Secretary in Lord Aberdeen's Coalition Government, carried a new Jewish Disabilities Bill through the Commons, but it was rejected. In 1855, Lord Russell tried another tactic. He attempted to gain his object by his Parliamentary Oaths Bill, which substituted a new single oath for the three formerly required. This did not mention Jews, but the words 'on the true faith of a Christian' was not included in the proposed new oath and, had it gone through, this bill would have automatically removed the barrier which had previously kept Jews out of Parliament. But, because the bill also abolished the special Roman Catholic oath which had been laid down by the Catholic Emancipation Act, it aroused great opposition from the Conservative benches and this, too, was thrown out, though by only a narrow margin. The struggle continued for three more years, with a number of sitting Members supporting the Jewish right not to have to swear a Christian oath. Eventually, in 1858, the Jewish Relief Act was passed, which, with its first important clause, opened Parliament to Jewish members:

> Where it shall appear to either House of Parliament that a Person professing the Jewish religion, otherwise entitled to sit and vote in the House, is prevented from so sitting and voting by his conscientious Objection to take the Oath which by an Act passed or to be passed in the present Session of Parliament has been or may be substituted for the Oaths of Allegiance, Supremacy, and Abjuration in the Form therein required, such House, if it thinks fit, may resolve that thenceforth any person professing the Jewish Religion, in taking the said Oath to entitle him to sit and vote as aforesaid, may omit the Words 'and I make this Declaration upon the true Faith of a Christian.

Baron Lionel de Rothschild took his seat in the House of Commons on 26 July 1858. Within two years, there were three other Jews in Parliament, including the doughty Sir David Salomons, who had also become the first Jewish Lord Mayor of London in 1855.

Almost exactly two hundred years after the death of Oliver Cromwell, the groundwork he and Menasseh ben Israel had done to resettle and achieve equality for Jews in Britain had come at last to fruition and, for the first time, British Jews were recognised as equal citizens of their native land. There were still some hurdles to be

Baron Lionel de Rothschild, the first Jewish Member of Parliament, being introduced into the House of Commons on 26 July 1858 – the moment of full emancipation of the Jews of Britain.

overcome, but, to all intents and purposes, Jewish emancipation in Britain was complete.

The Jews' position in Britain was very much enhanced by Queen Victoria's liking for them and although, of course, she was by no means an absolute monarch, she wielded a good deal of power. This was demonstrated when she raised Baron de Rothschild's son, Nathaniel, to the peerage and he took his seat in the Upper House without difficulty. By the turn of the 1860s, Jews were beginning to occupy quite high office. Indeed, in 1871, Sir George Jessel, MP, was appointed Solicitor-General – and was thus the first Jew to become a minister of the Crown.

Jews were not only making an impact on Britain's economy by Queen Victoria's reign, they were also contributing, in no small way, to the status of the British Empire overseas. One such family were the Sassoons – Sephardi Jews who had come originally from Baghdad where, for centuries, they had been princely merchants. They were direct descendants of Sheikh Sassoon ben Saleh, who had been the head of the Jewish community in Baghdad in the latter part of the eighteenth century and the start of the nineteenth.

In the 1850s, the Sassoons' business extended to India and the Treaty Ports of China and, in 1858, they established a London office and one part of the family moved to England. The head of the British settlers was Sassoon David Sassoon, who died in 1867 and was succeeded by his younger brother, Reuben. In 1876, Reuben was joined by an older brother, Abdullah, later to be knighted by the queen as Sir Albert Sassoon. The Sassoons became part of

The mausoleum which Sir Albert Sassoon built for himself at the corner of Paston Place and St George's Road, Brighton. Today, it forms part of a local public house and is called the Bombay Bar.

London society and, like others at the time, purchased 'holiday' properties in Brighton and Hove in Sussex, which had become very fashionable. After King Edward VII came to the throne, it is recorded that he quite often stayed with one of the family, Arthur Sassoon, who had a house at 8 King's Gardens in Hove. At the corner of Paston Place and St George's Road, Brighton, Sir Albert built himself a mausoleum which, very much in keeping with his family's origins in the Middle East, looked like a miniature copy of the Prince Regent's Brighton Pavilion. Sir Albert was buried in his mausoleum in 1896 and his son, Sir Edward, in 1912, but their remains were removed by the family in 1933. For a time, the building was used as a store by a firm of decorators. Today, fairly appropriately named the Bombay Bar, it forms part of a local public house. The Sassoons left their mark on the town in another way. On the western entrance to a small public park in Hove called St Ann's Well Gardens, there is a plaque which reads: 'The plots of land comprising the two croquet lawns with frontages north and south of the entrance were presented to the Borough of Hove by Mrs Flora Sassoon and opened to the public 1 May 1913 by Alderman Barnett Marks, JP, Mayor.' Mrs Flora Sassoon was the grandmother of Siegfried Sassoon, the poet. She had been born Fahra Reuben in Baghdad and, when she was fourteen was married to Sassoon David Sassoon, who was then eighteen. She lived much of her life in Hove and, after she died there, was remembered as 'an elegant little old lady who asked questions in a strange sing-song voice and rarely listened to the answers'.

At the beginning of the century, the number of Jews in Britain was estimated to be between 20,000 and 30,000, but this number was to rise significantly during the following years for a sad, but, to the Jews, inevitable, reason. While toleration and freedom for Jews was growing in Britiain, life was anything but easy for their co-religionists in Eastern Europe, especially in Russia and Poland. Indeed, by the late 1850s, Jewish immigrants, many of them of humble status, were entering Britain in relatively large numbers, as refugees from persecution in Russia, Poland and some of the Balkan States. By the time the first Jewish MP took his seat in 1858, it is believed that at least five thousand such immigrants had arrived on Britain's shores. But that was only the start. In 1881, a savage outbreak of Jewish persecution began in Russia, which was to continue unabated while the Tzars ruled Russia. This led to a wave of immigration unparalleled in previous Jewish history. Within a single generation, about a quarter of a million Eastern European Jews were forced to seek new homes overseas. The majority settled in the

The pogroms in Russia and Poland led to a wave of Jewish immigration unparallelled in Jewish history. Many of them came to Britain. This picture shows some Jewish families disembarking at Irongate Stairs.

United States, but almost all came via Britain, because the steam-driven ships which carried them refuelled in British ports. Consequently, quite a number of them decided to disembark in those ports and they stayed to increase Britain's Jewish population to at least 65,000.

This new wave of settlers brought with it a completely different way of life from that now enjoyed by native British Jewry. They arrived, on the whole, in such compact communities, mainly from the shtetels (Jewish villages) of Eastern Europe, that they were able to maintain, almost totally unchanged, their characteristic way of life, their institutions, even their Yiddish dialect. Many of them went into the clothing and allied industries and they were, in fact, the founders of today's off-the-peg tailoring and fashion industries, which, for the first time, brought to the general public inexpensive and fashionable garments. By 1890, as the persecuted continued to pour into Britain, the Jewish population had most probably more than doubled – to around 150,000. The majority of the new arrivals settled in London, but Leeds, Manchester and Glasgow also acquired communities which exceeded in number the entire Anglo-Jewish community of a century earlier.

The Eastern European immigration was to have a great influence on the Jews in Ireland, which, in 1861, had only 393 Jews, reduced to 285 ten years later and, by 1881, still had only 472 Jewish citizens – 394 of them in 'the twenty-six Counties' (now the Republic of Ireland) and 78 in 'the Six Counties' (now Northern Ireland). By 1891, however, the Jewish population in the whole of Ireland had risen to 1,779 (1,506 in the 26 Counties and 273 in the Six Counties). They set-

The immigrants from Eastern Europe brought with them a completely different way of life from that enjoyed by native British Jews. They came mainly from *shtetels* (Jewish villages) and spoke Yiddish. This family (whose names are not known) arrived from Odessa in Russia in 1890.

tled all over Ireland – many in Dublin and Belfast, both of which already had very small Jewish communities, and founded new congregations in Cork, Waterford, Londonderry, Dundalk, Lurgan and Limerick.

About twenty Lithuanian families settled in Limerick around the end of the 1870s and the beginning of the 1880s. As Louis Hyman explains in *The Jews of Ireland*: they lived in Edward Street and its environs and mostly traded in books and pictures. 'They kept to themselves, except for business, and the public knew little about them save insofar as minor congregational disputes came before the courts or were put to arbitration by M. King, President of the congregation.' It therefore came as a great shock to the little community on Easter Sunday morning in April, 1884, to find an angry crowd of Christians surrounding the house of Lieb Siev, a member of the synagogue. Not only angry words, but also stones were flung through the windows, injuring Siev's wife and child. Eventually, the rioters were dispersed by the local constables. Then the reason for the attack emerged – and it was not so far removed from the blood libel of earlier days. On Holy Thursday, a maidservant had seen her Jewish employer slaughtering chickens in the way the Jewish dietary laws prescribe – and which some of the townspeople considered to be cruel. She gossiped about what she had seen and this provoked an apparently spontaneous and probably unpremeditated onslaught on the Sievs' home. The two ringleaders of the riot were sentenced to a month's imprisonment with hard labour. The Mayor of Limerick, Alderman Lenihan, declared at the trial that there was no evidence that the Jews had offered any affront to their neighbours nor could the conduct to which they were subjected be tolerated in a civilised country. An important Irish newspaper, *The Cork Examiner*, wrote at the time:

> This country has long been honourably distinguished by its tolerance towards Jews. Its conduct in this respect was particularly creditable in a country in which Catholic enthusiasm is so strong. ... The Jews will never be convinced of the truth or beauty of Christianity by battering in their doors with stones. *Haud ignora mali* (Not ignorant of persecution and its evils), our own race ought to be especially careful to avoid its infliction.

A month later, there was another nasty anti-Semitic incident, this time in Cork, when, one Sunday afternoon, a newly arrived Lithuanian Jew, Jacob Sayers, was accused of preaching against the Catholics. He was so roughly used that he had to be escorted home by foot and mounted police. Louis Hyman reported that 'The crowd followed the party to the Hibernian Buildings and then returned to Parnell Bridge, and the police, thinking the disturbance at an end, went back to barracks. Thereupon, the crowd reassembled with wicked intent: any Jew they found was chased and assaulted and his house stoned; a Jewish shop was gutted.' The three ringleaders of this onslaught were sentenced to imprisonment.

There were, in the following years, a small number of petty anti-Semitic actions, but, on the whole, the Jews lived peacefully side by side with their Christian neighbours in Ireland. It was not until the early years of the twentieth century that something approaching a minor pogrom erupted in Limerick.

*   *   *   *

From quite early in the nineteenth century, the internal structure of British Jewry, and of its Judaism, changed and developed. Many of these changes would not have been either apparent or important to other British people, but for the now rapidly growing Jewish community, it was to set up the blueprint for the future of Jews and their welfare in the United Kingdom.

One of the earliest national Jewish benevolent societies was established in 1819 specifically to provide small regular pensions for needy Jewish blind people, which was called 'The Institute for the Relief of the Indiginent Blind of the Jewish Persuasion'. From this modest beginning, the Jewish Blind Society, to which its name was changed exactly a hundred years later, grew to be one of British Jewry's most active charitable bodies. The institute was started after Aaron Solomon, its first President, and his friends decided that something must be done for the blind within the Jewish community who, in the early nineteenth century, usually had little or no means of financial support. The institute offered help from its very meagre resources, but, for the few fortunate recipients, it at least meant they would not need to beg in the streets. The founders were soon convinced, however, that much more money had to be raised for them even to begin to tackle the problem of the Jewish blind. By the mid-1820s, the society had started a serious fund raising programme, with events commencing with river boat trips, followed by an annual ball, which quickly became very successful. The 1845 ball, for instance, with tickets at 10s. 6d. each, raised the considerable sum for those days of £360, which enabled each pensioner to receive a weekly payment of 6s. Five years later, as a result of the ball donations, including one of ten guineas from the Duke of Cambridge, subscriptions to the society reached £430 and, by 1858, it was able to provide thirty pensioners with a weekly stipend.

Until 1913, only those who were totally blind were eligible for financial help, but at the beginning of the First World War in 1914, the rules were amended so that those who 'for all practical purposes' were blind (i.e., the partially sighted) could qualify. Between the two world wars, development was relatively slow, though the number of pensioners had grown to 128. In the years immediately preceding the Second World War, however, great demands were put on the resources of the society, which began assisting blind and partially sighted refugees from Germany and Austria – and that included providing accommodation, education, training, rehabilitation and employment. At first, the refugees were housed in the Royal School for the Blind at Leatherhead, Surrey, but, in 1939, the first Jewish Blind Society residential home was opened specifically for them and, in the post-war years, several more residential and holiday homes were established in London and other areas. By the society's 150th anniversary year in 1969, 1,600 blind and partially sighted people were being cared for by the society, it had sixteen welfare officers, offered braille and audio services, educational and social facilities and a number of day centres, as well as its residential homes. Today, in its 170th year, the society assists a large number of elderly blind, partially sighted and physically handicapped Jewish men and women and shares the headquarters of the Jewish Welfare Board (see page 158). On 1 January 1990, the Jewish Blind Society and the Jewish Welfare Board joined together in an 'umbrella' organisation called Jewish Care. Many distinguished members of Britain's Jewish community have been connected with the Jewish Blind Society since its inception. Members of the Rothschild family have been among its Presidents, as have two Lord Mayors of London.

Although the first Jewish day school had been established in England as early as 1664, the school which was to make the greatest impact on Jewish junior education was the Jews' Free School (today the JFS Comprehensive School). What was clearly its forerunner had been opened by a group of German Jewish members of the Great Synagogue in 1732 in Ebenezer Square in the East End of London. Ebenezer Square was, as one pupil, who first entered the school in 1821, put it: '... little better than a den in those days. It was entirely shut out from the genial influences of the sun's rays'. By then, he reported, 'it consisted of little more than 100 boys'.

The Jews' Free School, as such, really dates from the opening of a purpose-built building in Bell Lane, near Aldgate, in 1822. Its syllabus was probably still fairly basic – mainly reading, writing, spel-

The Jews' Free School was started in the eighteenth century, but its positive establishment really dates from the opening of a purpose-built building in Bell Lane, near Aldgate, London, in 1822. This picture, taken at the turn of the century, shows school children in Bell Lane.

ling, the bare elements of Hebrew reading and 'the first four rules of arithmetic'. As time went on, however, the curriculum widened and it became co-educational at the turn of the century, by which time, it had no fewer than 3,500 pupils and was the largest school in Europe. As Jewish migration from the East End of London increased and the local community shrank, so did school numbers and it was much smaller by the outbreak of the First World War. The school remained in Bell Lane until the start of the Second World War in 1939, when it was evacuated to the Ely area in Cambridgeshire. The Bell Lane building was bombed during the London blitz. The 1944 Education Act ruled that schools could no longer provide combined primary and secondary education, as the Jews' Free School had and, for this reason and the fact that it no longer had a London building, the school ceased to function for thirteen years after the end of the war. Then, in 1958, it was re-opened as a secondary school in a new building in Camden Road, London, NW1, with Dr Edward Conway as its first head and with 350 pupils of both sexes. In the 1960s, it became a comprehensive school and its numbers increased considerably. Today, it has more than 1,400 pupils.

Since the Resettlement and even earlier, the Judaism practised by both Sephardis and Ashkenazis was in a form which today is called 'Orthodox'. It is true that the two factions differed slightly in their forms of worship and their sung liturgies, but basically their worship and belief was very similar and both, of course, prayed in Hebrew, though their pronunciation was different. As early as 1801, however, a 'reformed' movement had started in Germany – a movement created to examine and reform Jewish worship and practice, to modernise it and to bring it more into line with the way of life of the country in which Jews had now lived for many generations. As Jewish emancipation developed in Britain, the same desire arose among a number of the more integrated and well-established Jews. One of them was Francis Goldsmid (later Sir Francis), the first Jewish barrister, who had been born in the City of London, lived in the fashionable area of Regents Park and owned a large estate in Berkshire. Goldsmid came of a wealthy Ashkenazi family and was only one of a number of his contemporaries who felt the need to reform. It was, however, in the event, mainly a breakaway from the Bevis Marks Sephardi Synagogue which precipitated the start of Britain's Reform movement.

There had been rumblings of discontent in this community from some members for quite a long time, mainly on account of the lack of decorum during services, which was also one of the main complaints of those critics of London's three Ashkenazi synagogues. Another was dissatisfaction with one of the governing rules of the Bevis Marks Synagogue, which forbade the building of any other Sephardi synagogue within six miles of Bevis Marks. However, a proposal was put to the Elders of Bevis Marks that a branch synagogue should be opened in the West End of London. This was rejected in February, 1840, by the Mahamad (the governing body of Bevis Marks), which had previously made a condition that members of the new synagogue must remain members of Bevis Marks and that any changes in ritual must be approved by the ecclesiastical authorities of the whole community. The reformers (of both Sephardi and Ashkenazi persuasion) then decided to 'go it alone'

The first Reform synagogue, the West London Synagogue of British Jews, was founded in 1842 in Burton Street, near Euston. This engraving shows the interior of its present building in Upper Berkeley Street, when it was built in 1870. The *bimah* (reading desk) was in the middle of the synagogue and men and women were segregated for worship at either side. This is all changed today.

and, on 15 April 1840, at the Bedford Hotel, Southampton Row, twenty-four gentlemen (eighteen Sephardis and six Ashkenazis) resolved to form a new congregation 'under the denomination of British Jews', which would avoid the distinction between Ashkenazi and Sephardi. Amid a great deal of argument, anger and denunciation from the Orthodox Jewish authorities, plans went ahead and the first British Reform synagogue – the West London Synagogue of British Jews – opened its doors in Burton Street, near Euston, on 27 January 1842. In 1849, it moved to a building in Margaret Street, Cavendish Square, and, in 1870, went to its present premises in Upper Berkeley Street. In 1857, a Reform synagogue was

דבר בעתו מה טוב משלי טו כג׳ " A word in its season how good it is." Proverbs, chap. 15, ser 13.

No. 1.] כח׳ מרחשון תרב׳ לפק׳ November 12th. 5602.—1841. [Price 2d.

The first issue of *The Jewish Chronicle*, the world's first Jewish newspaper, was published on 12 November 1841. It appeared weekly (price 2d). With one or two interruptions in the very early days, it has done so ever since.

opened in Manchester and, in 1873, a similar congregation was created in Bradford. This was the start of what is today the Reform Synagogues of Great Britain, which did not develop much further until the 1930s. The early Reform movement had a slightly different and extended prayerbook from the Orthodox version and a somewhat different approach to the theology and practice of the faith, but it was not until after the First World War that it banished segregation for men and women at services – and until the 1970s, they remained segregated in the West London Synagogue on the Jewish High Holydays of New Year and the Day of Atonement. By the Second World War, there were six Reform congregations and today the Reform Synagogues of Great Britain is the parent body for thirty-eight synagogues.

A year after the crucial meeting of the creators of the Reform movement, on 12 November, 1841, the first issue of *The Jewish Chronicle*, the world's first Jewish newspaper, was published. It was founded by Isaac Vallentine, under joint editorship of Moses Angel, a University College graduate and a teacher at the Jews' Free School, and David Mendola, the spiritual leader of the Bevis Marks Synagogue. It was published to appear weekly from 132 Houndsditch, price 2d. a week. Until 1844, its publication was rather spasmodic and it fluctuated between weekly and fortnightly appearances, but on 18 October 1844, after being suspended for eighteen months, it appeared as a fortnightly under the auspices of a new proprietor, Joseph Mitchell, in collaboration with Isaac Vallentine. Its title was now *The Jewish Chronicle and Working Man's Friend*, but the last phrase was dropped after the twentieth issue. In April, 1846, the newspaper moved to new offices at 24 Houndsditch and the following year, on 8 October, it became weekly, which it remains today.

As the Jewish population increased and more and more congregations were formed, the demand for spiritual leaders of the synagogues became acute. The word 'rabbi' literally means 'my teacher' in Hebrew and, until about the beginning of the nineteenth century, that was the rabbi's role in a synagogue. For many, indeed most, rabbis, this was a spare time occupation and

Jews' College, set up by Orthodox Jews to train rabbis and ministers, was opened in this building in Finsbury Square, London, on 11 November 1855. It has moved several times since then and is now in purpose-built premises in Hendon in north-west London.

they earned their living in other ways. As the European communities developed, however, the need for a spiritual leader who would also act as a welfare advisor and helper to members of his congregation, became the norm. Rabbis in mainland Europe were trained in *yeshivas* (schools for studying and interpreting the Bible), but in the nineteenth century, there were no such institutions in Britain. Instead, on 11 November 1855, Jews' College opened in Finsbury Square in the City. It was set up by the Orthodox Jewish communities to train rabbis and ministers for Jewish congregations in Britain and the Commonwealth. The college soon outgrew its first home and moved, in 1881, to Bloomsbury into a house in Tavistock Square (the former home of Charles Dickens). In 1900, it removed to Queen Square, taking over a former Presbyterian College. After two more moves, it is now situated in Albert Road in Hendon in north-west London and has been, for some years, a recognised department of the University of London.

In the fifty-odd years since the Jews' Hospital had been opened in Mile End Road, specifically for the education and industrial employment of young Jewish boys and girls and for the 'reception and support of the aged poor', a good deal of other welfare work had been done by various synagogues (and specifically for the blind by the Jewish Blind Society), but it was not until the late 1850s that it became clear to the leaders of the Jewish community that financial help was urgently needed by many of the foreign immigrants who were, by then, beginning to arrive in Britain in fairly large – and mostly poverty-stricken – numbers.

Consequently, the following suggestions for the formation of an organisation to deal with this situation was put forward at a meeting of the committee of the Great Synagogue on 12 January 1858: 'That it is deemed advisable that a conjoint Board of Guardians be appointed to relieve the strange and foreign poor.' And 'that a copy of the foregoing resolution be transmitted to the President of the Hambro and New Synagogues requesting that their honorary officers will meet the honorary officers of this Synagogue as early as possible to confer on the matter.' A conference, with representatives of the three congregations, was held on 25 February and it was agreed to go ahead with setting up the Board of Guardians, although there was available from the three synagogues a total of less than £500 a year to 'disburse to a specific class of the Jewish Community'. But go ahead it did and its first meeting was held in the Great Synagogue chambers on 16 March 1859, under its founder and first President, Ephraim Alex, who remained in active office until 1909.

Over the intervening years, the considerable work of the Jewish

Board of Guardians has expanded and changed and its financial and staff resources have increased accordingly. This is best described by V.D. Lipman in *The Jewish Board of Guardians: A Centenary of Social Service*, which was published for the Board's centenary in 1959:

>...The Board began in 1859 with an avowed objective limited to the provision of monetary relief for a defined class – the strange or foreign poor Jews in London – and with a budget of £440 a year provided by the three synagogues in the City of London. In 1959, the Board provided for persons of the Jewish faith without restriction in Greater London and, indeed, in much of Southern England, a wide range of services, among which monetary relief played a relatively small part. Of their annual budget of a quarter of a million pounds a year on income and expenditure account, roughly half came from public authorities. Similar increases, both in scope and in size, are to be found in several aspects of the Board's history, whether in the increase in staff from a single clerk to nearly 300 headquarters staff and employees in the Board's homes or in building up, mostly in the last decade, of a chain of nearly 20 institutions in London and elsewhere in the Southern Counties. The past century has also seen many changes, perhaps even more important, in the spirit in which the Board's work has been undertaken, which can best be summed up as the change from relief to welfare.

In 1964, the Board of Guardians changed its name to the Jewish Welfare Board. In January, 1990, as has been said, it became part of Jewish Care.

Around this period and at the beginning of the twentieth century, more Jewish communal organisations were springing up, many of them specifically for young people, such as The Jewish Lads' and Girls' Brigade (established in 1895) and the Bernhard Baron Settlement in the East End of London.

Although the majority of synagogues in Britain were, by the 1860s, Ashkenazi, on the whole, they worked independently of one another, as many of them still do. By the late eighteenth century the spiritual head of the Great Synagogue in Duke's Place – the first and most important Ashkenazi synagogue – was recognised as the 'principal' or 'chief' rabbi of the Ashkenazi synagogues. (In the eighteenth century, in fact, he was known as the 'High Priest'.) The role of Chief Rabbi later became much more specific and far reaching. From the 1860s, there was a move to unite in one umbrella organisation the five London Ashkenazi synagogues then in existence, in order to ensure spiritual accord and administrative efficiency. In 1870, this plan came to fruition and, by the end of the century, fourteen London synagogues had become constituents of the organisation, which was called the United Synagogue. Sadly, the Great Synagogue in Duke's Place was bombed in the London blitz in the Second World War and not rebuilt because most of the large Jewish population had moved away from the City of London. By its centenary in 1970, the United Synagogue had eighty-one constituents or affiliated congregations in the London area and today many other Orthodox synagogues up and down the country and some in the Commonwealth accept the religious authority of the Chief Rabbi of the United Synagogue, now Lord Jakobovits, who does not, however, have any jurisdiction over Britain's other Jewish movements.

Under the administration of the Chief Rabbinate was (and still is) the London Bet Din or rabbinical court. Its function is to interpret the Jewish religious law, which is broken down, according to rabbinic tradition, into 613 mitzvot (obligatory religious observances) covering every function of Jewish life from birth to death and ranging from the dietary laws to conversion and divorce. Each Bet Din is really a local religious court and synagogues or groups of synagogues have always set up their own.

But the nineteenth century development of Britain's Jewish community was not just new places of worship, forms of prayer and 'good works'. Jews throughout the centuries have always been lovers of music and the theatre – and, indeed, have given to the world many distinguished instrumentalists, composers, playwrights and actors and actresses. One of the facets of theatre which particularly interested the Jewish immigrants from Eastern Europe (many of whom did not speak English) was seeing plays in their own Jewish language – Yiddish. By the early 1880s, a number of amateur actors in London's East End were already producing Yiddish plays in hired halls or theatres, but Britain's Yiddish theatre really started officially in December, 1883, when a company of professional Yiddish actors arrived in London from Riga in Latvia. They were soon playing to capacity houses, not only presenting drama, but also opera sung in Yiddish for their enthusiastic audiences. For a time, they, too, staged their productions in hired halls or theatres – until March, 1886, when the first purpose-built Yiddish theatre opened in Princes Street, just off Brick Lane in the East End. It was called The Princes Street Club and it soon became the leading venue for Yiddish theatre in western Europe. Other Yiddish theatres opened and closed during the following fifty-odd years, but, although there are still occasional visiting Yiddish theatre companies in London and the provinces, there has not been a full-time Yiddish theatre in London since 1961, when the Grand Palace in Commercial Road, which had been opened ten years earlier, started to run bingo sessions as

Yiddish theatre (with the plays all spoken in Yiddish) was very popular with Jews in the late nineteenth century. At first, Yiddish theatre companies from abroad staged their productions in hired halls or theatres. In March 1886, however, the first purpose-built Yiddish theatre was opened in the East End of London and, during the following fifty years, several others opened and closed. The Pavilion Theatre (top) in the East End was one of them. The Grand Palace (below) in Commercial Road survived longest – until 1970. There are no Yiddish theatres in Britain today.

well as Yiddish drama. It closed down completely in 1970.

Springing up in the East End and very much added to as the stream of refugees arrived from Russia, Poland and the Balkan States, were a number of fairly small 'minor' synagogues and/or Jewish local societies. By 1887, some eighteen such organisations were in existence, ranging in congregation numbers from 400 at the Sandys Row Synagogue to a handful in congregations such as those in Carter Street and Mansell Street. Just as the administrators of what had now become the United Synagogue saw the need for a parent organisation, so this group of synagogues decided the time had come to 'federate'. Accordingly, on 16 October 1887, a meeting of members of these synagogues was held at the Spital Square Synagogue in Spitalfields. The meeting was presided over by a local Member of Parliament, a Liberal and a Jew, Samuel Montagu (later the first Lord Swaithling). Two resolutions were passed unanimously at this meeting – that it was desirable for the congregations to be federated for certain clearly defined objects and that a representative of every 'minor' congregation in East London should be invited to attend a preliminary meeting to be held in the same venue on 6 November to discuss plans for the new federation. On 6 November, again under Samuel Montagu's chairmanship, representatives of the eighteen synagogues met and formally constituted these synagogues as the Federation of Minor Synagogues. It was further agreed that the new federation would be managed by a

Many middle class Jews were in the tobacco trade. This picture shows Maurice Simons, a cigar maker of Aldersgate Street, with his daughter, Rebecca, in 1885.

board of delegates and this met for the first time on 4 December. On 16 January 1888, a board meeting was held at which no less a personage than Lord Rothschild, the first Jewish MP, agreed to preside. It was clear by then that the Federation was anything but 'minor' and this word was soon dropped from the title of the organisation. During the following years, some 110 London synagogues joined the Federation – sited in areas as far apart as Croydon and Hendon, Leytonstone and Stamford Hill, Notting Hill and Woolwich – with about 16,000 members. By 1975, however, numbers had shrunk to about 10,000.

Many of the immigrants from Eastern Europe were to have a significant influence on the future of Britain's trade and prosperity. One of them was Michael Marks from Russia.

The story of the founding and subsequent history of the Marks & Spencer chain of stores must certainly be the prime example of Jewish trading at its best throughout the history of Britain's Jews. It is a company that has established a model for honest and efficient business methods, coupled with caring staff welfare, not only for the United Kingdom, but literally for the whole world. It is a story which, in the simplified form given here, may well sound rather like a fairy tale – but a fairy tale notwithstanding that has had a great deal of hard work and planning put into it to make the magic work the way it has for more than a hundred years.

Michael Marks, the firm's founder, was born in the little Russian town of Slonim in 1859. He emigrated to England in 1878, when he was nineteen, and settled in Hartlepool. He spoke Yiddish but no English, had no capital and was untrained, but he had heard that in Leeds there was a large Jewish community and a charitable firm called Barran's, which would help Jewish refugees. Accordingly, working as a pedlar, he eventually made his way, via Stockton on Tees, to Leeds and arrived there in 1884. In the event, he did not need to go to Barran's for help, because he was given a loan of £5 by a non-Jewish Leeds merchant named Isaac Dewhirst (who later also helped to teach him English). With the £5, he purchased goods from Dewhirst's warehouse and peddled them in the villages in the Leeds area. Despite poor English, he did well, but a combination of ambition and not very robust health spurred him to save up to take a stall in the local open market. Towards the end of 1884, he began to sell his wares from a trestle table, size six feet by three, in Kirkgate open market for the two days a week – probably Tuesdays and Saturdays – to which traders were restricted in that market. On the other days, it is probable he took his goods to nearby markets in the West Riding, such as Castleford and Wakefield. Kirkgate Market was only a hundred yards away from Dewhirst's warehouse, which he visited daily to purchase goods. He became well known to the staff there, particularly the cashier Tom Spencer, who, born in Skipton in Yorkshire, had moved to Leeds before he was twenty-one. During the next two years, Michael Marks made enough to get married – on 19 November 1886, to Hannah Cohen, aged twenty-two, whom he had first met in Stockton on Tees.

In 1857, a new covered market had been opened in Leeds and, in the year of his marriage, Michael hired a stall inside it at a low rent. Very soon – it may even have been before the move into the covered market – he attached a notice to a large number of goods on display: 'Don't ask the price, it's a penny'. It was a notice with a future – the start of the Penny Bazaars. The goods on sale were simple, but basic. They included nails, screws, pins, needles, buttons, handkerchiefs, mending wool, reels of cotton, soap, sponges, tumblers, cups and saucers, plates, egg cups, baking tins and so on. Soon, Michael opened two more penny bazaars – in Castleford and Wakefield – and, by about 1892, he had opened penny bazaars in Warrington, Birkenhead, Bolton and Manchester, to which he and his family had moved.

In 1894, when he acquired a permanent stall in Leeds covered market, he was ready to take a business partner – and he invited Tom Spencer to join him with an investment of £300 for his half-share in the business. Marks & Spencer, destined to become the most famous business partnership in British – and probably all – history, was born.

It was during this early period in the firm's development that the concern for sensible and sensitive staff welfare was first shown. As soon as he had more than one stall operating at the same time, Marks had to acquire some staff. Dewhirsts were able to provide two young girls to work for him. Very soon, Michael realised that standing on the stone floors of the markets could be a very cold business, so he had wooden platforms constructed on which the girls could stand and keep their feet warm. He often shared his food with his staff (soon enlarged to more than twenty). Later, when he opened 'penny bazaar' shops, he had gas rings provided on which the assistants could heat their lunches – and, early on, he began to give each member of his staff a Christmas present, which no British firm had ever done previously.

The partnership of Michael Marks and Tom Spencer thrived and, by 1895, four more penny bazaars were opened, as far distant from one another as Birmingham, Newcastle on Tyne, Bath and Cardiff.

Meanwhile, the Marks family was also growing. Michael's and

Michael Marks (left) and his partner, Tom Spencer, who together founded the firm of Marks & Spencer that was to have such an impact on British and later world retailing.

Hannah's first child had died in infancy. Their second, Simon, was born in 1888. In 1915, he married Miriam, daughter of Ephraim Sieff, born in Eiragolly in Kovno in Russia, who had come to England when he was twenty-five in about 1886 and had become a cotton and wool merchant in Manchester. Miriam's brother, Israel, married Simon's sister, Rebecca, in 1910. Simon had four daughters and three of them eventually married directors of the Marks & Spencer company.

The firm grew and spread. In 1899, it opened stores in London. By 1900, it had penny bazaars in twenty-three market halls up and down the country and branch establishments in eleven other places. By 1904, they were concentrating on opening shops, rather than market hall bazaars, and, by 1907, had seven in London. Though remaining a director of the company, Tom Spencer had taken what today would be regarded as early retirement in 1904, so that he could fulfil his dream of becoming a farmer. Sadly, he only lived one year to enjoy his hobby.

Now the increasing chain of stores were run by the Marks family, but Michael Marks, aged only forty-eight collapsed and died on 31 December 1907. After a period of management by non-family directors, Simon Marks was appointed to the board in 1911 and, in

Israel Sieff, a
manufacturer, joined
Marks & Spencer early in
the twentieth century.
This pedlar's certificate
was issued to his father,
Ephraim Sieff, in 1887,
the year after he landed
at Hull after fleeing from
the pogroms in Russia.

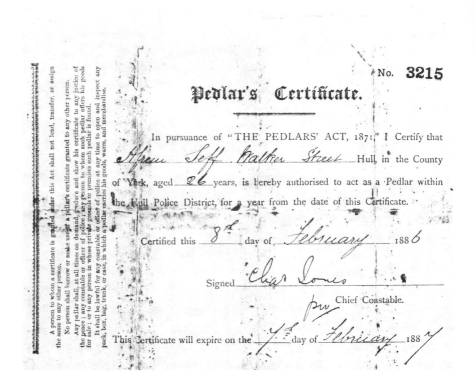

A Marks & Spencer
'Penny Bazaar'
photographed about
1912.

Simon Marks, later Lord Marks, who took over the firm after his father died and developed it considerably.

1916, when he was twenty-eight (a year before he was called up to join the army in the First World War), he was elected chairman of the firm.

By the beginning of the First World War, there were 145 Marks & Spencer stores in Britain, 56 of them in London. By the start of the Second World War, there were 234. When the firm reached its centenary in 1984, there were 262 stores in the United Kingdom, 213 in Canada and nine in Europe. Today, there are 660 stores worldwide. From that first turnover of a few pounds on a market stall, a total of over five billion pounds was spent in Marks & Spencer stores in 1989. From those two girl assistants in the 1880s, there are now over 70,000 employees. Though it became a public company as early as 1926, there is still a 'family feeling' to the business.

Simon Marks was knighted in 1944 and made a peer in 1961. He died in 1964. His brother-in-law, Israel Sieff, who was chairman from 1964 to 1967, was also raised to the peerage. Marcus Sieff, the present Lord Sieff, who has been chairman since 1972, succeeded his uncle, J. Edward Sieff. There are also two other members of the family on the firm's board.

The consolidation and development of Britain's Jewish community was not yet completed, however – there were to be more changes and additions in the twentieth century.

CHAPTER NINE
The Twentieth Century

By the turn of the century, a young woman, the Honorable Lily Montagu (daughter of the first Lord Swaithling, founder President of the Federation of Synagogues and a life member of the council of the United Synagogue), Dr Claude Montefiore, a distinguished scholar, several enlightened Orthodox rabbis and one Reform rabbi, concerned at the number of Jews drifting away from Judaism, had formed a committee to look into the matter. The first meeting of this committee was held in 1901 and the outcome of it was to form an organisation, to be called the Jewish Religious

The Honorable Lily Montagu (daughter of the first Lord Swaithling) who, with Dr Claude Montefiore and Rabbi Israel Mattuck, founded the Liberal Jewish Movement in 1902.

Union, set up to attract Jews back into modern Jewish observance. A good deal of Jewish interest in the project had been aroused by the following year, when, on 2 January, a meeting was held which attracted eighty-five people. The foundation of the Liberal (Progressive) movement was thus born and its first service was held the following October in a London hotel attended by more than three hundred people. The new movement did not segregate men and women at services, used an organ to accompany the singing (musical instruments are proscribed on the Sabbath in Orthodox Judaism 'until the Temple is rebuilt in Jerusalem'), included English as well as Hebrew in its services and, later, accepted children as Jewish if they came from either matrilineal or patrilineal descent (that is, unlike the Orthodox and Reform movements, Jewish descent is allowed through the father of the child, as well as the mother).

The movement's first synagogue, the Liberal Jewish Synagogue, was founded in 1910 in a disused chapel in Hill Street, St Marylebone, and, at that time, Rabbi Dr Israel Mattuck came from the United States, where Progressive Judaism was already established, to become the congregation's first spiritual leader. By the start of the Second World War in 1939, the Jewish Religious Union had grown quite rapidly and already had eight constituent congregations; five in London and three outside – in Brighton, Liverpool and Birmingham. In 1944, the title of the parent body was changed to the Union of Liberal and Progressive Synagogues, which today has twenty-six constituent congregations.

Notwithstanding the fact of Jewish emancipation and the Jewish

A contemporary sketch of the first service (held in a London hotel) of the Liberal Jewish Movement... and a scene during a consecration service of a new Ark to hold the Torah Scrolls in a modern Liberal synagogue – at Kingston in Surrey.

community's not inconsiderable contribution to British life, there were still pockets of anti-Semitism. In Limerick, for instance, where the Jews were mostly milk vendors, travelling drapers, small wholesalers and so on and were described at the time by the Chief Secretary for Ireland as 'a well-conducted section of the community engaged for the most part in small trades and dependent for their livelihood on the good-will of their customers'. Consequently, the small Jewish community was panic-stricken when, on 12 July 1904, Father John Creagh of the 'right wing' Redemptorist Order, preached a sermon, not only indicting their methods of business, but also accusing them of shedding Christian blood and even suggesting they would 'kidnap and slay Christian children, if they dared'. Arnold Griffith, leader of the Sinn Fein nationalists, supported Father Creagh in an article in the *United Irishman*, demanding freedom for the Irish peasantry from the international money-lenders and profiteers. A few days later, Father Creagh preached another, equally vicious sermon, and ordered his congregation 'not to deal with the Jews'. This was immediately interpreted to mean not only that the townspeople should not buy from Jewish traders, but that they should also repudiate previous debts they had incurred with them. The result, sadly, was that, with only one or two exceptions, the small Jewish community was very quickly impoverished. The Protestants of Limerick then opened relief funds for their poverty-stricken Jewish neighbours, but this unwittingly made the situation worse, because of the Catholic-Protestant feelings in Ireland at that time – and, indeed, most times – with the result that the small Jewish community became a kind of buffer between the two Christian communities and asked that fund-raising on their behalf should cease forthwith.

On 16 January, only six days after Father Creagh's first sermon, the Jews of Limerick were, as reported by the Reverend Elias Bere Levin: '... insulted, assaulted and threatened with the most menacing language'. Despite protests in the Irish press and by several Irish politicians and quite heavy penalties in the Irish courts for anyone physically assaulting Jews, the boycott on their livelihood which Father Creagh had instigated lasted two years and eventually drove out eighty members of the Jewish community from Limerick, leaving fewer than forty. The chief victim of the persecution was Rabbi Marcus Joseph Blond, who was born in Wexna, Lithuania, and ordained in his teens. When he settled in Limerick in the 1880s, he turned to trade. By April, 1904, his business was ruined and he had to sell stock fixtures and goodwill 'for a song'. In due time, Father Creagh's superiors realised that religious persecution had no place

A Jewish battalion fought in both France and the Middle East during the First World War. The top picture shows recruits for the 40th (Palestine) Battalion, Royal Fusiliers, in Jerusalem and below recruits are seen in a narrow gauge open truck train which took, them from Jaffa to Helmieh, their training centre, in 1918.

in Ireland; they disowned the priest and he was withdrawn from Limerick. But the damage was done and the pathetic remnants of Limerick's small Jewish community never recovered from the episode.

By the outbreak of the First World War, the Jewish refugees from eastern Europe who had settled in Britain had increased the total Jewish population to about 285,000, over two-thirds of whom lived in London and its environs. A few more were to arrive from the Balkan States and some from Western Europe over the following years, but the bulk of that wave of Jewish immigration was now virtually complete.

Jews took an active part in the fighting in the First World War.

A Jewish wedding group photographed in the garden of a house in Barnes in south-west London. It was the wedding of members of two old Sephardi families – Mr Daniel Hyams to Miss Elka Alvarez.

A typical 'sweat shop' of the early twentieth century. Jewish workers are seen in a badly lit and equipped mantle makers' workshop about 1913.

Two examples of Jewish shops in the early nineteenth century. Above, a confectioners and tobacconist in Liverpool Road, Islington, in 1911, and, below, Philip Barnett's 'steam works' about 1900. Mr Barnett is the bearded man outside the shop wearing a bowler hat and his son, Alf, also wearing a bowler, stands in the doorway. The others in the picture are the shop's staff.

There was, in fact, a complete Jewish battalion which fought in both France and the Middle East and Jews also served in other parts of the armed forces. This often meant that brother was fighting against brother. One of many such cases was that of the Reis (later Rees) family, who worked in Nuremberg's toy industry. Leon, the oldest of four brothers, came to England in 1896 to join a British toy firm. A few years later, he became naturalised and married his boss's daughter. During the war, Leon served in the British army for a time, while Fritz, one of his brothers, was a member of the German army. After the war, though one brother, Albert, emigrated to America, the other two, Fritz (later Fred) and Louis, settled in England, as had Leon some twenty years earlier. They were thus spared the terror that was to come in the 1930s to those many Jews who remained in Germany.

Up to the outbreak of the war, Zionism – the need and desire for a national home for Jews – had been growing all over Europe. The architect (though not the originator) of it was a brilliant young Austrian Jewish journalist and playwright named Theodor Herzl. Herzl had been very worried by the growth of anti-Semitism he had witnessed in Austria, while studying law in Vienna in the 1870s. His fears were crystallised after he covered the court martial of a Jewish staff officer of the French army in Paris in 1894, as a correspondent of the *Neue Freie Presse*. The officer, Captain Alfred Dreyfus, had been arrested on a charge of espionage. On trumped-up evidence, he was sentenced to life imprisonment and deported to French Guiana. The forgeries which had led to Dreyfus's conviction were soon made public and a number of leading Jewish and French people, led by the non-Jewish author, Emile Zola, demanded a retrial. This was refused for a long time by both the military and the reactionary administration and it was soon clear that anti-Semitism had been at the bottom of the whole thing, which was further demonstrated by a good deal of anti-Jewish violence after the case, the most serious outbreaks occurring in Algeria. At last, after two retrials, the verdict was reversed in 1906 and Dreyfus was reinstated as an officer, but, by then, he was a broken man.

So shocked was Herzl by the Dreyfus case, which had added 'tolerant' France to the other anti-Semitic countries, notably Russia and Germany, that it was clear to him that the only safe haven for Jews was a country of their own, back in the Middle East from whence they had originally come. Full of zeal, in 1896, Herzl wrote *Judenstaat* (*The Jewish State*), in which he elaborated his ideas for a Jewish autonomous nation. This was the first step in the launching of the Zionist movement, with its object (formulated officially at a

Notice of a mass meeting at a Jewish workingmen's club in East London, to welcome Theodore Herzl, the 'architect' of what was to become the State of Israel.

Zionist Congress held in Basle, Switzerland, in 1897) of 'securing for the Jewish people a home in Palestine guaranteed by public law'. It was the first of a series of Zionist congresses to discuss and formulate the creation of a new self-governing Jewish state. Herzl travelled the world meeting various European leaders, ranging from the German Kaiser to the Pope, trying, with varying success, to engage their interest in the project.

At this time, Palestine was part of the Turkish Empire and, during his negotiations, Herzl went to Constantinople, where he was cordially received by Sultan Abdul-Hamid II, but nevertheless a charter giving permission to set up the Jewish state was not forthcoming. In 1902, only two years before his early death at forty-four, Herzl came to London to give evidence before the Royal Commission on Alien Immigration, the purpose of which was to review the influx of Jews from Russia. He placed the following theory before the commission:

The main principle of Zionism is that the solution of the Jewish difficulty is the recognition of Jews as a people, and the finding by them of a legally recognised home, to which Jews in those parts of the world in which they are oppressed would naturally migrate, for they would arrive there as citizens just because they are Jews and not as aliens. This would mean the diverting of the stream of emigration from this country and from America, where as they form a perceptible number they become a trouble and burden to a land where the true interest would be served by accommodating as many as possible. Given to the Jews their rightful position as a people, I am convinced they would develop a distinctive Jewish cult – national characteristics and national aspirations – which would make for the progress of mankind.

Arthur (later Lord) Balfour who wrote a letter to Lord Rothschild expressing the British government's sympathy with the desire for a Jewish national home in Palestine. This letter, which came to be known as the Balfour Declaration, is looked on by many as the official start of the State of Israel.

The British government was impressed enough to offer Herzl territory in British East Africa for at least a temporary home for a Jewish state. This was refused, but it demonstrated Britain's view that Zionism was more than just an idealistic dream. In 1904, Chaim Weizmann, the man who was to follow Herzl in the creation of Israel and who was to become its first President, came to Manchester to work as a scientist and lecturer and thus the nerve centre of the Zionist movement moved to Britain.

When the First World War started, Zionist activity naturally diminished, but, in 1917, the British army under General Allenby ended four hundred years of Turkish rule in Palestine and Britain took charge of the country. Shortly afterwards, the British Foreign Secretary, Arthur (later Lord) Balfour, wrote to Lord Rothschild who was deeply involved in Zionist work:

I have much pleasure in conveying to you, on behalf of His Majesty's Government, the following declaration of sympathy with Jewish Zionist aspirations which have been submitted to, and approved by, the Cabinet. 'His Majesty's Government view with favour the establishment in Palestine of a national home for the Jewish people, and will use their best endeavours to facilitate the achievement of this object, it being clearly understood that nothing shall be done which may prejudice the civil and religious rights of existing non-Jewish communities in Palestine, or the rights and political status enjoyed by Jews in any other country.' I should grateful if you would bring this declaration to the knowledge of the Zionist Federation.

Three years after what came to be known as the Balfour Declaration

– and two years after the end of the war – the League of Nations gave Britain a formal mandate to administer Palestine. The first High Commissioner appointed was a Jew – Sir Herbert (later Lord) Samuel. It was, however, to be twenty-eight years before the State of Israel came into being.

The years between the two world wars were marked by the beginning of a new wave of anti-Semitism throughout Europe, culminating in the rise to power of Adolf Hitler and the National Socialist Party in Germany in 1933. It was the beginning of a systematic attempt at Jewish genocide, first in Germany itself and later in every country into which the Germans marched during the Second World War. By 1945, six million Jews – and one million other 'non-aryans' such as gipsies – had been horribly eradicated. In less than a generation, two-thirds of all European Jewry had perished and in countries such as Poland, Czechoslovakia and Greece, not more than a tenth of the Jewish population survived the Holocaust. In Germany itself, there were virtually no Jews left. When the Allied Armies marched into Europe at the end of the war, however, they found that some Jews *had* survived – the pathetic remnants of human beings in Hitler's concentration camps.

Unfortunately, there was a political group in England in the 1930s which was quite as anti-Semitic as the Nazis – and its growth was encouraged by what was happening in Germany and, to a slightly lesser degree, in Italy. The British Union of Fascists – or the Blackshirts, as they were soon called – were extremists of the most

Sir Oswald Mosley, leader of the British Union of Fascists, a virulent anti-Semitic group, passing down the ranks of his Blackshirts in June, 1933.

Police try to control the angry crowds in Cable Street in East London, who were demonstrating against a march of three thousand Blackshirts. 'They shall not pass' said the ordinary people of the area and they won 'The Battle of Cable Street' when Sir Oswald Mosley and his fascists were turned back by the police.

virulent kind. They were led by Sir Oswald Mosley, a minor member of the English aristocracy. Mosley, a great admirer of Hitler, whom he had met several times, led his thugs into the East End and the West End of London with the avowed intention of harassing Jewish people. Inevitably, the major marches and other less organised onslaughts included damaging as many Jewish homes and businesses as possible. The worst example was what came to be known as the Battle of Cable Street, when 3,000 Blackshirts mobilised in Royal Mint Street in the City, poised to march out in four columns by way of Cable Street in the East End. As William J. Fishman records in *The Streets of East London*:

Their flanks were to be protected *en route* by nearly 7,000 policemen recruited into the area and including the entire Metropolitan corps of mounted police. Radio vans patrolled and an autogyro flew overhead to monitor the opposing forces. At the confluence of Cable and Leman Street barricades were being erected and a huge crowd collected at Gardiners Corner – the real point of entry into East London. By mid-afternoon it was estimated that a hostile army of at least 100,000 had gathered along the proposed route. Anti-fascist placards hung from windows and walls; and the current slogan of the Spanish Republic 'They Shall Not Pass!' was proclaimed everywhere on a sea of banners. The 'Battle of Cable Street' broke out when a lorry dragged from a yard was overturned in the middle of the road, forming the base of a barricade. Police charges were met by a hail of stones and bricks from defenders on the ground and from the upper storeys of surrounding houses. It was the dockers of Wapping and St George's who constituted the vanguard of opposition here, thus preventing the march from taking off. After some police skirmishing and subsequent injuries and arrests, Sir Philip Game, Commissioner of Police, was convinced that it would be impossible for Mosley to proceed without mass riots and bloodshed. He ordered Mosley to turn about and the procession marched off to the music of pipes and drums, in the opposite direction, along the Embankment, where, in the absence of an audience, they quickly dispersed. That night there was dancing in the side streets as East Enders celebrated their victory and the birth of a 'heroic' legend.

The Battle of Cable Street had one rapid result – the Public Order Act, which prohibited political uniforms and gave the police powers to ban processions. The increasing troubles in Europe at the time, as well as the passing of this act, led to the decline of the British Union of Fascists, which, in addition to its anti-Semitic ethos, was also dedicated to the removal from Britain of what it saw as 'all other foreigners', including communists, gipsies, coloured people and so on. In the 1960s and 1970s, at least two other right-wing groups were formed in Britain. The most active of them was the National Front, which still exists, though, at present, it has little power. Mosley, however, had had his day. At the beginning of the Second World War, because of his known Nazi sympathies, he and his wife, a daughter of Lord Redesdale, were interned in the Isle of Man. After the war, they went to live in France, where he died, with his political and racist opinions unchanged.

From the start of the persecution of the Jews in Germany in 1933, refugees began to arrive in Britain, first as a trickle and later in considerable numbers. The Jewish population of Britain, which had been about 330,000 in 1932, had been increased by the end of 1939 by an estimated 75,000, most of whom were German or Austrian refugees. Many were offered temporary homes with British Jews, especially those who had arrived from persecution with few possessions but their lives. On the outbreak of war with Germany, there were calls, both from the general public and the chiefs of staff, for the internment of *all* aliens, despite the reason for the influx of refugees. So far as the British were concerned, anyone coming from Germany at that time was suspect. Consequently, about 5,000 German Jews were deported to Canada and Australia and another 15,000 were interned on the Isle of Man or in other internment camps in Britain. After a few months, however, there were many protests about the treatment of these unfortunate people, the internees were released and the majority went into war work or joined the armed forces, principally being drafted into the Pioneer Corps.

The need for somewhere for the survivors of the concentration camps and other stateless Jewish victims of the Nazis to live hastened the creation of the State of Israel by as much as ten years. As early as 1934, refugees from Germany had gone to Palestine to seek asylum. At the end of the war, the necessity for the Jewish State was obvious and Britain, because of its Mandate in Palestine, was very much involved. Many problems arose, both for the Jews struggling for their independent state against the surrounding Arab nations and for the British administrators. Finally, in 1947, the British Government referred the matter to the United Nations, which then made recommendations on how the partition of Palestine into two states – Jewish and Arab – was to be set up. On 29 November, the United Nations approved the recommendations. Great Britain, because the Arabs refused to accept the plan, declared it was unable to implement the recommendations and would therefore terminate its Mandate in Palestine. All British forces were withdrawn from Palestine on 15 May 1948, and the State of Israel was officially born the previous evening, though it was immediately involved in a war of independence against the Arabs. In addition, as D.R. Elston says in Israel – the Making of a Nation,

> It was one thing for the State of Israel to be proclaimed, even with such backing as remained from the United Nations' recommendations of 29 November 1947. It was quite another to obtain that degree of formal recognition without which no State can have any substantial being. ... By April 1949 the number of States recognizing Israel was fifty-three, including

the United Kingdom. Thereafter, one by one, most nations represented at the United Nations, with the exception, of course, of the Arab block and some of its Asian supporters, gave *de facto* or *de jure* recognition to Israel. The new State had 'arrived'. On 11 May 1949 the General Assembly of the United Nations, acting on the recommendation of the Security Council, admitted Israel to full membership.

The effect on Diaspora Jewry of the establishment of Israel was profound. Its very existence gave them a sense of identity, which many had previously lacked, and it also provided the assurance that, if anti-Semitism in the countries in which they lived should become unbearable, there was now somewhere safe to which they could go. Very soon after 1948, many, of course, made *aliyah* (in Hebrew, 'to go up', but now meaning to emigrate to Israel) – including some, though not a vast number, from Britain. Many young people – not all of them Jewish – from all parts of the world, including the United Kingdom, went – and still go – to Israel to spend months, or even years, working on the *kibbuzim* (the collective farms or industrial 'villages'). British Jews were among those who went willingly to help Israel fight its War of Independence and the two Israeli-Arab conflicts that followed – the Six-Day War in 1967 and the Yom Kippur War in 1973.

Although the number of Reform and Liberal synagogues increased before and soon after the end of the Second World War, there were no facilities in Britain for the training of Progressive rabbis. Before and after the war, they had either been students at Jews' College or had received their training at the Hebrew Union College in Cincinatti in the United States. This college had been established in 1875 in response to the need for rabbis to lead the increasing numbers of Reform congregations in America. After the war, it was the only seminary specifically for Liberal and Reform rabbis, because a rabbinical seminary in Germany, which had been opened in 1854 to train Progressive rabbis, had been wiped away during the Holocaust.

In 1954, the Reform movement decided that the call for rabbis in Britain was now so urgent that a theological college should be founded in London. After a good deal of work and fund raising, the Jewish Theological College opened its doors on 30 September 1956, in the premises of the West London Synagogue in Upper Berkeley Street, London, and the first five students began their studies there on 2 October. Great support and encouragement had been given to the founders of the college by Rabbi Dr Leo Baeck, one of the pioneers of German Liberal Judaism, who had spent two years during the war in Theresienstadt concentration camp and, after it was over, had come to live in England. It was planned that he should give regular lectures at the college, but he died on 2 November 1956, and, as a tribute to him, the college was renamed the Leo Baeck College. In 1964, the Union of Liberal and Progressive Synagogues joined with the Reform Synagogues of Great Britain in sustaining the Leo Baeck College and rabbis trained there were able to serve either Reform or Liberal synagogues. By 1989, nearly a hundred rabbis from all over the world, a proportion of them

An unusual view of London's famous Jewish market, Petticoat Lane in the East End, on a Sunday morning in the 1960s. The market is today run almost exclusively by members of the Asian community, many of whom now live in the area.

Dr Leo Baeck, one of the pioneers of German Liberal Judaism, who settled in England after the Second World War. The college, which was opened in 1956 for the training of Progressive Jewish rabbis, changed its name from the Jewish Theological College to the Leo Baeck College in his honour.

women, had been ordained, after five years of study and congregational practice, and a number of other students, including a Roman Catholic nun, had studied theology there for shorter terms. In 1983, the college moved to the Sternberg Centre in Finchley, London, at present the largest Jewish cultural centre in Europe.

The only Jewish missionary movement (directed solely at other Jews) arrived in Britain from America in 1959. The Lubavitch movement was founded in the eighteenth century by Rabbi Schneur Zalman. It is a form of Chassidism, the Jewish sect created by an eighteenth century rabbi in Poland (known affectionately by Jews as the *Baal Shem Tov*; in English, Master of the Good Name), which offered a simplified form of Judaism based entirely on the love of the Torah and its obligations. Male members of the various Chassidic sects, including the Lubavitch, still wear the same style of garments and facial hair and beards as the followers of the *Baal Shem Tov* did at the movement's inception. The headquarters of Britain's Lubavitch movement is in Stamford Hill, London. The movement has increased rapidly in numbers and now has twelve main centres up and down the country. It is a particularly separatist movement and its members are strongly discouraged from marrying even into mainstream Jewry.

By the early 1950s, the Jewish population of Britain had reached an estimated 430,000, but, since then, numbers have declined and it stands today at around 330,000 – quite a small proportion of Britain's population and now outstripped by other ethnic groups which have settled in the United Kingdom in recent years.

Nevertheless, the number of Jews in Britain today, contrasted with the numbers during medieval times and even with those who came just before the Resettlement, indicates a quite dramatic increase. An associated increase that is really out of all proportion to the relatively small Jewish population is the number of outstanding Jews who have made their mark on the twentieth century and, indeed, many continue to do so. They represent every walk of life and it would be impossible to list them all here.

Some, however, have, for one reason or another, made a particularly indelible impression on British life. Few in politics, for instance, will forget Lord Shinwell, who died, aged 101, in 1985. Emanuel Shinwell was born in the East End of London, but was taken by his family to live in Glasgow when he was quite young and he lived and worked there for over thirty years. Subsequently, his strong Scottish accent led people to think that he was born north of the border. He entered local and, later, national politics as a socialist very early in his career and was Member of Parliament for Lin-

Emanuel (later Lord) Shinwell, a leading Labour politician.

lithgow from 1922 to 1924 and again from 1928 to 1931. For fifteen years from 1935, he represented the Seaham Division of Durham and, from 1950 to 1970, was the Member for the Easington Division of Durham until he was created a Life Peer. He held various offices under successive Labour governments, including that of Minister of Fuel and Power, Secretary of State for War and Minister of Defence. He was also chairman of both the National Executive Committee of the Labour Party and of the Parliamentary Labour Party from 1964 to 1967. From the time he entered the House of Lords as Lord Shinwell of Easington, until a few weeks before this death, he took an active part in the proceedings. He was also the author of several books, including *Lead with the Left*, which he wrote when he was ninety-six. He was greatly respected by most people, even his political opponents – and was affectionately known by everyone as Manny Shinwell.

An impact on sport which was quite as definitive as Lord Shinwell's on politics was made by Bedford-born Harold Abrahams, one of the United Kingdom's earliest and most famous Olympic sprinters. After a distinguished athletics career at Cambridge University, Abrahams won the Olympic 100-metres in Paris in 1924, equalling the Olympic record three times. A month before the Olympics, on the same day that he ran 100 yards in record time, he

Harold Abrahams, Britain's great sprinter, winning the 100 metres race in the Paris Olympics in 1924.

long-jumped 7.38 metres – a jump that remained an English record for 32 years. His active career was unfortunately cut short in 1925 when he broke a leg while long-jumping. After his retirement from active athletics, he devoted himself to administration with the Amateur Athletics Association and also served on the British Amateur Athletics Board, becoming its honorary treasurer in 1948 and its chairman in 1968. He was a national newspaper athletics correspondent for forty years and a BBC radio athletics commentator for forty-five years. Shortly after this death at seventy-nine in 1978, although he was a professing Jew, a memorial service was held to honour him in the journalists' church, St Bride's, in Fleet Street.

Jews have always been eminent in medicine, but Sir Ludwig Guttmann, who was born in Tost, Upper Silesia (then in Poland), in 1899 and who died in Buckinghamshire in 1980, changed the way of life of many thousands of chairbound people throughout the world – and, in doing so, added a new dimension to international sport. A German doctor specialising in neurology, already with a distinguished career, Ludwig Guttmann had to leave Germany in 1939 to escape the Nazi regime, after he smuggled sixty Jews out of Germany through the Jewish hospital in which he was working. He and his family arrived at Harwich on 14 March 1939, with only ten German marks between them. After working at Oxford, where he had

Sir Ludwig Guttmann, founder of the Stoke Mandeville International Games.

been given a bursary, for about four years, he was offered, in 1944, what was little more than a huge barn at Stoke Mandeville in Buckinghamshire to house and treat service people who had sustained injuries to the spinal cord, which caused major paralysis, sometimes from the neck down. Previously, there would have been virtually nothing done for these patients, except to tend them until they died. Ludwig Guttmann thought otherwise and he had the skill, knowledge and foresight to put his ideas into practice. From the time he was appointed director of the National Spinal Injuries Centre at Stoke Mandeville, he worked, with a dedicated team, to set up treatment and training for paraplegic patients that would enable them to lead, if not completely normal lives, at least useful, active and happy ones. From the start, he realised that physical exercise from the waist upwards was very important and he soon introduced sport into the treatment.

In July, 1948, symbolically when the Olympic Games were opening in London, Dr Guttmann launched the International Stoke Mandeville Games for the Paralysed at Stoke Mandeville Hospital. It was the beginning of a worldwide movement. The Olympic Games for the Paralysed now take place every four years, in addition to annual paraplegic sports in spinal injury centres all over the world, including several in Germany. The Ludwig Guttmann Sports Centre in Aylesbury is the headquarters of the International Stoke Mandeville Games Federation. Two overseas spinal injury centres also bear his name – one in Barcelona and the other in Tel-Hashomer, Israel – and streets have been named after him in Germany, France and the Netherlands. He was made an OBE in 1950, a CBE in 1960 and was knighted six years later. The list of medical and other honours bestowed on him nationally and internationally is very long, but those who worked with him or knew the depth and dedication of his work for paralysed people, will understand that what mattered most to him was expressed in a comment he once made about his work: 'If I ever did one good thing in my medical career, it was to introduce sport into the treatment and rehabilitation programme of spinal cord sufferers and other severely disabled.'

Examples of the work of one of the most revolutionary sculptors of this century can be found all over the world. Jacob Epstein was born in 1880 on New York's Lower East Side into a family of Polish Jewish immigrants. He studied at the Art Students League and his first assignment in 1902 was from a non-Jew to illustrate a book about the Jewish quarter of New York. Epstein used the fee he received from the book publisher to study in Paris at the Ecole des Beaux Arts. In 1905, he came to London and stayed there for the rest

The great sculptor, Jacob Epstein, standing beside his sculpture of the playwright, George Bernard Shaw, at the Tate Gallery in London.

of his life. In 1907, he received his first important commission – from the British Medical Association to decorate the façade of its new building in the Strand in London. It was a series of eighteeen figures called 'The Birth of Energy', which caused controversy and protest, especially from religious bodies, because the figures were naked and explicit and one of them was of a pregnant woman. The nationwide protest made him famous. Epstein was a great admirer of the prehistoric carvers, the archaic Greek sculptors and the African, Polynesian and pre-Columbian image-makers. In creating his varied and often massive works, he drew on his knowledge of the sculpture of all periods and places, yet he always retained the powerful imprint of his own style. His output was enormous and his works included both Jewish and Christian religious subjects, ranging from Genesis, Adam and Jacob to Christ in Majesty (in Llandaff Cathedral in Wales) and St Michael and the Devil (for the fascia of the post-war Coventry Cathedral). He also created many portrait sculptures of famous people and a number of public statues. He received the KBE in 1954 and was still working when he died five years later.

A woman with dedication that equalled Epstein's, though in a very different field, was born Miriam Rambach in Warsaw in Poland in 1888. Marie Rambert, considered to be the mother of British ballet, started her career by studying eurythmics and, in 1913, was invited by the great ballet impresario, Serge Diaghilev, to teach the

Dalcroze method of eurythmics to his company. This she did for a time, but soon found that she preferred to concentrate on classical ballet. She became a pupil of Enrico Cecchetti, the distinguished Italian ballet dancer and teacher, and she followed his principles when she opened her own school in London in 1920. By 1930, the school had developed into a prestigious ballet club, which, as Ballet Rambert, became famous for its performances at the Mercury Theatre in Notting Hill. Rambert had a great flair for discovering new talent and an ability to inspire the artistes in her company. Many dancers, designers and choreographers who became famous in national and international ballet started in Ballet Rambert, which became Britain's first permanent ballet company and school. Madame Rambert was awarded the CBE in 1954, the French Legion of Honour in 1957 and was made a Dame in 1962. Mim, as she was affectionately called by the ballet world, continued to give ballet classes up to the end of her life in 1982.

A convert who brought her unique musical gift to British Jewry in 1967 and who died tragically of multiple sclerosis when she was only forty-two, was the great cellist, Jacqueline du Pré.

The recipient of many cello prizes and educational grants from her extreme youth, she studied under William Preeth, Pablo Casals, Paul Tortelier and Mstislav Rostropovich. She made her debut at

Dame Marie Rambert, pioneer of British ballet.

Jacqueline du Pré,
Britain's greatest cellist,
who died from multiple
sclerosis in 1987.

Wigmore Hall in London when she was sixteen and, after that performance, offers for recitals and orchestral engagements flooded in from all over the world. In 1962, she first appeared at the Royal Festival Hall and, performing for the first time with a full orchestra, was the soloist in Elgar's Cello Concerto, a work with which she was always to be associated. At the beginning of 1967, she became engaged to Daniel Barenboim, the Israeli pianist and conductor, and thereafter often performed and made recordings with him. When the Six-Day War in Israel was imminent, she and Barenboim cancelled their professional engagements and went to Israel to entertain the troops, giving two concerts a day all over the country. After the war, she converted to Judaism and they were married on 15 June 1967, in a rabbi's house near the Western Wall in the Old City of Jerusalem.

By the time she was twenty-five, Jacqueline du Pré had played and recorded all the major cello works in the repertoire with orchestras of great distinction. It was an achievement that was to be a comfort to her in the tragic years that followed. Early in 1970, it became clear that something very serious was wrong with her. Three years later, multiple sclerosis was diagnosed. It was the effective end of her performing career, because the disease progressed rapidly and she was soon confined to a wheelchair. After two years' virtual seclusion, she emerged in public again to conduct cello master classes and she also gave private tuition to a few students. She fought the disease bravely, even when she could hardly move her limbs or enunciate clearly. Both before and after the onset of her illness, she received many musical and intellectual honours and she was made an OBE in 1976.

From the time of her marriage, she was sincerely committed to

Judaism, though she was not, in the full sense, religious. This commitment continued until the end of her life on 19 October 1987. In fact, she asked her rabbi and her nurse to play to her her own recording of Max Bruch's Kol Nidrei (which is based on the most holy music of Yom Kippur – the Day of Atonement) and her rabbi came on the day before Yom Kippur and played the music to her. They then talked and prayed together. Two hours before she died, her rabbi sat by her bed and the nurse again played the record of the Kol Nidrei as her final music.

It is not coincidental that this book is published in the year which marks not only the 700th anniversary of the Expulsion of the Jews from Britain by King Edward I, but also the 800th anniversary of the mass suicide of the majority of the Jews besieged in Clifford's Tower in York. Despite that medieval tragedy, British Jewry is today a permanent part of the British way of life, with an uninterrupted history of settlement since the middle-1650s. Once the largest religious minority in the United Kingdom, the Anglo-Jewish community is now probably among the smaller religious movements. Nevertheless, the distinguished contribution many of its members have made to the general community, coupled with the preservation of the Jewish way of life, makes both it and its history integral to British society.

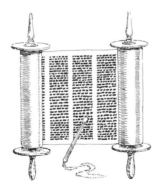

Works Consulted

Abrahams, B.L. *The Expulsion of the Jews in 1290* Blackwell. 1894.

Abrahams, Israel. *Jewish Life in the Middle Ages* Goldston. 1932.

Adler, Michael. *The Jews of Medieval England* Jewish Historical Society of England. 1939.

Alderman, Geoffrey. *The Federation of Synagogues: 1887–1987* Federation of Synagogues. 1987.

Barnett, Richard D. and Levy, Abraham. *The Bevis Marks Synagogue* Booklet issued by the Bevis Marks Synagogue, London.

Briggs, Asa. *Marks & Spencer: A Centenary History* Octopus Books. 1984.

Bookbinder, Paul. *Marks & Spencer: the War Years 1939–1945* Century Benham. 1989.

Brook, Stephen. *The Club – the Jews of Modern Britain* Constable. 1989.

Conway, Edward S., MA, PhD. *The Origins of the Jewish Orphanage* Transaction of the Jewish Historical Society of England. 1934.

Dobson, R.B. *The Jews of Medieval York and the Massacre of March 1290* Borthwick Papers No. 45. 1974.

Elson, D.R. *Israel – the making of a nation* Oxford. 1963.

Encyclopaedia Judaica (various authors)

Endelman, Todd M. *The Jews of Georgian England: 1714–1830* Jewish Publication Society of America. 1979.

Ewald, Alexander Charles. *The Right Hon. the Earl of Beaconsfield, KG, and his Times* William Mackenzie. 1881.

Fraser, Antonia. *Cromwell: Our Chief of Men* Weidenfeld and Nicolson. 1974.

Gilbert, Martin. *Exile and Return – the Emergence of Jewish Statehood* Weidenfeld and Nicolson. 1978.

Gilbert, Martin. *Jewish History Atlas* (revised edition) Weidenfeld and Nicolson. 1976.

Green, Geoffrey L. *The Royal Navy and Anglo-Jewry: 1740–1820* Geoffrey Green. 1989.

Hill, J.W.F. *Medieval Lincoln* Cambridge University Press. 1948.

Howitt, Arthur. *Richmond and its Jewish Connections* Privately printed. 1930.

Hyamson, Albert M. *The Sephardim of England* Methuen. 1951.

Hyman, Louis. *The Jews of Ireland: from earliest times to the year 1910* Jewish Historical Society and Israel Universities Press. 1972.

Jacobs, Joseph. *The Jews of Angevin England* David Nutt. 1893.

Jews in England, The (An exhibition of records). Public Record Office. 1957.

WORKS CONSULTED

Lipman, V.D. *The Jews of Medieval Norwich* Jewish Historical Society of England. 1967.

Lipman, V.D. *Jews and Castles in Medieval England* Transactions of the Jewish Historical Society of England. 1981–1982.

Mazower, David. *Yiddish Theatre in London* Museum of the Jewish East End. 1987.

Newman, Aubrey. *The United Synagogue: 1870–1970* Routledge and Kegan Paul. 1977.

Newman, Aubrey *The Board of Deputies of British Jews: 1760–1985* Vallentine Mitchell. 1987.

Reform Judaism (essays) Reform Synagogues of Great Britain. 1973.

Reitlinger, Gerald. *The Changing Face of English Jewry at the End of the Eighteenth Century* Jewish Historical Society transaction.

Richardson, H.G. *The English Jewry under the Angevin Kings* Jewish Historical Society of England/Methuen. 1939.

Romain, Jonathan A. *Anglo-Jewry in Evidence* (now retitled *The Jews of England*) The Michael Goulston Educational Foundation. 1985 (first edition).

Roth, Cecil. *A Life of Menasseh Ben Israel* The Jewish Publication Society of America. 1934.

Roth, Cecil. *A History of the Jews of England* Clarenden Press, Oxford. 1964 (third edition).

Roth, Cecil. *A Short History of the Jewish People* The East and West Library. 1969.

Shinwell, Manny. *Lead with the Left* Cassell. 1981.

Sieff, Marcus. *Don't Ask the Price* Weidenfeld and Nicolson. 1987.

Stenton, Doris Mary. *English Society in the Early Middle Ages* Penguin Books. 1965.

Stokes, H.P. *A Short History of the Jews in England* S.P.C.K. 1921.

Underwood, Eric. *Brighton* BT Batsford. 1978.

Waterman, Stanley, and Kosmin, Barry. *British Jewry in the Eighties* Routledge and Kegan Paul. 1977.

Wolf, Lucien. *Essays in Jewish History* Jewish Historical Society of England. 1934.

Wolf, Lucien. *Crypto-Jews under the Commonwealth* Jewish Historical Society of England transaction.

Wolf, Lucien. *The Jewry of the Restoration* Jewish Historical Society of England transaction.

Wurmbrand, Max, and Roth, Cecil. *The Jewish People – 4000 Years of Survival* Cassell. 1966.

Index

INDEX